LIFE AND LETTERS OF WALTER H. PAGE

BY
BURTON J. HENDRICK

VOLUME
II

London
William Heinemann, Ltd.
1923

PRINTED IN THE UNITED STATES OF AMERICA

CONTENTS

VOLUME II

LIST OF ILLUSTRATIONS

THE
LIFE AND LETTERS
OF
WALTER H. PAGE

THE LIFE AND LETTERS OF WALTER H. PAGE

CHAPTER XIV

THE "LUSITANIA"—AND AFTER

I

THE news of the *Lusitania* was received at the American Embassy at four o'clock on the afternoon of May 7, 1915. At that time preparations were under way for a dinner in honour of Colonel and Mrs. House; the first *Lusitania* announcement declared that only the ship itself had been destroyed and that all the passengers and members of the crew had been saved; there was, therefore, no good reason for abandoning this dinner.

At about seven o'clock, the Ambassador came home; his manner showed that something extraordinary had taken place; there were no outward signs of emotion, but he was very serious. The first news, he now informed Mrs. Page, had been a mistake; more than one thousand men, women, and children had lost their lives, and more than one hundred of these were American citizens. It was too late to postpone the dinner but that affair was one of the most tragic in the social history of London. The Ambassador was constantly receiving bulletins from his Chancery, and these, as quickly as they were received, he read to his guests. His voice was quiet and subdued; there were no indications of excitement in his manner or in that of his friends, and hardly of suppressed emotion.

1

The atmosphere was rather that of dumb stupefaction. The news seemed to have dulled everyone's capacity for thought and even for feeling. If any one spoke, it was in whispers. Afterward, in the drawing room, this same mental state was the prevailing one; there was little denunciation of Germany and practically no discussion as to the consequences of the crime; everyone's thought was engrossed by the harrowing and unbelievable facts which the Ambassador was reading from the little yellow slips that were periodically brought in. An irresistible fascination evidently kept everybody in the room; the guests stayed late, eager for every new item. When they finally left, one after another, their manner was still abstracted and they said their good-nights in low voices. There were two reasons for this behaviour. The first was that the Ambassador and his guests had received the details of the greatest infamy which any supposedly civilized state had perpetrated since the massacre of Saint Bartholomew. The second was the conviction that the United States would at once declare war on Germany.

On this latter point several of the guests expressed their ideas and one of the most shocked and outspoken was Colonel House. For a month the President's personal representative had been discussing with British statesmen possible openings for mediation, but all his hopes in this direction now vanished. That President Wilson would act with the utmost energy Colonel House took for granted. This act, he evidently believed, left the United States no option. "We shall be at war with Germany within a month," he declared.

The feeling that prevailed in the Embassy this evening was the one that existed everywhere in London for several days. Emotionally the event acted like an anæsthetic. This was certainly the condition of all Americans associated with the American Embassy, especially Page himself. A day or two after the sinking the Ambassador went to Euston Station, at an early hour in the morning, to receive the American survivors. The hundred or more men and women who shambled from the train made a listless and bedraggled gathering. Their grotesque clothes, torn and unkempt—for practically none had had the opportunity of obtaining a change of dress—their expressionless faces, their lustreless eyes, their uncertain and bewildered walk, faintly reflected an experience such as comes to few people in this world. The most noticeable thing about these unfortunates was their lack of interest in their surroundings; everything had apparently been reduced to a blank; the fact that practically none made any reference to their ordeal, or could be induced to discuss it, was a matter of common talk in London. And something of this disposition now became noticeable in Page himself. He wrote his dispatches to Washington in an abstracted mood; he went through his duties almost with the detachment of a sleep-walker; like the *Lusitania* survivors, he could not talk much at that time about the scenes that had taken place off the coast of Ireland. Yet there were many indications that he was thinking about them, and his thoughts, as his letters reveal, were concerned with more things than the tragedy itself. He believed that his country was now face to face with its destiny. What would Washington do?

Page had a characteristic way of thinking out his problems. He performed his routine work at the Chancery in the daytime, but his really serious thinking he did in his own room at night. The picture is still a vivid one in the recollection of his family and his other intimates. Even at this time Page's health was not good, yet he frequently spent the evening at his office in Grosvenor

Gardens, and when the long day's labours were finished, he would walk rather wearily to his home at No. 6 Grosvenor Square. He would enter the house slowly—and his walk became slower and more tired as the months went by—go up to his room and cross to the fireplace, so apparently wrapped up in his own thoughts that he hardly greeted members of his own family. A wood fire was kept burning for him, winter and summer alike; Page would put on his dressing gown, drop into a friendly chair, and sit there, doing nothing, reading nothing, saying nothing —only thinking. Sometimes he would stay for an hour; not infrequently he would remain till two, three, or four o'clock in the morning; occasions were not unknown when his almost motionless figure would be in this same place at daybreak. He never slept through these nights, and he never even dozed; he was wide awake, and his mind was silently working upon the particular problem that was uppermost in his thoughts. He never rose until he had solved it or at least until he had decided upon a course of action. He would then get up abruptly, go to bed, and sleep like a child. The one thing that made it possible for a man of his delicate frame, racked as it was by anxiety and over work, to keep steadily at his task, was the wonderful gift which he possessed of sleeping.

Page had thought out many problems in this way. The tension caused by the sailing of the *Dacia*, in January, 1915, and the deftness with which the issue had been avoided by substituting a French for a British cruiser, has already been described. Page discovered this solution on one of these all-night self-communings. It was almost two o'clock in the morning that he rose, said to himself, "I've got it!" and then went contentedly to bed. And during the anxious months that followed the *Lusitania*, the *Arabic*, and those other outrages which have now taken their place in history, he spent night after night turning the matter over in his mind. But he found no way out of the humiliations presented by the policy of Washington.

"Here we are swung loose in time," he wrote to his son Arthur, a few days after the first *Lusitania* note had been sent to Germany, "nobody knows the day or the week or the month or the year—and we are caught on this island, with no chance of escape, while the vast slaughter goes on and seems just beginning, and the degradation of war goes on week by week; and we live in hope that the United States will come in, as the only chance to give us standing and influence when the reorganization of the world must begin. (Beware of betraying the word 'hope'!) It has all passed far beyond anybody's power to describe. I simply go on day by day into unknown experiences and emotions, seeing nothing before me very clearly and re-membering only dimly what lies behind. I can see only one proper thing: that all the world should fall to and hunt this wild beast down.

"Two photographs of little Mollie[1] on my mantelpiece recall persons and scenes and hopes unconnected with the war: few other things can. Bless the baby, she couldn't guess what a sweet purpose she serves."

The sensations of most Americans in London during this crisis are almost indescribable. Washington's failure promptly to meet the situation affected them with aston-ishment and humiliation. Colonel House was confident that war was impending, and for this reason he hurried his preparations to leave England; he wished to be in the United States, at the President's side, when the declara-tion was made. With this feeling about Mr. Wilson,

---

[1] The Ambassador's granddaughter.

Colonel House received a fearful shock a day or two after the *Lusitania* had gone down: while walking in Piccadilly, he caught a glimpse of one of the famous sandwich men, bearing a poster of an afternoon newspaper. This glaring broadside bore the following legend: "We are too proud to fight—Woodrow Wilson." The sight of that placard was Colonel House's first intimation that the President might not act vigorously. He made no attempt to conceal from Page and other important men at the American Embassy the shock which it had given him. Soon the whole of England was ringing with these six words; the newspapers were filled with stinging editorials and cartoons, and the music halls found in the Wilsonian phrase materials for their choicest jibes. Even in more serious quarters America was the subject of the most severe denunciation. No one felt these strictures more poignantly than President Wilson's closest confidant. A day or two before sailing home he came into the Embassy greatly depressed at the prevailing revulsion against the United States. "I feel," Colonel House said to Page, "as though I had been given a kick at every lamp post coming down Constitution Hill." A day or two afterward Colonel House sailed for America.

II

And now came the period of distress and of disillusionment. Three *Lusitania* notes were sent and were evasively answered, and Washington still seemed to be marking time. The one event in this exciting period which gave Page satisfaction was Mr. Bryan's resignation as Secretary of State. For Mr. Bryan personally Page had a certain fondness, but as head of the State Department the Nebraska orator had been a cause of endless vexation. Many of Page's letters, already printed, bear evidence of the utter demoralization which existed in this branch of the Administration and this demoralization became especially glaring during the *Lusitania* crisis. No attempt was made even at this momentous period to keep the London Embassy informed as to what was taking place in Washington; Page's letters and cablegrams were, for the most part, unacknowledged and unanswered, and the American Ambassador was frequently obliged to obtain his information about the state of feeling in Washington from Sir Edward Grey. It must be said, in justice to Mr. Bryan, that this carelessness was nothing particularly new, for it had worried many ambassadors before Page. Readers of Charles Francis Adams's correspondence meet with the same complaints during the Civil War; even at the time of the *Trent* crisis, when for a fortnight Great Britain and the United States were living on the brink of war, Adams was kept entirely in the dark about the plans of Washington.[1] The letters of John Hay show a similar condition during his brief ambassadorship to Great Britain in 1897–1898.[2]

But Mr. Bryan's incumbency was guilty of diplomatic vices which were peculiarly its own. The "leaks" in the State Department, to which Page has already referred, were constantly taking place; the Ambassador would send the most confidential cipher dispatches to his superior, cautioning the Department that they must be held inviolably secret, and then he would pick up the London newspapers the next morning and find that everything had been cabled from Washington. To most readers, the informal method of conducting foreign business, as it is disclosed in these letters, probably comes as something of

[1] "A Cycle of Adams Letters, 1861–1865," edited by Worthington Chauncey Ford. Vol. I, p. 84.

[2] "The Life and Letters of John Hay," by William Roscoe Thayer. Vol. II, p. 166.

a shock. Page is here discovered discussing state matters, not in correspondence with the Secretary of State, but in private unofficial communications to the President, and especially to Colonel House—the latter at that time not an official person at all. All this, of course, was extremely irregular and, in any properly organized State Department, it would have been even reprehensible. But the point is that there was no properly organized State Department at that time, and the impossibility of conducting business through the regular channels compelled Page to adopt other means. "There is only one way to reform the State Department," he informed Colonel House at this time. "That is to raze the whole building, with its archives and papers, to the ground, and begin all over again."

This state of affairs in Washington explains the curious fact that the real diplomatic history of the United States and Great Britain during this great crisis is not to be found in the archives of the State Department, for the official documents on file there consist of the most routine telegrams, which are not particularly informing, but in the Ambassador's personal correspondence with the President, Colonel House, and a few other intimates. The State Department did not have the first requisite of a properly organized foreign office, for it could not be trusted with confidential information. The Department did not tell Page what it was doing, but it apparently told the whole world what Page was doing. It is an astonishing fact that Page could not write and cable the most important details, for he was afraid that they would promptly be given to the reporters.

"I shall not send another confidential message to the State Department," Page wrote to Colonel House,

September 15, 1914; "it's too dangerous. Time and time again now the Department has leaked. Last week, I sent a dispatch and I said in the body of it, *'this is confidential and under no condition to be given out or made public, but to be regarded as inviolably secret.'* The very next morning it was telegraphed from Washington to the London newspapers. Bryan telegraphed me that he was sure it didn't get out from the Department and that he now had so fixed it that there could be no leak. He's said that at least four times before. The Department swarms with newspaper men, I hear. But whether it does or not the leak continues. I have to go with my tail between my legs and apologize to Sir Edward Grey and to do myself that shame and to do my very best to keep his confidence— against these unnecessary odds. The only way to be safe is to do the job perfunctorily, to answer the questions the Department sends and to do nothing on your own account. That's the reason so many of our men do their jobs in that way—or *one* reason and a strong one. We can never have an alert and energetic and powerful service until men can trust the Department and until they can get necessary information from it. I wrote the President that of course I'd go on till the war ended and all the questions growing out of it were settled, and that then he must excuse me, if I must continue to be exposed to this danger and humiliation. In the meantime, I shall send all my confidential matter in private letters to him."

Page did not regard Mr. Bryan's opinions and attitudes as a joke: to him they were a serious matter and, in his eyes, Bryan was most interesting as a national menace. He regarded the Secretary as the extreme expression of an irrational sentimentalism that was in danger of undermining the American character, especially as the kind of thought he represented was manifest in many phases of American life. In a moment of exasperation, Page gave expression to this feeling in a letter to his son:

To Arthur W. Page

London, June 6, 1915.

DEAR ARTHUR:

. . . We're in danger of being feminized and fad-ridden—grape juice (God knows water's good enough: why grape juice?); pensions; Christian Science; peace cranks; efficiency-correspondence schools; aid-your-memory; women's clubs; co-this and co-t'other and coddling in general; Billy Sunday; petticoats where breeches ought to be and breeches where petticoats ought to be; white livers and soft heads and milk-and-water;—I don't want war: nobody knows its horrors or its degradations or its cost. But to get rid of hyphenated degenerates perhaps it's worth while, and to free us from 'isms and soft folk. That's the domestic view of it. As for being kicked by a sauerkraut caste—O Lord, give us backbone!

Heartily yours,

W. H. P.

In the bottom of this note, Page has cut a notch in the paper and against it he has written: "This notch is the place to apply a match to this letter."

"Again and ever I am reminded," Page also wrote in reference to Bryan's resignation, "of the danger of having to do with cranks. A certain orderliness of mind and conduct seems essential for safety in this short life. Spiritualists, bone-rubbers, anti-vivisectionists, all sort of anti's in fact, those who have fads about education or fads against it, Perfectionists, Daughters of the Dove of Peace, Sons of the Roaring Torrent, itinerant peace-mongers—all these may have a real genius among them once in forty years; but to look for an exception to the common run of yellow dogs and damfools among them is like opening oysters with the hope of finding pearls. It's the common man we want and the uncommon common man when we can find him—never the crank. This is the lesson of Bryan."

At one time, however, Mr. Bryan's departure seemed likely to have important consequences for Page. Colonel House and others strongly urged the President to call him home from London and make him Secretary of State. This was the third position in President Wilson's Cabinet for which Page had been considered. The early plans to make him Secretary of the Interior or Secretary of Agriculture have already been described. Of all cabinet posts, however, the one that would have especially attracted him would have been the Department of State. But President Wilson believed that the appointment of an Ambassador at one of the belligerent capitals, especially of an Ambassador whose sympathies for the Allies were so pronounced as were Page's, would have been an "unneutral" act, and, therefore, Colonel House's recommendation was not approved.

From Edward M. House

Roslyn, Long Island,
June 25th, 1915.

DEAR PAGE:

The President finally decided to appoint Lansing to succeed Mr. Bryan. In my opinion, he did wisely, though I would have preferred his appointing you.

The argument against your appointment was the fact that you are an Ambassador at one of the belligerent

capitals.   The President did not think it would do, and
from what I read, when your name was suggested I take
it there would have been much criticism.   I am sorry—
sorrier than I can tell you, for it would have worked ad-
mirably in the general scheme of things.

However, I feel sure that Lansing will do the job, and
that you will find your relations with him in every way
satisfactory.

The President spent yesterday with me and we talked
much of you.   He is looking well and feeling so.

I read the President your letter and he enjoyed it as
much as I did.

I am writing hastily, for I am leaving for Manchester,
Massachusetts, where I shall be during July and August.

Your sincere friend,

E. M. House.

III

But, in addition to the *Lusitania* crisis, a new terror now
loomed on the horizon.   Page's correspondence reveals
that Bryan had more reasons than one for his resignation;
he was now planning to undertake a self-appointed mission
to Europe for the purpose of opening peace negotiations
entirely on his own account.

From Edward M. House

Manchester, Massachusetts,
August 12th, 1915.

DEAR PAGE:

The Bryans have been stopping with the X's. X
writes me that Bryan told him that he intended to go to
Europe soon and try peace negotiations. He has Lloyd
George in mind in England, and it is then his purpose to
go to Germany.

I take it he will want credentials from the President which, of course, he will not want to give, but just what he will feel obliged to give is another story. I anticipated this when he resigned. I knew it was merely a matter of time when he would take this step.

He may find encouragement in Germany, for he is in high favour now in that quarter. It is his purpose to oppose the President upon the matter of "preparedness," and, from what we can learn, it will not be long before there will be open antagonism between the Administration and himself.

It might be a good thing to encourage his going to Europe. He would probably come back a sadder and wiser man. I take it that no one in authority in England would discuss the matter seriously with him, and, in France, I do not believe he could even get a hearing.

Please let me have your impressions upon this subject.

I wish I could be near you to-day for there are so many things I could tell that I cannot write.

Your friend,
E. M. House.

To Edward M. House

American Embassy, London [Undated].

DEAR HOUSE:

Never mind about Bryan. Send him over here if you wish to get rid of him. He'll cut no more figure than a tar-baby at a Negro camp-meeting. If he had come while he was Secretary, I should have jumped off London Bridge and the country would have had one ambassador less. But I shall enjoy him now. You see some peace crank from the United States comes along every week— some crank or some gang of cranks. There've been two this week. Ever since the Daughters of the Dove of

Peace met at The Hague, the game has become popular in America; and I haven't yet heard that a single one has been shot—so far. I think that some of them are likely soon to be hanged, however, because there are signs that they may come also from Germany. The same crowd that supplies money to buy labour-leaders and the press and to blow up factories in the United States keeps a good supply of peace-liars on tap. It'll be fun to watch Bryan perform and never suspect that anybody is lying to him or laughing at him; and he'll go home convinced that he's done the job and he'll let loose doves all over the land till they are as thick as English sparrows. Not even the President could teach him anything permanently. He can do no harm on this side the world. It's only your side that's in any possible danger; and, if I read the signs right, there's a diminishing danger there.

No, there's never yet come a moment when there was the slightest chance of peace. Did the Emperor not say last year that peace would come in October, and again this year in October? Since he said it, how can it come?

The ambitions and the actions of men, my friend, are determined by their antecedents, their surroundings, and their opportunities—the great deeds of men before them whom consciously or unconsciously they take for models, the codes they are reared by, and the chances that they think they see. These influences shaped Alexander and Cæsar, and they shaped you and me. Now every monarch on the Continent has behind him the Napoleonic example. "Can I do that?" crosses the mind of every one. Of course every one thinks of himself as doing it beneficently—for the good of the world. Napoleon, himself, persuaded himself of his benevolent intentions, and the devil of it was he persuaded other people also. Now the only monarch in Europe in our time who thought he had a chance is your friend in Berlin. When he told you last year (1914) that of course he didn't want war, but that he was "ready," that's what he meant. A similar ambition, of course, comes into the mind of every professional soldier of the continent who rises to eminence. In Berlin you have both—the absolute monarch and the military class of ambitious soldiers and their fighting machine. Behind these men walks the Napoleonic ambition all the time, just as in the United States we lie down every night in George Washington's feather-bed of no entangling alliances.

Then remember, too, that the German monarchy is a cross between the Napoleonic ambition and its inheritance from Frederick the Great and Bismarck. I suppose the three damnedest liars that were ever born are these three—old Frederick, Napoleon, and Bismarck—not, I take it, because they naturally loved lying, but because the game they played constantly called for lying. There was no other way to play it: they *had* to fool people all the time. You have abundant leisure—do this: Read the whole career of Napoleon and write down the startling and exact parallels that you will find there to what is happening to-day. The French were united and patriotic, just as the Germans now are. When they invaded other people's territory, they said they were attacked and that the other people had brought on war. They had their lying diplomats, their corruption funds; they levied money on cities and states; they took booty; and they were God's elect. It's a wonderful parallel—not strangely, because the game is the same and the moral methods are the same. Only the tools are somewhat different—the submarine, for example. Hence the *Lusitania* disaster (not disavowed, you will observe), the *Arabic* disaster, the propaganda, underground and above, in the United States. And there'll be more.   The Napoleonic Wars were about eleven years long.   I fancy that we shall have war and wars from this attempt to dominate Europe, for perhaps as long a period.   The Balkans can't be quieted by this war only, nor Russia and Italy perhaps.   And Germany may have a series of earthquakes herself—internal explosions. Then Poland and perhaps some of the Scandinavian States.   Nobody can tell.

I cannot express my admiration of the President's management, so far at least, of his colossal task of leading us right.   He has shown his supreme wisdom up to this point and I have the profoundest confidence in his judgment.   But I hope he doesn't fool himself about the future; I'm sure he doesn't.   I see no possible way for us to keep out, because I know the ignorance and falseness of the German leaders.   They'll drown or kill more Americans—on the sea and in America.   They *may* at last even attack one of our own passenger ships, or do something that will dramatically reveal them to the whole American people.   Then, of course, the tune will be called.   It's only a question of time; and I am afraid the war will last long enough to give them time.   An early peace is all that can prevent them from driving us at last into war; and I can see no chance of an early peace.   You had as well prepare as fast as the condition of public opinion will permit.

There could be no better measure of the immeasurable moral advance that the United States has made over Europe than the incredulity of our people.   They simply can't comprehend what the Napoleonic legend can do, nor the low political morality of the Continent—of Berlin in particular.   Hence they don't believe it.   We have gone on for 100 years working might and main to better our condition and the condition of people about us—the greatest effort made by the largest number of people since the world began to further the mood and the arts of peace. There is no other such chapter in human history as our work for a hundred years.   Yet just a hundred years ago the Capitol at Washington was burned by—a political oligarchy in the freest country of Europe—as damnable an atrocity as you will find in history.   The Germans are a hundred years behind the English in political development and political morality.

So, let Willum J. come.   He can't hurt Europe—nor help it; and you can spare him.   Let all the Peace-gang come.   You can spare *them*, too; and they can do no harm here.   Let somebody induce Hoke Smith to come, too. You have hit on a great scheme—friendly deportation.

And Bryan won't be alone.   Daughters of the Dove of Peace and Sons of the Olive Branch come every week. The latest Son came to see me to-day.   He said that the German Chancellor told him that he wanted peace— wants it now and wants it bad, and that only one thing stood in the way—if England would agree not to take Belgium, Germany would at once make peace!   This otherwise sensible American wanted me to take him to see Sir Edward to tell him this, and to suggest to him to go over to Holland next week to meet the German Chancellor and fix it up.   A few days ago a pious preacher chap (American) who had come over to "fix it all up," came back from France and called on me.   He had seen something in France—he was excited and he didn't quite make it clear what he had seen; but he said that if they'd only let him go home safely and quickly he'd promise not to mention peace any more—did I think the American boats *entirely* safe?—So, you see, I do have some fun even in these dark days.

Yours heartily,

W. H. PAGE.

IV

This letter discloses that Page was pinning his faith in President Wilson, and that he still had confidence in the President's determination to uphold the national honour. Page was not one of those who thought that the United States should declare war immediately after the *Lusitania*. The President's course, in giving Germany a chance to make amends, and to disavow the act, met with his approval, and he found, also, much to admire in Mr. Wilson's first *Lusitania* note. His judgment in this matter was based first of all upon the merits of the case; besides this, his admiration for Mr. Wilson as a public man was strong. To think otherwise of the President would have been a great grief to the Ambassador and to differ with his chief on the tremendous issue of the war would have meant for Page the severance of one of the most cherished associations of his life. The interest which he had shown in advocating Wilson's presidential candidacy has already been set forth; and many phases of the Wilson administration had aroused his admiration. The President's handling of domestic problems Page regarded as a masterpiece in reconciling statesmanship with practical politics, and his energetic attitude on the Panama Tolls had introduced new standards into American foreign relations. Page could not sympathize with all the details of the Wilsonian Mexican policy, yet he saw in it a high-minded purpose and a genuine humanitarianism. But the outbreak of war presented new aspects of Mr. Wilson's mind. The President's attitude toward the European struggle, his conception of "neutrality," and his failure to grasp the meaning of the conflict, seemed to Page to show a lack of fundamental statesmanship; still his faith in Wilson was deep-seated, and he did not abandon hope that the

President could be brought to see things as they really were.   Page even believed that he might be instrumental in his conversion.

But in the summer and autumn of 1915 one agony followed another.   The "too proud to fight" speech was in Page's mind nothing less than a tragedy.   The president's first *Lusitania* note for a time restored the Ambassador's confidence; it seemed to show that the President intended to hold Germany to that "strict accountability" which he had threatened.   But Mr. Wilson's course now presented new difficulties to his Ambassador.   Still Page believed that the President, in his own way and in his own time, would find a path out of his dilemma that would protect the honour and the safety of the United States.   If any of the Embassy subordinates became impatient over the procedure of Washington, he did not find a sympathetic listener in the Ambassador. The whole of London and of Europe might be resounding with denunciations of the White House, but Page would tolerate no manifestations of hostility in his presence. "The problem appears different to Washington than it does to us," he would say to his confidants.   "We see only one side of it; the President sees all sides.   If we give him all the facts, he will decide the thing wisely."   Englishmen with whom the Ambassador came into contact soon learned that they could not become flippant or critical about Mr. Wilson in his presence; he would resent the slightest hostile remark, and he had a way of phrasing his rebukes that usually discouraged a second attempt. About this time Page began to keep closely to himself, and to decline invitations to dinners and to country houses, even those with which he was most friendly.   The reason was that he could not meet Englishmen and Englishwomen, or even Americans who were resident in England, on his old easy familiar terms; he knew the ideas which everybody entertained about his country, and he knew also what they were saying, when he was not among them; the restraint which his presence necessarily put upon his friends produced an uncongenial atmosphere, and the Ambassador therefore gave up, for a time, those distractions which had ordinarily proved such a delightful relief from his duties. For the first time since he had come to England he found himself a solitary man. He even refused to attend the American Luncheon Club in London because, in speeches and in conversation, the members did not hesitate to assail the Wilson policies.

Events, however, eventually proved too strong for the most devoted supporter of President Wilson. After the *Arabic* and the *Hesperian*, Page's official intimates saw signs that the Ambassador was losing confidence in his old friend. He would discuss Mr. Wilson occasionally, with those secretaries, such as Mr. Laughlin, in whom his confidence was strongest; his expressions, however, were never flippant or violent. That Page could be biting as well as brilliant in his comments on public personages his letters abundantly reveal, yet he never exercised his talent for sarcasm or invective at the expense of the White House. He never forgot that Mr. Wilson was President and that he was Ambassador; he would still defend the Administration; and he even now continued to find consolation in the reflection that Mr. Wilson was living in a different atmosphere and that he had difficulties to confront of which a man in London could know nothing. The Ambassador's emotion was rather one of disappointment and sorrow, mingled with anxiety as to the plight into which his country was being led. As to his duty in this situation, however, Page never hesitated. In his relations with his Embassy and with the

British world he maintained this non-critical attitude; but in his letters to President Wilson and Colonel House, he was describing the situation, and expressing his convictions, with the utmost freedom and frankness. In both these attitudes Page was consistent and absolutely loyal. It was his duty to carry out the Wilson instructions and he had too high a conception of the Ambassadorial office to show to the world any unfavourable opinions he may have held about his country's course. His duty to his post made it just as imperative that he set forth to the President the facts exactly as they were. And this the Ambassador now proceeded to do. For the mere ornamental dignities of an Ambassadorship Page cared nothing; he was wasting his health in his duties and exhausting his private resources; much as he loved the English and congenial as were his surroundings, the fear of being recalled for "disloyalty" or insubordination never influenced him. The letters which he now wrote to Colonel House and to President Wilson himself are probably without parallel in the diplomatic annals of this or of any other country. In them he told the President precisely what Englishmen thought of him and of the extent to which the United States was suffering in European estimation from the Wilson policy. His boldness sometimes astounded his associates. One day a friend and adviser of President Wilson's came into the Ambassador's office just as Page had finished one of his communications to Washington.

"Read that!" the Ambassador said, handing over the manuscript to his visitor.

As the caller read, his countenance displayed the progressive stages of his amazement. When he had finished, his hands dropped helplessly upon his knees.

"Is that the way you write to the President?" he gasped.

"Of course," Page replied, quietly. "Why not? Why shouldn't I tell him the truth? That is what I am here for."

"There is no other person in the world who dare talk to him like that!" was the reply.

This is unquestionably the fact. That President Wilson did not like people about him whose views were opposed to his own is now no secret, and during the period when his policy was one of the great issues of the world there was probably no one except Page who intruded upon his solitude with ideas that so abruptly disagreed with the opinions of the White House. The letters which Page wrote Colonel House were intended, of course, for the President himself, and practically all of them Colonel House read aloud to the head of the nation. The two men would closet themselves in the old cabinet room on the second floor of the White House—that same room in which Lincoln had met his advisers during Civil War days; and here Colonel House would quietly read the letters in which Page so mercilessly portrayed the situation as it appeared in English and European eyes. The President listened impassively, giving no sign of approval or disapproval, and hardly, at times, of much interest. In the earlier days, when Page's letters consisted of pictures of English life and English men, and colourful descriptions of England under the stress of war, the President was vastly entertained; he would laugh loudly at Page's wit, express his delight at his graphic and pungent style and feel deeply the horrors of war as his Ambassador unfolded them. "I always found Page compelling on paper," Mr. Wilson remarked to Mr. Laughlin, during one of the latter's visits to Washington. "I could never resist him—I get more information from his letters than from any other single source. Tell him to keep it up." It was during this period that the President used occasionally to read Page's letters to the Cabinet, expressing his great appreciation of their charm and historical importance. "The President quoted from one of the Ambassador's letters to the Cabinet to-day," a member of the Cabinet wrote to Mrs. Page in February, 1915. "'Some day,' the President said, 'I hope that Walter Page's letters will be published. They are the best letters I have ever read. They make you feel the atmosphere in England, understand the people, and see into the motives of the great actors.'" The President repeated this statement many times, and his letters to Page show how greatly he enjoyed and profited from this correspondence. But after the sinking of the *Lusitania* and the *Arabic* his attitude toward Page and his letters changed.

He now found little pleasure or satisfaction in the Page communications. When Mr. Wilson found that one of his former confidants had turned out to be a critic, that man instantaneously passed out of his life. And this was now Page's fate; the friendship and associations of forty years were as though they had never been. Just why Mr. Wilson did not recall his Ambassador is a question that has puzzled Page's friends. He would sometimes refer to him as a man who was "more British than the British," as one who had been taken completely captive by British blandishments, but he never came to the point of dismissing him. Perhaps he did not care to face the public scandal that such an act would have caused; but a more plausible reason is that Page, despite the causes which he had given for irritation, was indispensable to him. Page's early letters had furnished the President ideas which had taken shape in Wilson's policies, and, disagreeable as the communications now became, there are evidences that they influenced the solitary statesman in the White House, and that they had much to do in finally forcing Mr. Wilson into the war. The alternative question, as to why Page did not retire when he found himself so out of sympathy with the President, will be sufficiently answered in subsequent chapters; at present it may be said that he did resign and only consented to remain at the urgent request of Washington. In fact, all during 1915 and 1916, there seemed to be a fear in Washington that Page would definitely abandon the London post. On one occasion, when the newspapers published rumours to this effect, Page received an urgent despatch from Mr. Lansing. The message came at a time—the date was October 26, 1915—when Page was especially discouraged over the Washington policy. "Representatives of the press," said Mr. Lansing, "have repeated rumours that you are planning to resign. These have been brought to the President's attention, and both he and I have denied them. Still these rumours persist, and they cause both the President and me great anxiety. We cannot believe that they are well founded.

"In view of the fact that they are so persistent, we have thought it well to inform you of them and to tell you how earnestly we hope that they are baseless. We trust that you will set both our minds at rest."

If Page had ever had any compunction about addressing the President in blunt phrases these expressions certainly convinced him that he was a free agent.

Yet Page himself at times had his doubts as to the value of this correspondence. He would frequently discuss the matter with Mr. Laughlin. "That's a pretty harsh letter," he would say. "I don't like to talk that way to the President, yet it doesn't express half what I feel."

"It's your duty to tell the President the real state of affairs," Mr. Laughlin would urge.

"But do you suppose it does any good?" Page would ask.

"Yes, it's bound to, and whether it does or not, it's your business to keep him informed."

If in these letters Page seems to lay great stress on the judgment of Great Britain and Europe on American policy, it must be remembered that that was his particular province. One of an Ambassador's most important duties is to transmit to his country the public opinion of the country to which he is accredited. It was Page's place to tell Washington what Great Britain thought of it; it was Washington's business to formulate policy, after giving due consideration to this and other matters.

To Edward M. House

July 21, 1915.

DEAR HOUSE:

I enclose a pamphlet in ridicule of the President. I don't know who wrote it, for my inquiries so far have brought no real information. I don't feel like sending it to him. I send it to you—to do with as you think best. This thing alone is, of course, of no consequence. But it is symptomatic. There is much feeling about the slowness with which he acts. One hundred and twenty people (Americans) were drowned on the *Lusitania* and we are still writing notes about it—to the damnedest pirates that ever blew up a ship. Anybody who knows the Germans knows, of course, that they are simply playing for time, that they are not going to "come down," that Von Tirpitz is on deck, that they'd just as lief have war with us as not —perhaps had rather—because they don't want any large nation left fresh when the war ends. They'd like to have the whole world bankrupt. There is a fast growing feeling here, therefore, that the American Government is pusillanimous —dallies with 'em, is affected by the German propaganda, etc., etc. Of course, such a judgment is not fair.

It is formed without knowing the conditions in the United States.   But I think you ought to realize the strength of this sentiment.   No doubt before you receive this, the President will send something to Germany that will amount to an ultimatum and there will be at least a momentary change of sentiment here.   But looking at the thing in a long-range way, we're bound to get into the war. For the Germans will blow up more American travellers without notice.   And by dallying with them we do not change the ultimate result, but we take away from ourselves the spunk and credit of getting in instead of being kicked and cursed in.   We've got to get in: they won't play the game in any other way.   I have news direct from a high German source in Berlin which strongly confirms this. . . .

It's a curious thing to say.   But the only solution that I see is another *Lusitania* outrage, which would force war.

W. H. P.

P. S.   The London papers every day say that the President will send a strong note, etc.   And the people here say, "Damn notes: hasn't he written enough?"   Writing notes hurts nobody—changes nothing.   The Washington correspondents to the London papers say that Burleson, the Attorney-General, and Daniels are Bryan men and are holding the President back.

The prophecy contained in this letter was quickly fulfilled.   A week or two after Colonel House had received it, the *Arabic* was sunk with loss of American life.

Page was taking a brief holiday with his son Frank in Rowsley, Derbyshire, when this news came.   It was telegraphed from the Embassy.

"That settles it," he said to his son.   "They have sunk the *Arabic*.   That means that we shall break with Germany and I've got to go back to London."

To Edward M. House

American Embassy, London, August 23, 1915.

DEAR HOUSE:

The sinking of the *Arabic* is the answer to the President and to your letter to me. And there'll be more such answers. You said to me one day after you had got back from your last visit to Berlin: "They are impossible." I think you told the truth, and surely you know your German and you know your Berlin—or you did know them when you were here.

The question is not what we have done for the Allies, not what any other neutral country has done or has failed to do—such comparisons, I think, are far from the point. The question is when the right moment arrives for us to save our self-respect, our honour, and the esteem and fear (or the contempt) in which the world will hold us.

Berlin has the Napoleonic disease. If you follow Napoleon's career—his excuses, his evasions, his inventions, the wild French enthusiasm and how he kept it up—you will find an exact parallel. That becomes plainer every day. Europe may not be wholly at peace in five years—may be ten.

Hastily and heartily,

W. H. P.

I have your note about Willum J. . . . Crank once, crank always. My son, never tie up with a crank. W. H. P.

To Edward M. House

London, September 2nd, 1915.

DEAR HOUSE:

You write me about pleasing the Allies, the big Ally in particular. That doesn't particularly appeal to me. We don't owe them anything. There's no obligation. I'd never confess for a moment that we are under any obligation to any of them nor to anybody. I'm not out to "please" anybody, as a primary purpose: that's not my game nor my idea—nor yours either. As for England in particular, the account was squared when she twice sent an army against us—in her folly—especially the last time when she burnt our Capitol. There's been no obligation since. The obligation is on the other foot. We've set her an example of what democracy will do for men, an example of efficiency, an example of freedom of opportunity. The future is ours, and she may follow us and profit by it. Already we have three white English-speaking men to every two in the British Empire: we are sixty per cent. of the Anglo-Saxons in the world. If there be any obligation to please, the obligation is on her to please us. And she feels and sees it now.

My point is not that, nor is it what we or any other neutral nation has done or may do—Holland or any other. This war is the direct result of the over-polite, diplomatic, standing-aloof, bowing-to-one-another in gold lace, which all European nations are guilty of in times of peace—castes and classes and uniforms and orders and such folderol, instead of the proper business of the day. Every nation in Europe knew that Germany was preparing for war. If they had really got together—not mere Hague Sunday-school talk and resolutions—but had really got together for business and had said to Germany, "The moment you fire a shot, we'll all fight against you; we have so many millions of men, so many men-of-war, so many billions of money; and we'll increase all these if you do not change your system and your building-up of armies"—then there would have been no war.

My point is not sentimental.   It is:

(1)   We must maintain our own self-respect and safety.   If we submit to too many insults, *that* will in time bring Germany against us.   We've got to show at some time that we don't believe, either, in the efficacy of Sunday-School resolves for peace—that we are neither Daughters of the Dove of Peace nor Sons of the Olive Branch, and

(2)   About nagging and forever presenting technical legal points as lawyers do to confuse juries—the point is the point of efficiency.   If we do that, we can't carry our main points.   I find it harder and harder to get answers now to important questions because we ask so many unimportant and nagging ones.

I've no sentiment—perhaps not enough.   My gushing days are gone, if I ever had 'em.   The cutting-out of the "100 years of peace" oratory, etc., etc., was one of the blessings of the war.   But we must be just and firm and preserve our own self-respect and keep alive the fear that other nations have of us; and we ought to have the courage to make the Department of State more than a bureau of complaints.   We must learn to say "No" even to a Gawdamighty independent American citizen when he asks an improper or impracticable question.   Public opinion in the United States consists of something more than the threats of Congressmen and the bleating of newspapers; it consists of the judgment of honourable men on courageous and frank actions—a judgment that cannot be made up till action is taken.

Heartily yours,

W. H. P.

To Edward M. House

American Embassy, London, Sept. 8, 1915.
(This is not prudent.   It is only true—nothing more.)
DEAR HOUSE:

I take it for granted that Dumba[1] is going, of course.
But I must tell you that the President is being laughed
at by our best friends for his slowness in action.   I hardly
ever pick up a paper without seeing some sarcastic remark.   I don't mean they expect us to come into the war.
They only hoped we would be as good as our word—
would regard another submarine attack on a ship carrying Americans as an unfriendly act and would send Bernstorff home.   Yet the *Arabic* and now the *Hesperian* have
had no effect in action.   Bernstorff's personal *note to
Lansing,*[2] *even as far as it goes, does not bind his Government.*

The upshot of all this is that the President is fast losing
in the minds of our best friends here all that he gained
by his courageous stand on the Panama tolls.   They feel
that if he takes another insult—keeps taking them—and
is satisfied with Bernstorff's personal word, which is
proved false in four days—he'll take anything.   And the
British will pay less attention to what we say.   That's
inevitable.   If the American people and the President
accept the *Arabic* and the *Hesperian* and do nothing to
Dumba till the Government here gave out his letter,
which the State Department had (and silently held) for

---

[1] On September 6th, certain documents seriously compromising Dr. Constantin
Dumba, Austro-Hungarian Ambassador to the United States, were published in
the British press.   They disclosed that Dr. Dumba was fomenting strikes in the
United States and conducting other intrigues.   The American Government gave
Dr. Dumba his passports on September 17th.

[2] On August 26th, Count Bernstorff gave a pledge to the United States Government, that, in future, German submarines would not attack liners without warning.   This promise was almost immediately violated.

several days—then nobody on this side the world will pay much heed to anything we say hereafter.

This, as I say, doesn't mean that these (thoughtful) people wish or expect us to go to war. They wish only that we'd prove ourselves as good as the President's word. That's the conservative truth; we're losing influence more rapidly than I supposed it were possible.

Dumba's tardy dismissal will not touch the main matter, which is the rights of neutrals at sea, and keeping our word in action.

Yours sincerely,

W. H. P.

P. S. They say it's Mexico over again—watchful waiting and nothing doing. And the feeling grows that Bryan has really conquered, since his programme seems to prevail.

To Edward M. House

London, Tuesday night, Sept. 8, 1915.

DEAR HOUSE:

The Germans seem to think it a good time to try to feel about for peace. They have more to offer now than they may have again. That's all. A man who seriously talks peace now in Paris or in London on any terms that the Germans will consider, would float dead that very night in the Seine or in the Thames. The Germans have for the time being "done-up" the Russians; but the French have shells enough to plough the German trenches day and night (they've been at it for a fortnight now); Joffre has been to see the Italian generalissimo; and the English destroy German submarines now almost as fast as the Germans send them out. I am credibly told that several weeks ago a group of Admiralty men who are in the secret had a little dinner to celebrate the destruction of the 50th submarine.

While this is going on, you are talking on your side of the water about a change in German policy! The only change is that the number of submarines available becomes smaller and smaller, and that they wish to use Uncle Sam's broad, fat back to crawl down on when they have failed.

Consequently, they are laughing at Uncle Sam here—it comes near to being ridicule, in fact, for seeming to jump at Bernstorff's unfrank assurances. And, as I have telegraphed the President, English opinion is—well, it is very nearly disrespectful. Men say here (I mean our old friends) that with no disavowal of the *Lusitania*, the *Falaba*, the *Gulflight*, or the *Arabic* or of the *Hesperian*, the Germans are "stuffing" Uncle Sam, that Uncle Sam is in the clutches of the peace-at-any-price public opinion, that the United States will suffer any insult and do nothing. I hardly pick up a paper that does not have a sarcastic paragraph or cartoon. We are on the brink of convincing the English that we'll not act, whatever the provocation. By the English, I do not mean the lighter, transitory public opinion, but I mean the thoughtful men who do not wish us or expect us to fire a gun. They say that the American democracy, since Cleveland's day, has become a mere agglomeration of different races, without national unity, national aims, and without courage or moral qualities. And (I deeply regret to say) the President is losing here the high esteem he won by his Panama tolls repeal. They ask, why on earth did he raise the issue if under repeated provocation he is unable to recall Gerard or to send Bernstorff home? The *Hesperian* follows the *Arabic;* other "liners" will follow the *Hesperian*, if the Germans have submarines.

And, when Sackville-West[1] was promptly sent home for answering a private citizen's inquiry about the two political parties, Dumba is (yet awhile) retained in spite of a far graver piece of business. There is a tone of sad disappointment here—not because the most thoughtful men want us in the war (they don't), but because for some reason, which nobody here understands, the President, having taken a stand, seems unable to do anything.

All this is a moderate interpretation of sorrowful public opinion here. And the result will inevitably be that they will pay far less heed to anything we may hereafter say. In fact men now say here every day that the American democracy has no opinion, can form no opinion, has no moral quality, and that the word of its President never gets as far as action even of the mildest form. The atmosphere is very depressing. And this feeling has apparently got beyond anybody's control. I've even heard this said: "The voice of the United States is Mr. Wilson's: its actions are controlled by Mr. Bryan."

So, you see, the war will go on a long long time. So far as English opinion is concerned, the United States is useful to make ammunition and is now thought of chiefly in this connection. Less and less attention is paid to what we say. Even the American telegrams to the London papers have a languid tone.

Yet recent revelations have made it clearer than ever that the same qualities that the English accuse us of having are in them and that these qualities are directly to blame for this war. I recall that when I was in Germany a few weeks, six years ago, I became convinced that

[1]Sir Lionel Sackville-West was British Minister to the United States from 1881 to 1888. In the latter year a letter was published which he had written to an American citizen of British origin, the gist of which was that the reëlection of President Cleveland would be of advantage to British interests. For this gross interference in American domestic affairs, President Cleveland immediately handed Sir Lionel his passports. The incident ended his diplomatic career.

Germany had prepared to fight England; I didn't know when, but I did know that was what the war-machine had in mind. Of course, I had no opportunities to find out anything in particular. You were told practically that same thing by the Kaiser, before the war began. "We are ready," said he. Of course the English feared it and Sir Edward put his whole life into his effort to prevent it. The day the war began, he told me with tears that it seemed that his life had been wasted—that his life work had gone for naught.—Nobody could keep from wondering why England didn't——

(Here comes a parenthesis. Word came to me a little while ago that a Zeppelin was on its way to London. Such a remark doesn't arouse much attention. But just as I had finished the fifth line above this, Frank and Mrs. Page came in and challenged me to play a game of cards before we should go to bed. We sat down, the cards were dealt, and bang! bang!—with the deep note of an explosion. A third, a fourth shot. We went into the street. There the Zeppelin was revealed by a searchlight —sailing along. I think it had probably dropped its bombs; but the aircraft guns were cracking away at it. Some of them shot explosive projectiles to find the range. Now and then one such explosive would almost reach the Zeppelin, but it was too high for them and it sailed away, the air guns doing their ineffectual best. I couldn't see whether airplanes were trying to shoot it or not. The searchlight revealed the Zeppelin but nothing else.— While we were watching this battle in the air, the maids came down from the top of the house and went into the cellar. I think they've already gone back. You can't imagine how little excitement it caused. It produces less fright than any other conceivable engine of war.

We came back as soon as the Zeppelin was out of sight

and the firing had ceased; we played our game of cards; and here I am writing you the story—all within about half an hour.—There was a raid over London last night, too, wherein a dozen or two women and children and a few men were killed. I haven't the slightest idea what harm this raid to-night has done. For all I know it may not be all done. But of all imaginable war-experiences this seems the most futile. It interrupted a game of cards for twenty minutes!)

Now—to go on with my story: I have wondered ever since the war began why the Allies were not better pre-pared—especially England on land. England has just one *big* land gun—no more. Now it has turned out, as you have doubtless read, that the British Government were as good as told by the German Government that Germany was going to war pretty soon—this in 1912 when Lord Haldane[1] was sent to make friends with Germany.

The only answer he brought back was a proposition that England should in any event remain neutral—stand aside while Germany whipped Russia and France. This insulting proposal was kept secret till the other day. Now, why didn't the British Cabinet inform the people and get ready? They were afraid the English people wouldn't believe it and would accuse them of fomenting war. The English people were making money and pur-suing their sports. Probably they wouldn't have be-lieved it. So the Liberal Cabinet went on in silence, knowing that war was coming, but not exactly when it was coming, and they didn't make even a second big gun.

---

[1] In this passage the Ambassador touches on one of the bitterest controversies of the war. In order completely to understand the issues involved and to obtain Lord Haldane's view, the reader should consult the very valuable book recently published by Lord Haldane: "Before the War." Chapter II tells the story of Lord Haldane's visit to the Kaiser, and succeeding chapters give the reasons why the creation of a huge British army in preparation for the war was not a simple matter.

Now here was the same silence in this "democracy" that they now complain of in ours. Rather an interesting and discouraging parallel—isn't it? Public opinion has turned Lord Haldane out of office because he didn't tell the public what he declares they wouldn't have believed. If the English had raised an army in 1912, and made a lot of big guns, Austria would not have trampled Serbia in the earth. There would have been no war now; and the strong European Powers might have made then the same sort of protective peace-insurance combine that they will try to make after this war is ended. Query: A democracy's inability to *act*—how much is this apparently inherent quality of a democracy to blame for this war and for—other things?

When I am asked every day "Why the United States doesn't *do* something—send Dumba and Bernstorff home?"—Well, it is not the easiest question in the world to answer.

Yours heartily,

W. H. P.

P. S. This is the most comical of all worlds: While I was writing this, it seems the maids went back upstairs and lighted their lights without pulling their shades down —they occupy three rooms, in front. The doorbell rang furiously. Here were more than half a dozen policemen and special constables—must investigate! "One light would be turned on, another would go out; another one on!"—etc., etc. Frank tackled them, told 'em it was only the maids going to bed, forgetting to pull down the shades. Spies and signalling were in the air! So, in the morning, I'll have to send over to the Foreign Office and explain. The Zeppelin did more "frightfulness" than I had supposed, after all. Doesn't this strike you as comical?

W. H. P.

Friday, September 10, 1915.

P. S.   The news is just come that Dumba is dismissed. That will clear the atmosphere—a little, but only a little. Dumba committed a diplomatic offence.   The German Government has caused the death of United States citizens, has defied us, has declared it had changed its policy and yet has gone on with the same old policy.   Besides, Bernstorff has done everything that Dumba did except employ Archibald, which was a mere incident of the game.   The President took a strong stand: they have disregarded it—no apology nor reparation for a single boat that has been sunk.   Now the English opinion of the Germans is hardly a calm, judicial opinion—of course not.   There may be facts that have not been made known.   There must be good reasons that nobody here can guess, why the President doesn't act in the long succession of German acts against us.   *But I tell you with all solemnity that British opinion and the British Government have absolutely lost their respect for us and their former high estimate of the President.   And that former respect is gone for good unless he acts now very quickly.*[1]   They will pay nothing more than formal and polite attention to anything we may hereafter say.   This is not resentful. They don't particularly care for us to get into the war. Their feeling (I mean among our best old friends) is not resentful.   It is simply sorrowful.   They had the highest respect for our people and our President.   The Germans defy us; we sit in silence.   They conclude here that we'll submit to anything from anybody.   We'll write strong notes—nothing more.

I can't possibly exaggerate the revulsion of feeling. Members of the Government say (in private, of course) that we'll submit to any insult.   The newspapers refuse

[1]The italics are Page's.

to publish articles which attempt to make the President's silence reasonable. "It isn't defensible," they say, "and they would only bring us thousands of insulting letters from our readers." I can't think of a paper nor of a man who has a good word to say for us—except, perhaps, a few Quaker peace-at-any-price people. And our old friends are disappointed and sorrowful. They feel that we have dropped out of a position of influence in the world.

I needn't and can't write more. Of course there are more important things than English respect. But the English think that every Power has lost respect for us— the Germans most of all. And (unless the President acts very rigorously and very quickly) we'll have to get along a long time without British respect.

W. H. P.

P. S. The last Zeppelin raid—which interrupted the game of cards—killed more than twenty persons and destroyed more than seven million dollars' worth of private business property—all non-combatants'!

W. H. P.

To Edward M. House

21st of September, 1915.

DEAR HOUSE:

The insulting cartoon that I enclose (destroy it without showing it) is typical of, I suppose, five hundred that have appeared here within a month. This represents the feeling and opinion of the average man. They say we wrote brave notes and made courageous demands, to none of which a satisfactory reply has come, but only more outrages and no guarantee for the future. Yet we will not even show our displeasure by sending Bernstorff home. We've simply "gone out," like a snuffed candle, in the regard and respect of the vast volume of British opinion. (The last *Punch* had six ridiculing allusions to our "fall.")

It's the loneliest time I've had in England. There's a tendency to avoid me.

They can't understand here the continued declaration in the United States that the British Government is trying to take our trade—to use its blockade and navy with the direct purpose of giving British trade profit out of American detentions. Of course, the Government had no such purpose and has done no such thing—with any such purpose. It isn't thinking about trade but only about war.

The English think they see in this the effect on our Government and on American opinion of the German propaganda. I have had this trade-accusation investigated half a dozen times—the accusation that this Government is using its military power for its own trade advantage to our detriment: it simply isn't true. They stop our cargoes, not for their advantage, but wholly to keep things from the enemy. Study our own trade reports.

In a word, our importers are playing (so the English think) directly into the hands of the Germans. So matters go on from bad to worse.

Bryce[1] is very sad. He confessed to me yesterday the utter hopelessness of the two people's ever understanding one another.

The military situation is very blue—very blue. The general feeling is that the long war will begin next March and end—nobody dares predict.

W. H. P.

---

[1]Viscount Bryce, author of "The American Commonwealth" and British Ambassador to the United States, 1907–1913.

P. S.   There's not a moral shadow of a doubt (1) that the commander of the submarine that sunk the *Arabic* is dead—although he makes reports to his government! nor (2) that the *Hesperian* was torpedoed.   The State Department has a piece of the torpedo.

V

The letters which Page sent directly to the President were just as frank.   "Incidents occur nearly every day," he wrote to President Wilson in the autumn of 1915, "which reveal the feeling that the Germans have taken us in.   Last week one of our naval men, Lieutenant McBride, who has just been ordered home, asked the Admiralty if he might see the piece of metal found on the deck of the *Hesperian*.   Contrary to their habit, the British officer refused.   'Take my word for it,' he said. 'She was torpedoed.   Why do you wish to investigate? Your country will do nothing—will accept any excuse, any insult and—do nothing.'   When McBride told me this, I went at once to the Foreign Office and made a formal request that this metal should be shown to our naval attaché, who (since Symington is with the British fleet and McBride has been ordered home) is Lieutenant Towers.   Towers was sent for and everything that the Admiralty knows was shown to him and I am sending that piece of metal by this mail.   But to such a pass has the usual courtesy of a British naval officer come. There are many such instances of changed conduct. They are not hard to endure nor to answer and are of no consequence in themselves but only for what they denote. They're a part of war's bitterness.   But my mind runs ahead and I wonder how Englishmen will look at this subject five years hence, and it runs afield and I wonder how the Germans will regard it.   A sort of pro-German

American newspaper correspondent came along the other day from the German headquarters; and he told me that one of the German generals remarked to him: 'War with America? Ach no! Not war. If trouble should come, we'd send over a platoon of our policemen to whip your little army.' (He didn't say just how he'd send 'em.)"

To the President

American Embassy, London, Oct. 5, 1915.

DEAR MR. PRESIDENT:

I have two letters that I have lately written to you but which I have not sent because they utterly lack good cheer. After reading them over, I have not liked to send them. Yet I should fail of my duty if I did not tell you bad news as well as good.

The high esteem in which our Government was held when the first *Lusitania* note to Germany was sent seems all changed to indifference or pity—not hatred or hostility, but a sort of hopeless and sad pity. That ship was sunk just five months ago; the German Government (or its Ambassador) is yet holding conversations about the principle involved, making "concessions" and promises for the future, and so far we have done nothing to hold the Germans to accountability.[1] In the meantime their submarine fleet has been so reduced that probably the future will take care of itself and we shall be used as a sort of excuse for their failure. This is what the English think and say; and they explain our failure to act by concluding that the peace-at-any-price sentiment dominates the Government and paralyzes it. They have now, I think, given up hope that we will ever take any action.

---

[1] In a communication sent February 10, 1915, President Wilson warned the German Government that he would hold it to a "strict accountability" for the loss of American lives by illegal submarine attack.

So deeply rooted (and, I fear, permanent) is this feeling that every occurrence is made to fit into and to strengthen this supposition. When Dumba was dismissed, they said: "Dumba, merely the abject tool of German intrigue. Why not Bernstorff?" When the Anglo-French loan[1] was oversubscribed, they said: "The people's sympathy is most welcome, but their Government is paralyzed." Their respect has gone—at least for the time being.

It is not that they expect us to go to war: many, in fact, do not wish us to. They expected that we would be as good as our word and hold the Germans to accountability. Now I fear they think little of our word. I shudder to think what our relations might be if Sir Edward Grey were to yield to another as Foreign Minister, as, of course, he must yield at some time.

The press has less to say than it had a few weeks ago. *Punch*, for instance, which ridiculed and pitied us in six cartoons and articles in each of two succeeding numbers, entirely forgets us this week. But they've all said their say. I am, in a sense, isolated—lonely in a way that I have never before been. I am not exactly avoided, I hope, but I surely am not sought. They have a polite feeling that they do not wish to offend me and that to make sure of this the safest course is to let me alone. There is no mistaking the great change in the attitude of men I know, both in official and private life.

It comes down and comes back to this—that for five months after the sinking of the *Lusitania* the Germans are yet playing with us, that we have not sent Bernstorff home, and hence that we will submit to any rebuff or any indignity. It is under these conditions—under this judgment of us—that we now work—the English respect for

---

[1] A reference to the Anglo-French loan for $500,000,000, placed in the United States in the autumn of 1915.

our Government indefinitely lessened and instead of the old-time respect a sad pity. I cannot write more.

Heartily yours,

WALTER H. PAGE.

"I have authoritatively heard," Page writes to President Wilson in early September, "of a private conversation between a leading member of the Cabinet and a group of important officials all friendly to us in which all sorrowfully expressed the opinion that the United States will submit to any indignity and that no effect is now to be hoped for from its protests against unlawful submarine attacks or against anything else. The inactivity of our Government, or its delay, which they assume is the same as inactivity, is attributed to domestic politics or to the lack of national, consciousness or unity.

"No explanation has appeared in the British press of our Government's inactivity or of any regret or promise of reparation by Germany for the sinking of the *Lusitania*, the *Falaba*, the *Gulflight*, the *Nebraskan*, the *Arabic*, or the *Hesperian*, nor any explanation of a week's silence about the Dumba letter; and the conclusion is drawn that, in the absence of action by us, all these acts have been practically condoned.

"I venture to suggest that such explanations be made public as will remove, if possible, the practically unanimous conclusion here that our Government will permit these and similar future acts to be explained away. I am surprised almost every hour by some new evidence of the loss of respect for our Government, which, since the sinking of the *Arabic*, has become so great as to warrant calling it a complete revulsion of English feeling toward the United States. There is no general wish for us to enter the war, but there is genuine sorrow that we are thought to submit to any indignity, especially after having taken a firm stand. I conceive I should be lacking in duty if I did not report this rapid and unfortunate change in public feeling, which seems likely to become permanent unless facts are quickly made public which may change it."

There are many expressions of such feelings in Page's letters of this time. They brought only the most perfunctory acknowledgment from the White House. On January 3, 1916, Page sent the President a mass of clippings from the British press, all criticizing the Wilson Administration in unrestrained terms. In his comment on these, he writes the President:

"Public opinion, both official and unofficial, is expressed by these newspaper comments, with far greater restraint than it is expressed in private conversation. Ridicule of the Administration runs through the programmes of the theatres; it inspires hundreds of cartoons; it is a staple of conversation at private dinners and in the clubs. The most serious class of Englishmen, including the best friends of the United States, feel that the Administration's reliance on notes has reduced our Government to a third- or fourth-rate power. There is even talk of spheres of German influence in the United States as in China. No government could fall lower in English opinion than we shall fall if more notes are sent to Austria or to Germany. The only way to keep any shred of English respect is the immediate dismissal without more parleying of every German and Austrian official at Washington. Nobody here believes that such an act would provoke war.

"I can do no real service by mincing matters. My previous telegrams and letters have been purposely restrained as this one is. We have now come to the parting of the ways. If English respect be worth preserving at all, it can be preserved only by immediate action. Any other course than immediate severing of diplomatic relations with both Germany and Austria will deepen the English opinion into a conviction that the Administration was insincere when it sent the *Lusitania* notes and that its notes and protests need not be taken seriously on any subject. And English opinion is allied opinion. The Italian Ambassador[1] said to me, 'What has happened? The United States of to-day is not the United States I knew fifteen years ago, when I lived in Washington.' French officers and members of the Government who come here express themselves even more strongly than do the British. The British newspapers to-day publish translations of ridicule of the United States from German papers."

To the President

London,
January 5, 1916.

DEAR MR. PRESIDENT:

I wish—an impossible thing of course—that some sort of guidance could be given to the American correspondents of the English newspapers. Almost every day they telegraph about the visits of the Austrian Chargé or the German Ambassador to the State Department to assure Mr. Lansing that their governments will of course make a satisfactory explanation of the latest torpedo-act in the Mediterranean or to "take one further step in reaching a satisfactory understanding about the *Lusitania*." They usually go on to say also that more notes are in preparation to Germany or to Austria. The impression made upon the European mind is that the German and Austrian officials in Washington are leading the Administration on

---

[1]The Marquis Imperiali.

to endless discussion, endless notes, endless hesitation. Nobody in Europe regards their pledges or promises as worth anything at all: the *Arabic* follows the *Lusitania*, the *Hesperian* follows the *Arabic*, the *Persia* follows the *Ancona*. "Still conferences and notes continue," these people say, "proving that the American Government, which took so proper and high a stand in the *Lusitania* notes, is paralyzed—in a word is hoodwinked and 'worked' by the Germans." And so long as these diplomatic representatives are permitted to remain in the United States, "to explain," "to parley" and to declare that the destruction of American lives and property is disavowed by their governments, atrocities on sea and land will of course continue; and they feel that our Government, by keeping these German and Austrian representatives in Washington, condones and encourages them and their governments.

This is a temperate and even restrained statement of the English feeling and (as far as I can make out) of the whole European feeling.

It has been said here that every important journal published in neutral or allied European countries, daily, weekly, or monthly, which deals with public affairs, has expressed a loss of respect for the United States Government and that most of them make continuous severe criticisms (with surprise and regret) of our failure by action to live up to the level of our *Lusitania* notes. I had (judiciously) two American journalists, resident here— men of judgment and character—to inquire how true this declaration is. After talking with neutral and allied journalists here and with men whose business it is to read the journals of the Continent, they reported that this declaration is substantially true—that the whole European press (outside Germany and its allies) uses the same tone

toward our Government that the English press uses—
to-day, disappointment verging on contempt; and many
of them explain our keeping diplomatic intercourse with
Germany by saying that we are afraid of the German vote,
or of civil war, or that the peace-at-any-price people really
rule the United States and have paralyzed our power to
act—even to cut off diplomatic relations with governments
that have insulted and defied us.

Another (similar) declaration is that practically all men
of public influence in England and in the European allied
and neutral countries have publicly or privately expressed
themselves to the same effect. The report that I have
about this is less definite than about the newspapers, for,
of course, no one can say just what proportion of men of
public influence have so expressed themselves; but the
number who have so expressed themselves is overwhelming.

In this Kingdom, where I can myself form some opinion
more or less accurate, and where I can check or verify my
opinion by various methods—I am afraid, as I have frequently already reported, that the generation now living
will never wholly regain the respect for our Government
that it had a year ago. I will give you three little indications of this feeling; it would be easy to write down hundreds of them:

(One)   The governing class: Mr. X [a cabinet member]
told Mrs. Page a few nights ago that for sentimental reasons only he would be gratified to see the United States in
the war along with the Allies, but that merely sentimental
reasons were not a sufficient reason for war—by no means;
that he felt most grateful for the sympathetic attitude of
the large mass of the American people, that he had no
right to expect anything from our Government, whose
neutral position was entirely proper. Then he added;
"But what I can't for the life of me understand is your

Government's failure to express its disapproval of the German utter disregard of its *Lusitania* notes. After eight months, it has done nothing but write more notes. My love for America, I must confess, is offended at this inaction and—puzzled. I can't understand it. You will pardon me, I am sure."

(Two) "Middle Class" opinion: A common nickname for Americans in the financial and newspaper districts of London is "Too-prouds."

(Three) The man in the street: At one of the moving picture shows in a large theatre a little while ago they filled in an interval by throwing on the screen the picture of the monarch, or head of state, and of the flag of each of the principal nations. When the American picture appeared, there was such hissing and groaning as caused the managers hastily to move that picture off the screen.

Some time ago I wrote House of some such incidents and expressions as these; and he wrote me that they were only part and parcel of the continuous British criticism of their own Government—in other words, a part of the passing hysteria of war. This remark shows how House was living in an atmosphere of illusion.

As the matter stands to-day our Government has sunk lower, as regards British and European opinion, than it has ever been in our time, not as a part of the hysteria of war but as a result of this process of reasoning, whether it be right or wrong:

We said that we should hold the Germans to strict accountability on account of the *Lusitania*. We have not settled that yet and we still allow the German Ambassador to discuss it after the *Hesperian* and other such acts showed that his *Arabic* pledge was worthless.

The *Lusitania* grows larger and larger in European memory and imagination. It looks as if it would become the great type of war atrocities and barbarities. I have seen pictures of the drowned women and children used even on Christmas cards. And there is documentary proof in our hands that the warning, which was really an advance announcement, of that disaster was paid for by the German Ambassador and charged to his Government. It is the *Lusitania* that has caused European opinion to regard our foreign policy as weak. It is not the wish for us to go to war. No such general wish exists.

I do not know, Mr. President, who else, if anybody, puts these facts before you with this complete frankness. But I can do no less and do my duty.

No Englishman—except two who were quite intimate friends—has spoken to me about our Government for months, but I detect all the time a tone of pity and grief in their studied courtesy and in their avoidance of the subject. And they talk with every other American in this Kingdom. It is often made unpleasant for Americans in the clubs and in the pursuit of their regular business and occupations; and it is always our inaction about the *Lusitania*. Our controversy with the British Government causes little feeling and that is a sort of echo of the *Lusitania*. They feel that we have not lived up to our promises and professions.

That is the whole story.

Believe me always heartily,

WALTER H. PAGE.

This dismissal of Dumba and of the Attachés has had little more effect on opinion here than the dismissal of the Turkish Ambassador.[1] Sending these was regarded as

---

[1] Rustem Bey, the Turkish Ambassador to the United States, was sent home early in the war, for publishing indiscreet newspaper and magazine articles.

merely kicking the dogs of the man who had stolen our sheep.

VI

One of the reasons why Page felt so intensely about American policy at this time was his conviction that the severance of diplomatic relations, in the latter part of 1915, or the early part of 1916, in itself would have brought the European War to an end. This was a conviction from which he never departed. Count Bernstorff was industriously creating the impression in the United States that his dismissal would immediately cause war between Germany and the United States, and there is little doubt that the Administration accepted this point of view. But Page believed that this was nothing but Prussian bluff. The severance of diplomatic relations at that time, in Page's opinion, would have convinced the Germans of the hopelessness of their cause. In spite of the British blockade, Germany was drawing enormous quantities of food supplies from the United States, and without these supplies she could not maintain indefinitely her resistance. The severance of diplomatic relations would naturally have been accompanied by an embargo suspending trade between the United States and the Fatherland. Moreover, the consideration that was mainly leading Germany to hope for success was the belief that she could embroil the United States and Great Britain over the blockade. A break with Germany would of course mean an end to that manœuvre. Page regarded all Mr. Wilson's attempts to make peace in 1914 and early 1915—before the *Lusitania*—as mistakes, for reasons that have already been set forth. Now, however, he believed that the President had a real opportunity to end the war and the unparalleled suffering which it was causing. The mere dismissal of Bernstorff, in the Ambassador's opinion, would accomplish this result.

In a communication sent to the President on February 15, 1916, he made this plain.

To the President

February 15, 7 P. M.

The Cabinet has directed the Censor to suppress, as far as he can with prudence, comment which is unfavourable to the United States. He has taken this action because the public feeling against the Administration is constantly increasing. Because the *Lusitania* controversy has been going on so long, and because the Germans are using it in their renewed U-boat campaign, the opinion of this country has reached a point where only prompt action can bring a turn in the tide. Therefore my loyalty to you would not be complete if I should refrain from sending, in the most respectful terms, the solemn conviction which I hold about our opportunity and our duty.

If you immediately refuse to have further parley or to yield one jot or tittle of your original *Lusitania* notes, and if you at once break diplomatic relations with the German Empire, and then declare the most vigorous embargo of the Central Powers, you will quickly end the war. There will be an immediate collapse in German credit. If there are any Allies who are wavering, such action will hold them in line. Certain European neutrals—Sweden, Rumania, Greece, and others—will put up a firm resistance to Germanic influences and certain of them will take part with Great Britain and France. There will be an end at once to the German propaganda, which is now worldwide. The moral weight of our country will be a determining influence and bring an early peace. The credit you will receive for such a decision will make you immortal and even the people of Germany will be forever grateful.

It is my conviction that we would not be called upon to fire a gun or to lose one human life.

Above all, such an action will settle the whole question of permanent peace. The absolute and grateful loyalty of the whole British Empire, of the British Fleet, and of all the Allied countries will be ours. The great English-speaking nations will be able to control the details of the peace and this without any formal alliance. There will be an incalculable saving of human life and of treasure. Such an act will make it possible for Germany to give in honourably and with good grace because the whole world will be against her. Her bankrupt and blockaded people will bring such pressure to bear that the decision will be hastened.

The sympathies of the American people will be brought in line with the Administration.

If we settle the *Lusitania* question by compromising in any way your original demands, or if we permit it to drag on longer, America can have no part in bringing the war to an end. The current of allied opinion will run so strongly against the Administration that no censorship and no friendly interference by an allied government can stem the distrust of our Government which is now so strong in Europe.

We shall gain by any further delay only a dangerous, thankless, and opulent isolation. The *Lusitania* is the turning point in our history. The time to act is now.

PAGE.

CHAPTER XV

THE AMBASSADOR AND THE LAWYERS

REFERENCES in the foregoing letters show that Page was still having his troubles over the blockade. In the latter part of 1915, indeed, the negotiations with Sir Edward Grey on this subject had reached their second stage. The failure of Washington to force upon Great Britain an entirely new code of naval warfare—the Declaration of London—has already been described. This failure had left both the British Foreign Office and the American State Department in an unsatisfactory frame of mind. The Foreign Office regarded Washington with suspicion, for the American attempt to compel Great Britain to adopt a code of naval warfare which was exceedingly unfavourable to that country and exceedingly favourable to Germany, was susceptible of a sinister interpretation. The British rejection of these overtures, on the other hand, had evidently irritated the international lawyers at Washington. Mr. Lansing now abandoned his efforts to revolutionize maritime warfare and confined himself to specific protests and complaints. His communications to the London Embassy dealt chiefly with particular ships and cargoes. Yet his persistence in regarding all these problems from a strictly legalistic point of view Page regarded as indicating a restricted sense of statesmanship.

To Edward M. House

London, August 4, 1915.

MY DEAR HOUSE:

. . . The lawyer-way in which the Department goes on in its dealings with Great Britain is losing us the only great international friendship that we have any chance of keeping or that is worth having. Whatever real principle we have to uphold with Great Britain—that's all right. I refer only to the continuous series of nagging incidents—always criticism, criticism, criticism of small points—points that we have to yield at last, and never anything constructive. I'll illustrate what I mean by a few incidents that I can recall from memory. If I looked up the record, I should find a very, very much larger list.

(1) We insisted and insisted and insisted, not once but half a dozen times, at the very beginning of the war, on England's adoption of the Declaration of London entire in spite of the fact that Parliament had distinctly declined to adopt it. Of course we had to give in—after we had produced a distinctly unfriendly atmosphere and much feeling.

(2) We denied the British right to put copper on the contraband list—much to their annoyance. Of course we had at last to acquiesce. They were within their rights.

(3) We protested against bringing ships into port to examine them. Of course we had to give in—after producing irritation.

(4) We made a great fuss about stopped telegrams. We have no case at all; but, even after acknowledging that we have no case, every pouch continues to bring telegrams with the request that I ask an explanation why

they were stopped. Such explanations are practically refused. I have 500 telegrams. Periodically I wire the state of the case and ask for more specific instructions. I never get an answer to these requests. But the Department continues to send the telegrams! We confessedly have no case here; and this method can produce nothing but irritation.

I could extend this list to 100 examples—of mere lawyer-like methods—mere useless technicalities and objections which it is obvious in the beginning cannot be maintained. A similar method is now going on about cotton. Now this is not the way Sir Edward Grey takes up business. It's not the way I've done business all my life, nor that you have, nor other frank men who mean what they say and do not say things they do not mean. The constant continuation of this method is throwing away the real regard and confidence of the British Government and of the British public—very fast, too.

I sometimes wish there were not a lawyer in the world. I heard the President say once that it took him twenty years to recover from his legal habit of mind. Well, his Administration is suffering from it to a degree that is pathetic and that will leave bad results for 100 years.

I suspect that in spite of all the fuss we have made we shall at last come to acknowledge the British blockade; for it is pretty nearly parallel to the United States blockade of the South during our Civil War. The only difference is—they can't make the blockade of the Baltic against the traffic from the Scandinavian neutral states effective. That's a good technical objection; but, since practically all the traffic between those States and Germany is in our products, much of the real force of it is lost.

If a protest is made against cotton being made contraband—it'll amount to nothing and give only irritation. It will only play into Hoke Smith-German hands and accomplish nothing here. We make as much fuss about points which we have silently to yield later as about a real principle. Hence they all say that the State Department is merely captious, and they pay less and less attention to it and care less and less for American opinion—if only they can continue to get munitions. We are reducing English regard to this purely mercenary basis. . . .

We are—under lawyers' quibbling—drifting apart very rapidly, to our complete isolation from the sympathy of the whole world.

Yours forever sincerely,

W. H. P.

Page refers in this letter to the "blockade"; this was the term which the British Government itself used to describe its restrictive measures against German commerce, and it rapidly passed into common speech. Yet the truth is that Great Britain never declared an actual blockade against Germany. A realization of this fact will clear up much that is obscure in the naval warfare of the next two years. At the beginning of the Civil War, President Lincoln laid an interdict on all the ports of the Confederacy; the ships of all nations were forbidden entering or leaving them: any ship which attempted to evade this restriction, and was captured doing so, was confiscated, with its cargo. That was a blockade, as the term has always been understood. A blockade, it is well to keep in mind, is a procedure which aims at completely closing the blockaded country from all commercial intercourse with the world. A blockading navy, if the blockade is

---

[1]Senator Hoke Smith, of Georgia, was at this time—and afterward—conducting a bitter campaign against the British blockade and advocating an embargo as a retaliation.

successful, or "effective," converts the whole country into a beleaguered fortress, just as an army, surrounding a single town, prevents goods and people from entering or leaving it. Precisely as it is the purpose of a besieging army to starve a particular city or territory into submission, so it is the aim of a blockading fleet to enforce the same treatment on the nation as a whole. It is also essential to keep in mind that the question of contraband has nothing to do with a blockade, for, under this drastic method of making warfare, everything is contraband. Contraband is a term applied to cargoes, such as rifles, machine guns, and the like, which are needed in the prosecution of war.

That a belligerent nation has the right to intercept such munitions on the way to its enemy has been admitted for centuries. Differences of opinion have raged only as to the extent to which this right could be carried—the particular articles, that is, that constituted contraband, and the methods adopted in exercising it. But the important point to be kept in mind is that where there is a blockade, there is no contraband list—for everything automatically becomes contraband. The seizure of contraband on the high seas is a war measure which is availed of only in cases in which the blockade has not been established.

Great Britain, when she declared war on Germany, did not follow President Lincoln's example and lay the whole of the German coast under interdict. Perhaps one reason for this inaction was a desire not unduly to offend neutrals, especially the United States; but the more impelling motive was geographical. The fact is that a blockade of the German seacoast would accomplish little in the way of keeping materials out of Germany. A glance at the map of northwestern Europe will make this fact clear. In the first place the seacoast of Germany is a small affair. In the North Sea the German coast is a little indentation, not more than two hundred miles long, wedged in between the longer coastlines of Holland and Denmark; in the Baltic it is somewhat more extensive, but the entrances to this sea are so circuitous and treacherous that the suggestion of a blockade here is not a practicable one. The greatest ports of Germany are located on this little North Sea coastline or on its rivers—Hamburg and Bremen. It might therefore be assumed that any nation which successfully blockaded these North Sea ports would have strangled the commerce of Germany. That is far from being the case. The point is that the political boundaries of Germany are simply fictions, when economic considerations are involved. Holland, on the west, and Denmark, on the north, are as much a part of the German transportation system as though these two countries were parts of the German Empire. Their territories and the territories of Germany are contiguous; the railroad and the canal systems of Germany, Holland, and Denmark are practically one. Such ports as Rotterdam, Amsterdam, and Copenhagen are just as useful to Germany for purposes of commerce as are Hamburg and Bremen, and, in fact, a special commercial arrangement with Rotterdam has made that city practically a port of Germany since 1868. These considerations show how ineffective would be a blockade of the German coast which did not also comprehend the coast of Holland and Denmark. Germany could still conduct her commerce through these neighbouring countries. And at this point the great difficulty arose. A blockade is an act of war and can be applied only to a country upon which war has been declared. Great Britain had declared war on Germany and could therefore legally close her ports; she had not declared war on Holland and Denmark, and therefore could not use the same measure against those friendly countries. Consequently the blockade was useless to Great Britain; and so, in the first six months of the war, the Admiralty fell back upon the milder system of declaring certain articles contraband of war and seizing ships that were suspected of carrying them to Germany.

A geographical accident had apparently largely destroyed the usefulness of the British fleet and had guaranteed Germany an unending supply of those foodstuffs without which she could not maintain her resistance for any extended period. Was Great Britain called upon to accept this situation and to deny herself the use of the blockade in this, the greatest struggle in her history? Unless the British fleet could stop cargoes which were really destined to Germany but which were bound for neutral ports, Great Britain could not win the war; if the British fleet could intercept such cargoes, then the chances strongly favoured victory. The experts of the Foreign Office searched the history of blockades and found something which resembled a precedent in the practices of the American Navy during the Civil War. In that conflict Nassau, in the Bahamas, and Matamoros, in Mexico, played a part not unlike that played by Rotterdam and Copenhagen in the recent struggle. These were both neutral ports and therefore outside the jurisdiction of the United States, just as Rotterdam and Copenhagen were outside the jurisdiction of Great Britain. They were the ports of powers with which the United States was at peace, and therefore they could not be blockaded, just as Amsterdam and Copenhagen were ports of powers with which Great Britain was now at peace.

Trade from Great Britain to the Bahamas and Mexico was ostensibly trade from one neutral port to another

neutral port in the same sense as was trade from the
United States to Holland and Denmark.   Yet the fact is
that the "neutrality" of this trade, in the Civil War, from
Great Britain to the Bahamas and Mexico, was the most
transparent subterfuge; such trade was not "neutral" in
the slightest degree.   It consisted almost entirely of
contraband of war and was intended for the armies of the
Confederate States, then in arms against the Federal
Government.   What is the reason, our Government
asked, that these gentle and unwarlike inhabitants of the
Bahamas have so suddenly developed such an enormous
appetite for percussion caps, rifles, cannon, and other instruments of warfare?   The answer, of course, lay upon
the surface; the cargoes were intended for reshipment into
the Southern States, and they were, in fact, immediately
so reshipped.   The American Government, which has
always regarded realities as more important than logic,
brushed aside the consideration that this trade was con-
ducted through neutral ports, unhesitatingly seized these
ships and condemned both the ships and their cargoes.
Its action was without legal precedent, but our American
courts devised a new principle of international law to
cover the case—that of "continuous voyage" or "ultimate
destination."   Under this new doctrine it was maintained
that cargoes of contraband could be seized anywhere upon
the high seas, even though they were going from one neutral port to another, if it could be demonstrated that this
contraband was really on its way to the enemy.   The
mere fact that it was transshipped at an intermediate
neutral port was not important; the important point was
the "ultimate destination."   British shippers naturally
raged over these decisions, but they met with little sympathy from their own government.   Great Britain filed
no protest against the doctrine of "continuous voyage,"

but recognized its fundamental soundness, and since 1865 this doctrine has been a part of international law.

Great Britain's good sense in acquiescing in our Civil War practices now met its reward; for these decisions of American courts proved a godsend in her hour of trial. The one neutral from which trouble was anticipated was the United States. What better way to meet this situation than to base British maritime warfare upon the decisions of American courts? What more ideal solution of the problem than to make Chief Justice Chase, of the United States Supreme Court, really the author of the British "blockade" against Germany? The policy of the British Foreign Office was to use the sea power of Great Britain to crush the enemy, but to do it in a way that would not alienate American sympathy and American support; clearly the one way in which both these ends could be attained was to frame these war measures upon the pronouncements of American prize courts. In a broad sense this is precisely what Sir Edward Grey now proceeded to do. There was a difference, of course, which Great Britain's enemies in the American Senate—such men as Senator Hoke Smith, of Georgia, and Senator Thomas Walsh, of Montana—proceeded to point out; but it was a difference of degree. Great Britain based her blockade measures upon the American principle of "ultimate destination," but it was necessary considerably to extend that doctrine in order to meet the necessities of the new situation. President Lincoln had applied this principle to absolute contraband, such as powder, shells, rifles, and other munitions of war. Great Britain now proceeded to apply it to that nebulous class of commodities known as "conditional contraband," the chief of which was foodstuffs. If the United States, while a war was pending, could evolve the idea of "ultimate destination" and apply it to absolute contraband, could not Great Britain, while another war was pending, carry it one degree further and make it include conditional contraband? Thus reasoned the British Foreign Office. To this Mr. Lansing replied that to stop foodstuffs on the way to Germany through a neutral port was simply to blockade a neutral port, and that this was something utterly without precedent. Seizing contraband is not an act of war against the nation whose ships are seized; blockading a port is an act of war; what right therefore had Great Britain to adopt measures against Holland, Denmark, and Sweden which virtually amounted to a blockade?

This is the reason why Great Britain, in the pronouncement of March 1, 1915, and the Order in Council of March 11, 1915, did not describe these measures as a "blockade." President Wilson described his attack on Mexico in 1914 as "measures short of war," and now someone referred to the British restrictions on neutral commerce as "measures short of blockade." The British sought another escape from their predicament by justifying this proceeding, not on the general principles of warfare, but on the ground of reprisal. Germany declared her submarine warfare on merchant ships on February 4, 1915; Great Britain replied with her announcement of March 1st, in which she declared her intention of preventing "commodities of any kind from reaching or leaving Germany." The British advanced this procedure as a retaliation for the illegal warfare which Germany had declared on merchant shipping, both that of the enemy and of neutrals. "The British and French governments will therefore hold themselves free to detain and take into port ships carrying goods of presumed enemy destination, ownership, and origin." This sentence accurately describes the purposes of a blockade—to cut the enemy off from all commercial relations with the outside world; yet the procedure Great Britain now proposed to follow was not that of a blockade. When this interdict is classically laid, any ship that attempts to run the lines is penalized with confiscation, along with its cargo; but such a penalty was not to be exacted in the present instance. Great Britain now proposed to purchase cargoes of conditional contraband discovered on seized ships and return the ships themselves to their owners, and this soon became the established practice. Not only did the Foreign Office purchase all cotton which was seized on its way to Germany, but it took measures to maintain the price in the markets of the world. In the succeeding months Southern statesmen in both Houses of Congress railed against the British seizure of their great staple, yet the fact was that cotton was all this time steadily advancing in price. When Senator Hoke Smith made a long speech advocating an embargo on the shipment of munitions as a punishment to Great Britain for stopping American cotton on the way to Germany, the acute John Sharp Williams, of Mississippi, arose in the Senate and completely annihilated the Georgia politician by demonstrating how the Southern planters were growing rich out of the war.

That the so-called "blockade" situation was a tortuous one must be apparent from this attempt to set forth the salient facts. The basic point was that there could be no blockade of Germany unless the neutral ports of contiguous countries were also blockaded, and Great Britain believed that she had found a precedent for doing this in the operations of the American Navy in the Civil War. But it is obvious that the situation was one which would provide a great feast for the lawyers. That Page sympathized with this British determination to keep foodstuffs out of Germany, his correspondence shows. Day

after day the "protests" from Washington rained upon
his desk. The history of our foreign relations for 1915
and 1916 is largely made up of an interminable correspondence dealing with seized cargoes, and the routine of
the Embassy was an unending nightmare of "demands,"
"complaints," "precedents," "cases," "notes," "detentions" of Chicago meats, of Southern cotton, and the like.
The American Embassy in London contains hundreds of
volumes of correspondence which took place during Page's
incumbency; more material has accumulated for those five
years than for the preceding century and a quarter of the
Government's existence. The greater part of this mass
deals with intercepted cargoes.

The following extract from a letter which Page wrote
at this time gives a fair idea of the atmosphere that prevailed in London while this correspondence was engaging
the Ambassador's mind:

The truth is, in their present depressed mood, the
United States is forgotten—everything's forgotten but
the one great matter in hand. For the moment at least,
the English do not care what we do or what we think or
whether we exist—except those critics of things-in-general
who use us as a target since they must take a crack at
somebody. And I simply cannot describe the curious
effect that is produced on men here by the apparent utter
lack of understanding in the United States of the phase
the war has now entered and of the mood that this phase
has brought. I pick up an American paper eight days old
and read solemn evidence to show that the British Government is interrupting our trade in order to advance
its own at our expense, whereas the truth is that the
British Government hasn't given six seconds' thought in
six months to anybody's trade—not even its own.

When I am asked to inquire why Pfister and Schmidt's telegram from New York to Schimmelpfenig and Johann in Holland was stopped (the reason is reasonably obvious), I try to picture to myself the British Minister in Washington making inquiry of our Government on the day after Bull Run, why the sailing boat loaded with persimmon blocks to make golf clubs is delayed in Hampton Roads.

I think I have neither heard nor read anything from the United States in three months that didn't seem so remote as to suggest the captain of the sailing ship from Hongkong who turned up at Southampton in February and had not even heard that there was a war. All day long I see and hear women who come to ask if I can make inquiry about their sons and husbands, "dead or missing," with an interval given to a description of a man half of whose body was splashed against a brick wall last night on the Strand when a Zeppelin bomb tore up the street and made projectiles of the pavement; as I walk to and from the Embassy the Park is full of wounded and their nurses; every man I see tells me of a new death; every member of the Government talks about military events or of Balkan venality; the man behind the counter at the cigar store reads me part of a letter just come from his son, telling how he advanced over a pile of dead Germans and one of them grunted and turned under his feet—they (the English alone) are spending $25,000,000 a day to keep this march going over dead Germans; then comes a telegram predicting blue ruin for American importers and a cheerless Christmas for American children if a cargo of German toys be not quickly released at Rotterdam, and I dimly recall the benevolent unction with which American children last Christmas sent a shipload of toys to this side of the world—many of them for German children —to the tune of "God bless us all"—do you wonder we

often have to pinch ourselves to find out if we are we; and
what year of the Lord is it? What *is* the vital thing—
the killing of fifty people last night by a Zeppelin within
sight of St. Paul's on one side and of Westminster Abbey
on the other, or is it making representations to Sir Edward Grey, who has hardly slept for a week because his
despatches from Sofia, Athens, Belgrade, and Salonika
come at all hours, each possibly reporting on which side
a new government may throw its army—to decide perhaps
the fate of the canal leading to Asia, the vast British
Asiatic empire at stake—is it making representations to
Sir Edward while his mind is thus occupied, that it is of
the greatest importance to the United States Government
that a particular German who is somewhere in this Kingdom shall be permitted to go to the United States because
he knows how to dye sealskins and our sealskins are
yet undyed and the winter is coming? There will be no
new sealskins here, for every man and woman must give
half his income to keep the cigarman's son marching over
dead Germans, some of whom grunt and turn under his
feet. Dumba is at Falmouth to-day and gets just two
lines in the newspapers. Nothing and nobody gets three
lines unless he or it in some way furthers the war. Every
morning the Washington despatches say that Mr. Lansing is about to send a long note to England. England
won't read it till there comes a lull in the fighting or in
the breathless diplomatic struggle with the Balkans.
London and the Government are now in much the same
mood that Washington and Lincoln's administration
were in after Lee had crossed the Potomac on his way to
Gettysburg. Northcliffe, the Lord of Yellow Journals,
but an uncommonly brilliant fellow, has taken to his bed
from sheer nervous worry. "The revelations that are
imminent," says he, "will shake the world—the incom-

petence of the Government, the losses along the Dardanelles, the throwing away of British chances in the Balkans, perhaps the actual defeat of the Allies." I regard
Lord Northcliffe less as an entity than as a symptom.
But he is always very friendly to us and he knows the
United States better than any Englishman that I know
except Bryce. He and Bryce are both much concerned
about our Note's coming just "at this most distressing
time." "If it come when we are calmer, no matter; but
now it cannot receive attention and many will feel that
the United States has hit on a most unhappy moment—
almost a cruel moment—to remind us of our sins."—
That's the substance of what they say.

Overwork, or perhaps mainly the indescribable strain
on the nerves and vitality of men, caused by this experience, for which in fact men are not built, puts one of
our staff after another in bed. None has been seriously
sick: the malady takes some form of "grip." On the
whole we've been pretty lucky in spite of this almost
regular temporary breakdown of one man after another.
I've so far escaped. But I am grieved to hear that
Whitlock is abed—"no physical ailment whatever—just
worn out," his doctor says. I have tried to induce him
and his wife to come here and make me a visit; but one
characteristic of this war-malady is the conviction of the
victim that he is somehow necessary to hold the world
together. About twice a week I get to the golf links and
take the risk of the world's falling apart and thus escape
both illness and its illusions.

"I cannot begin to express my deep anxiety and even
uneasiness about the relations of these two great governments and peoples," Page wrote about this time.
"The friendship of the United States and Great Britain

is all that now holds the world together.   It is the greatest asset of civilization left.   All the cargoes of copper and oil in the world are not worth as much to the world.   Yet when a shipper's cargo is held up he does not think of civilization and of the future of mankind and of free government; he thinks only of his cargo and of the indignity that he imagines has been done him; and what is the American Government for if not to protect his rights? Of course he's right; but there must be somebody somewhere who sees things in their right proportion.   The man with an injury rushes to the Department of State— quite properly.   He is in a mood to bring England to book.   Now comes the critical stage in the journey of his complaint.   The State Department hurries it on to me— very properly; every man's right must be guarded and defended—a right to get his cargo to market, a right to get on a steamer at Queenstown, a right to have his censored telegram returned, any kind of a right, if he have a right. Then the Department, not wittingly, I know, but humanly, almost inevitably, in the great rush of overwork, sends his 'demands' to me, catching much of his tone and apparently insisting on the removal of his grievance as a right, without knowing all the facts in the case.   The telegrams that come to me are full of 'protests' and 'demands'—protest and demand this, protest and demand that.   A man from Mars who should read my book of telegrams received during the last two months would find it difficult to explain how the two governments have kept at peace.   It is this serious treatment of trifling grievances which makes us feel here that the exactions and dislocations and necessary disturbances of this war are not understood at home.

"I assure you (and there are plenty of facts to prove it) that this Government (both for unselfish and selfish reasons) puts a higher value on our friendship than on any similar thing in the world. They will go—they are going—the full length to keep it. But, in proportion to our tendency to nag them about little things will the value set on our friendship diminish and will their confidence in our sincerity decline."

The note which Lord Bryce and Lord Northcliffe so dreaded reached the London Embassy in October, 1915. The State Department had spent nearly six months in preparing it; it was the American answer to the so-called blockade established by the Order in Council of the preceding March. Evidently its contents fulfilled the worst forebodings:

To Edward M. House

London, November 12, 1915.

DEAR HOUSE:

I have a great respect for the British Navy. Admiral Jellicoe now has under his command 3,000 ships of all sorts—far and away the biggest fleet, I think, that was ever assembled. For the first time since the ocean was poured out, one navy practically commands all the seas: nothing sails except by its grace. It is this fleet of course that will win the war. The beginning of the end—however far off yet the end may be—is already visible by reason of the economic pressure on Germany. But for this fleet, by the way, London would be in ruins, all its treasure looted; every French seacoast city and the Italian peninsula would be as Belgium and Poland are; and thousands of English women would be violated—just as dead French girls are found in many German trenches that have been taken in France. Hence I greatly respect the British fleet.

We have a good navy, too, for its size, and a naval personnel as good as any afloat. I hear—with much joy—that we are going to make our navy bigger—as much bigger (God save the mark!) as Bryan will permit.

Now, whatever the future bring, since any fighting enterprise that may ever be thrust on us will be just and justified, we must see to it that we win, as doubtless we shall and as hitherto we always have won. We must be dead sure of winning. Well, whatever fight may be thrust on us by anybody, anywhere, at any time, for any reason—if it only be generally understood beforehand that our fleet and the British fleet shoot the same language, there'll be no fight thrust upon us. The biggest bully in the world wouldn't dare kick the sorriest dog we have.

Here, therefore, is a Peace Programme for you—the only basis for a permanent peace in the world. There's no further good in having venerable children build houses of sand at The Hague; there's no further good in peace organizations or protective leagues to enforce peace. We had as well get down to facts. So far as ensuring peace is concerned the biggest fact in the world is the British fleet. The next biggest fact is the American fleet, because of itself and still more because of the vast reserve power of the United States which it implies. If these two fleets perfectly understand one another about the undesirability of wars of aggression, there'll be no more big wars as long as this understanding continues. Such an understanding calls for no treaty—it calls only for courtesy.

And there is no other peace-basis worth talking about—by men who know how the world is governed.

Since I have lived here I have spent my days and nights, my poor brain, and my small fortune all most freely and gladly to get some understanding of the men who rule this Kingdom, and of the women and the customs and the traditions that rule these men—to get their trick of thought, the play of their ideals, the working of their imagination, the springs of their instincts. It is impossible for any man to know just how well he himself does such a difficult task—how accurately he is coming to understand the sources and character of a people's actions. Yet, at the worst, I do know something about the British: I know enough to make very sure of the soundness of my conclusion that they are necessary to us and we to them. Else God would have permitted the world to be peopled in some other way. And when we see that the world will be saved by such an artificial combination as England and Russia and France and Japan and Serbia, it calls for no great wisdom to see the natural way whereby it must be saved in the future.

For this reason every day that I have lived here it has been my conscious aim to do what I could to bring about a condition that shall make sure of this—that, whenever we may have need of the British fleet to protect our shores or to prevent an aggressive war anywhere, it shall be ours by a natural impulse and necessity—even without the asking.

I have found out that the first step toward that end is courtesy; that the second step is courtesy, and the third step—such a fine and high courtesy (which includes courage) as the President showed in the Panama tolls controversy. We have—we and the British—common aims and character. Only a continuous and sincere courtesy—over periods of strain as well as of calm—is necessary for as complete an understanding as will be required for the automatic guidance of the world in peaceful ways.

Now, a difference is come between us—the sort of difference that handled as between friends would serve only to bind us together with a sturdier respect. We

send a long lawyer's Note, not discourteous but wholly
uncourteous, which is far worse.   I am writing now only
of the manner of the Note, not of its matter.   There is
not a courteous word, nor a friendly phrase, nor a kindly
turn in it, not an allusion even to an old acquaintance, to
say nothing of an old friendship, not a word of thanks for
courtesies or favours done us, not a hint of sympathy in
the difficulties of the time.   There is nothing in its tone
to show that it came from an American to an Englishman:
it might have been from a Hottentot to a Fiji-Islander.

I am almost sure—I'll say quite sure—that this uncourteous manner is far more important than its endless
matter.   It has greatly hurt our friends, the real men of
the Kingdom.   It has made the masses angry—which is
of far less importance than the severe sorrow that our
discourtesy of manner has brought to our friends—I fear
to all considerate and thoughtful Englishmen.

Let me illustrate: When the Panama tolls controversy
arose, Taft ceased to speak the language of the natural
man and lapsed into lawyer's courthouse zigzagging mut-
terings.   Knox wrote a letter to the British Government
that would have made an enemy of the most affectionate
twin brother—all mere legal twists and turns, as agreeable
as a pocketful of screws.   Then various bovine "international lawyers" wrote books about it.   I read them and
became more and more confused the further I went: you
always do.   It took me some time to recover from this
word-drunk debauch and to find my own natural intelligence again, the common sense that I was born with.
Then I saw that the whole thing went wrong from the place
where that Knox legal note came in.   Congressmen in the
backwoods quoted cryptic passages from it, thought they
were saying something, and proceeded to make their
audiences believe that somehow England had hit us with

a club—or would have hit us but for Knox. That pure discourtesy kept us apart from English sympathy for something like two years.

Then the President took it up. He threw the legal twaddle into the gutter. He put the whole question in a ten-minutes' speech to Congress, full of clearness and fairness and high courtesy. It won even the rural Congressmen. It was read in every capital and the men who conduct every government looked up and said, "This is a real man, a brave man, a just man." You will recall what Sir Edward Grey said to me: "The President has taught us all a lesson and set us all a high example in the noblest courtesy."

This one act brought these two nations closer together than they had ever been since we became an independent nation. It was an act of courtesy. . . .

My dear House, suppose the postman some morning were to leave at your door a thing of thirty-five heads and three appendices, and you discovered that it came from an old friend whom you had long known and greatly valued—this vast mass of legal stuff, without a word or a turn of courtesy in it—what would you do? He had a grievance, your old friend had. Friends often have. But instead of explaining it to you, he had gone and had his lawyers send this many-headed, much-appendiced ton of stuff. It wasn't by that method that you found your way from Austin, Texas, to your present eminence and wisdom. Nor was that the way our friend found his way from a little law-office in Atlanta, where I first saw him, to the White House.

More and more I am struck with this—that governments are human. They are not remote abstractions, nor impersonal institutions. Men conduct them; and they do not cease to be men. A man is made up of six parts of human nature and four parts of facts and other things—a little reason, some prejudice, much provincialism, and of the particular fur or skin that suits his habitat. When you wish to win a man to do what *you* want him to do, you take along a few well-established facts, some reasoning and such-like, but you take along also three or four or five parts of human nature—kindliness, courtesy, and such things—sympathy and a human touch.

If a man be six parts human and four parts of other things, a government, especially a democracy, is seven, or eight, or nine parts human nature. It's the most human thing I know. The best way to manage governments and nations—so long as they are disposed to be friendly— is the way we manage one another. I have a confirmation of this in the following comment which came to me to-day. It was made by a friendly member of Parliament.

"The President himself dealt with Germany. Even in his severity he paid the Germans the compliment of a most courteous tone in his Note. But in dealing with us he seems to have called in the lawyers of German importers and Chicago pork-packers. I miss the high Presidential courtesy that we had come to expect from Mr. Wilson."

An American banker here has told me of the experience of an American financial salesman in the city the day after our Note was published. His business is to make calls on bankers and other financial men, to sell them securities. He is a man of good address who is popular with his clients. The first man he called on, on that day, said: "I don't wish to be offensive to you. But I have only one way to show my feeling of indignation toward the United States, and that is, to have nothing more to do with Americans."

The next man said: "No, nothing to-day, I thank you. No—nor to-morrow either; nor the next day. Good morning."

After four or five such greetings, the fellow gave it up and is now doing nothing.

I don't attach much importance to such an incident as this, except as it gives a hint of the general feeling. These financial men probably haven't even read our Note. Few people have. But they have all read the short and sharp newspaper summary which preceded it in the English papers. But what such an incident does indicate is the prevalence of a state of public feeling which would prevent the Government from yielding any of our demands even if the Government so wished. It has now been nearly a week since the Note was published. I have seen most of the neutral ministers. Before the Note came they expressed great eagerness to see it: it would champion their cause. Since it came not one of them has mentioned it to me. The Secretary of one of them remarked, after being invited to express himself: "It is too—too—long!" And, although I have seen most of the Cabinet this week, not a man mentioned it to me. People seem studiously to avoid it, lest they give offense.

I have, however, got one little satisfaction. An American—a half-expatriated loafer who talks "art"—you know the intellectually affected and degenerate type— screwed his courage up and told me that he felt ashamed of his country. I remarked that I felt sure the feeling was mutual. That, I confess, made me feel better.

As nearly as I can make out, the highwater mark of English good-feeling toward us in all our history was after the President's Panama tolls courtesy. The low-water mark, since the Civil War, I am sure, is now. The Cleveland Venezuela message came at a time of no nervous strain and did, I think, produce no long-lasting effect. A part of the present feeling is due to the English conviction that we have been taken in by the Germans in the submarine controversy, but a large part is due to the lack of courtesy in this last Note—the manner in which it was written even more than its matter. As regards its matter, I have often been over what I conceive to be the main points with Sir Edward Grey—very frankly and without the least offense. He has said: "We may have to arbitrate these things," as he might say, "We had better take a cab because it is raining." It is easily possible—or it was—to discuss anything with this Government without offense. I have, in fact, stood up before Sir Edward's fire and accused him of stealing a large part of the earth's surface, and we were just as good friends afterward as before. But I never drew a lawyer's indictment of him as a land-thief: that's different.

I suppose no two peoples or governments ever quite understand one another. Perhaps they never will. That is too much to hope for. But when one government writes to another it ought to write (as men do) with some reference to the personality of the other and to their previous relations, since governments are more human than men. Of course I don't know who wrote the Note. Hence I can talk about it freely to you without implying criticism of anybody in particular. But the man who wrote it never saw the British Government and wouldn't know it if he met it in the road. To him it is a mere legal entity, a wicked, impersonal institution against which he has the task of drawing an indictment—not the task of trying to persuade it to confess the propriety of a certain course of conduct. In his view, it is a wicked enemy to start with —like the Louisiana lottery of a previous generation or the Standard Oil Company of our time.

One would have thought, since we were six months in preparing it, that a draft of the Note would have been sent to the man on the ground whom our Government keeps in London to study the situation at first hand and to make the best judgment he can about the most effective methods of approach on delicate and difficult matters. If that had been done, I should have suggested a courteous short Note saying that we are obliged to set forth such and such views about marine law and the rights of neutrals, to His Majesty's Government; and that the contention of the United States Government was herewith sent—etc., etc.—Then this identical Note (with certain court-house, strong, shirt-sleeve adjectives left out) could have come without arousing any feeling whatsoever. Of course I have no personal vanity in saying this to you. I am sure I outgrew that foible many years ago. But such a use of an ambassador—of any ambassador—is obviously one of the best and most natural uses he could be put to; and all governments but ours do put their ambassadors to such a use: that's what they have 'em for.

Per contra: a telegram has just come in saying that a certain Lichtenstein in New York had a lot of goods stopped by the British Government, which (by an arrangement made with their attorney here) agreed to buy them at a certain price: will I go and find out why the Government hasn't yet paid Lichtenstein and when he may expect his money? Is it an ambassadorial duty to collect a private bill for Lichtenstein, in a bargain with which our Government has had nothing to do? I have telegraphed the Department, quite calmly, that I don't think it is. I venture to say no ambassador ever had such a request as that before from his Government.

My dear House, I often wonder if my years of work here—the kind of high good work I've tried to do—have

not been thrown away. I've tried to take and to busy
myself with a long-range view of great subjects. The
British Empire and the United States will be here long
after we are dead, and their relations will continue to be
one of the most important matters—perhaps the most
important matter—in the world. Well, now think of
Lichtenstein's bill!

To get back where I started—I fear, therefore, that,
when I next meet the Admiral of the Grand Fleet (with
whom I used to discuss everything quite freely before he
sailed away to the war), he may forget to mention that
we may have his 3,000 ships at our need.

Since this present difference is in danger of losing the
healing influence of a kindly touch—has become an uncourteous monster of 35 heads and 3 appendices—I see no
early end of it. The British Foreign Office has a lot of
lawyers in its great back offices. They and our lawyers
will now butt and rebut as long as a goat of them is left
alive on either side. The two governments—the two
human, kindly groups—have retired: they don't touch, on
this matter, now. The lawyers will have the time of their
lives, each smelling the blood of the other.

If more notes must come—as the English papers report
over and over again every morning and every afternoon—
the President might do much by writing a brief, human
document to accompany the Appendices. If it be done
courteously, we can accuse them of stealing sheep and of
dyeing the skins to conceal the theft—without provoking
the slightest bad feeling; and, in the end, they'll pay
another *Alabama* award without complaint and frame
the check and show it to future ambassadors as Sir Edward
shows the *Alabama* check to me sometimes.

And it'll be a lasting shame (and may bring other Great
Wars) if lawyers are now permitted to tear the garments

with which Peace ought to be clothed as soon as she can escape from her present rags and tatters.

Yours always heartily,

W. H. P.

P. S. My dear House: Since I have—in weeks and months past—both telegraphed and written the Department (and I presume the President has seen what I've sent) about the feeling here, I've written this letter to you and not to the President nor Lansing. I will not run the risk of seeming to complain—nor even of seeming to seem to complain. But if you think it wise to send or show this letter to the President, I'm willing you should. This job was botched: there's no doubt about that. We shall not recover for many a long, long year. The identical indictment could have been drawn with admirable temper and the way laid down for arbitration and for keeping our interpretation of the law and precedents intact—all done in a way that would have given no offense.

The feeling runs higher and higher every day—goes deeper and spreads wider.

Now on top of it comes the *Ancona*.[1] The English press, practically unanimously, makes sneering remarks about our Government. After six months it has got no results from the *Lusitania* controversy, which Bernstorff is allowed to prolong in secret session while factories are blown up, ships supplied with bombs, and all manner of outrages go on (by Germans) in the United States. The English simply can't understand why Bernstorff is allowed to stay. They predict that nothing will come of the *Ancona* case, nor of any other case. Nobody wants us to get into the war—nobody who counts—but they are

---

[1]Torpedoed off Sardinia on Nov. 7, 1915, by the Austrians. There was a large loss of life, including many Americans.

losing respect for us because we seem to them to submit to anything.

We've simply dropped out. No English person ever mentions our Government to me. But they talk to one another all the time about the political anæmia of the United States Government. They think that Bernstorff has the State Department afraid of him and that the Pacifists dominate opinion—the Pacifists-at-any-price. I no longer even have a chance to explain any of these things to anybody I know.

It isn't the old question we used to discuss of our having no friend in the world when the war ends. It's gone far further than that. It is now whether the United States Government need be respected by anybody.

W. H. P.

CHAPTER XVI

DARK DAYS FOR THE ALLIES

To Edward M. House

June 30, 1915.

MY DEAR HOUSE:

There's a distinct wave of depression here—perhaps I'd better say a period of setbacks has come. So far as we can find out only the Germans are doing anything in the war on land. The position in France is essentially the same as it was in November, only the Germans are much more strongly entrenched. Their great plenty of machine guns enables them to use fewer men and to kill more than the Allies. The Russians also lack ammunition and are yielding more and more territory. The Allies —so you hear now—will do well if they get their little army away from the Dardanelles before the German-Turks eat 'em alive, and no Balkan state comes in to help the Allies. Italy makes progress—slowly, of course, over almost impassable mountains—etc., etc. Most of this doleful recital I think is true; and I find more and more men here who have lost hope of seeing an end of the war in less than two or three years, and more and more who fear that the Germans will never be forced out of Belgium. And the era of the giant aeroplane seems about to come—a machine that can carry several tons and several men and go great distances—two engines, two propellers, and the like. It isn't at all impossible, I am told, that these machines may be the things that will at last end the war—possibly, but I doubt it.

At any rate, it is true that a great wave of discouragement is come.   All these events and more seem to prove to my mind the rather dismal failure the Liberal Government made—a failure really to grasp the problem.   It was a dead failure.   Of course they are waking up now, when they are faced with a certain dread lest many soldiers prefer frankly to die rather than spend another winter in practically the same trenches.   You hear rumours, too, of great impending military scandals—God knows whether there be any truth in them or not.

In a word, while no Englishman gives up or will ever give up—that's all rot—the job he has in hand is not going well.   He's got to spit on his hands and buckle up his belt two holes tighter yet.   And I haven't seen a man for a month who dares hope for an end of the fight within any time that he can foresee.

I had a talk to-day with the Russian Ambassador.[1]   He wished to know how matters stood between the United States and Great Britain.   I said to him: "I'll give you a task if you have leisure.   Set to and help me hurry up your distinguished Ally in dealing with our shipping troubles."

The old man laughed—that seemed a huge joke to him; he threw up his hands and exclaimed—"My God! He is slow about his own business—has always been slow —can't be anything else."

After more such banter, the nigger in his wood-pile poked his head out: "Is there any danger," he asked, "that munitions may be stopped?"

The Germans have been preparing northern France for German occupation.   No French are left there, of course, except women and children and old men.   They must be fed or starved or deported.   The Germans put them on

---

[1] Count Beckendorff.

trains—a whole village at a time—and run them to the Swiss frontier. Of course the Swiss pass them on into France. The French have their own and—the Germans will have northern France without any French population, if this process goes on long enough.

The mere bang! bang! frightful era of the war is passed. The Germans are settling down to permanent business with their great organizing machine. Of course they talk about the freedom of the seas and such mush-mush; of course they'd like to have Paris and rob it of enough money to pay what the war has cost them, and London, too. But what they really want for keeps is seacoast—Belgium and as much of the French coast as they can win. That's really what they are out gunning for. Of course, somehow at some time they mean to get Holland, too, and Denmark, if they really need it. Then they'll have a very respectable seacoast—the thing that they chiefly lack now.

More and more people are getting their nerves knocked out. I went to a big hospital on Sunday, twenty-five miles out of London. They showed me an enormous, muscular Tommy sitting by himself in a chair under the trees. He had had a slight wound which quickly got well. But his speech was gone. That came back, too, later. But then he wouldn't talk and he'd insist on going off by himself. He's just knocked out—you can't find out just how much gumption he has left. That's what the war did for him: it stupefied him. Well, it's stupefied lots of folks who have never seen a trench. That's what's happened. Of all the men who started in with the game, I verily believe that Lloyd George is holding up best. He organized British finance. Now he's organizing British industry.

It's got hot in London—hotter than I've ever known

it.   It gets lonelier (more people going away) and sadder
—more wounded coming back and more visible sorrow.
We seem to be settling down to something that is more
or less like Paris—so far less, but it may become more and
more like it.   And the confident note of an earlier period
is accompanied by a dull undertone of much less cheerfulness.   The end is—in the lap of the gods.

W. H. P.

To Arthur W. Page

American Embassy, London,
July 25, 1915.

DEAR ARTHUR:

.   .   .   Many men here are very active in their
thought about the future relations of the United States
and Great Britain.   Will the war bring or leave them
closer together?   If the German machine be completely
smashed (and it may not be completely smashed) the
Japanese danger will remain.   I do not know how to
estimate that danger accurately.   But there is such a
danger.   And, if the German wild beast ever come to life
again, there's an eternal chance of trouble with it.   For
defensive purposes it may become of the very first importance that the whole English-speaking world should
stand together—not in entangling alliance, but with a
much clearer understanding than we have ever yet had.
I'll indicate to you some of my cogitations on this subject by trying to repeat what I told Philip Kerr[1] a fortnight ago—one Sunday in the country.   I can write this
to you without seeming to parade my own opinions.—
Kerr is one of "The Round Table," perhaps the best
group of men here for the real study and free discussion
of large political subjects.   Their quarterly, *The Round*

[1]Afterward private secretary to Premier Lloyd George.

Table, is the best review, I dare say, in the world. Kerr is red hot for a close and perfect understanding between Great Britain and the United States. I told him that, since Great Britain had only about forty per cent. of the white English-speaking people and the United States had about sixty per cent., I hoped in his natural history that the tail didn't wag the dog. I went on:

"You now have the advantage of us in your aggregation of three centuries of accumulated wealth—the spoil of all the world—and in the talent that you have developed for conserving it and adding to it and in the institutions you have built up to perpetuate it—your merchant ships, your insurance, your world-wide banking, your mortgages on all new lands; but isn't this the only advantage you have? This advantage will pass. You are now shooting away millions and millions, and you will have a debt that is bound to burden industry. On our side, we have a more recently mixed race than yours; you've begun to inbreed. We have also (and therefore) more adaptability, a greater keenness of mind in our masses; we are Old-World men set free—free of classes and traditions and all that they connote. Your so-called democracy is far behind ours. Your aristocracy and your privileges necessarily bring a social and economic burden. Half your people look backward.

"Your leadership rests on your wealth and on the power that you've built on your wealth."

When he asked me how we were to come closer together—"closer together, with your old-time distrust of us and with your remoteness?"—I stopped him at "remoteness."

"That's the reason," I said. "Your idea of our 're-moteness.' 'Remoteness' from what? From you? Are you not betraying the only real difficulty of a closer sym-

pathy by assuming that you are the centre of the world?
When you bring yourself to think of the British Empire
as a part of the American Union—mind you, I am not
saying that you would be formally admitted—but when
you are yourselves in close enough sympathy with us to
wish to be admitted, the chief difficulty of a real union
of thought will be gone. You recall Lord Rosebery's
speech in which he pictured the capital of the British
Empire being moved to Washington if the American
Colonies had been retained under the Crown? Well, it
was the Crown that was the trouble, and the capital of
English-speaking folk has been so moved and you still
remain 'remote.' Drop 'remote' from your vocabulary and your thought and we'll actually be closer together."

It's an enormous problem—just how to bring these
countries closer together. Perhaps nothing can do it but
some great common danger or some great common adventure. But this is one of the problems of your life-
time. England can't get itself clean loose from the continent nor from continental mediævalism; and with that
we can have nothing to do. Men like Kerr think that
somehow a great push toward democracy here will be
given by the war. I don't quite see how. So far the
aristocracy have made perhaps the best showing in defense of English liberty. They are paying the bills of
the war; they have sent their sons; these sons have died
like men; and their parents never whimper. It's a fine
breed for such great uses as these. There was a fine incident in the House of Lords the other day, which gave
the lie to the talk that one used to hear here about "de-
generacy." Somebody made a perfectly innocent proposal to complete a list of peers and peers' sons who had
fallen in the war—a thing that will, of course, be done,

just as a similar list will be compiled of the House of Commons, of Oxford and Cambridge Universities. But one peer after another objected vigorously lest such a list appear immodest. "We are but doing our duty. Let the matter rest there."

In a time like this the aristocracy proves its worth. In fact, all aristocracies grew chiefly out of wars, and perhaps they are better for wars than a real democracy. Here, you see, you run into one of those contradictions in life and history which make the world so hard to change. . . .

You know there are some reasons why peace, whenever it may come, will bring problems as bad as the problems of the war itself. I can think of no worse task than the long conferences of the Allies with their conflicting interests and ambitions. Then must come their conferences with the enemy. Then there are sure to be other conferences to try to make peace secure. And, of course, many are going to be dissatisfied and disappointed, and perhaps out of these disappointments other wars may come. The world will not take up its knitting and sit quietly by the fire for many a year to come. . . .

Affectionately,

W. H. P.

One happiness came to Mr. and Mrs. Page in the midst of all these war alarums. On August 4, 1915, their only daughter, Katharine, was married to Mr. Charles G. Loring, of Boston, Massachusetts. The occasion gave the King an opportunity of showing the high regard in which Page and his family were held. It had been planned that the wedding should take place in Westminster Abbey, but the King very courteously offered Miss Page the Royal chapel in St. James's Palace. This was a distinguished compliment, as it was the first time that any marriage, in which both bride and bridegroom were foreigners, had ever been celebrated in this building, which for centuries has been the scene of royal weddings. The special place which his daughter had always held in the Ambassador's affections is apparent in the many letters that now followed her to her new home in the United States. The unique use Page made of the initials of his daughter's name was characteristic.

To Mrs. Charles G. Loring

London, September 1, 1915.

My dear K. A. P-tain:

Here's a joke on your mother and Frank: We three (and Smith) went up to Broadway in the car, to stay there a little while and then to go on into Wales, etc. The hotel is an old curiosity shop; you sit on Elizabethan chairs by a Queen Anne table, on a drunken floor, and look at the pewter platters on the wall or do your best to look at them, for the ancient windows admit hardly any light. "Oh! lovely," cries Frank; and then he and your mother make out in the half-darkness a perfectly wonderful copper mug on the mantelpiece; and you go out and come in the ramshackle door (stooping every time) after you've felt all about for the rusty old iron latch, and then you step down two steps (or fall), presently to step up two more. Well, for dinner we had six kinds of meat and two meat pies and potatoes and currants! My dinner was a potato. I'm old and infirm and I have many ailments, but I'm not so bad off as to be able to live on a potato a day. And since we were having a vacation, I didn't see the point. So I came home where I have seven courses for dinner, all good; and Mrs. Leggett took my place in the car. That carnivorous company

Col. Edward M. House. From a painting by P. A. Laszlo

The Rt. Hon. Herbert Henry Asquith, Prime Minister
of Great Britain, 1908–1916

went on. They've got to eat six kinds of meat and two meat pies and—currants! I haven't. Your mother calls me up on the phone every morning—me, who am living here in luxury, seven courses at every dinner—and asks anxiously, "And how *are* you, dear?" I answer: " Prime, and how are *you*?" We are all enjoying ourselves, you see, and I don't have to eat six kinds of meat and two meat pies and—currants! They do; and may Heaven save 'em and get 'em home safe!

It's lovely in London now—fine, shining days and showers at night and Ranelagh beautiful, and few people here; but I don't deny its loneliness—somewhat. Yet sleep is good, and easy and long. I have neither an ocean voyage nor six kinds of meat and two meat pies and currants. I congratulate myself and write to you and mother.

You'll land to-morrow or next day—good; I congratulate you. Salute the good land for me and present my respectful compliments to vegetables that have taste and fruit that is not sour—to the sunshine, in fact, and to everything that ripens and sweetens in its glow.

And you're now (when this reaches you) fixing up your home—your *own* home, dear Kitty. Bless your dear life, you left a home here—wasn't it a good and nice one?—left it very lonely for the man who has loved you twenty-four years and been made happy by your presence. But he'll love you twenty-five more and on and on—always. So you haven't lost that—nor can you. And it's very fit and right that you should build your own nest; that adds another happy home, you see. And I'm very sure it will be very happy always. Whatever I can do to make it so, now or ever, you have only to say. But —your mother took your photograph with her and got it out of the bag and put it on the bureau as soon as she went to her room—a photograph taken when you were a little girl.

Hodson[1] came up to see me to-day and with tears of gratitude in his voice told me of the present that you and Chud had made him. He is very genuinely pleased. As for the rest, life goes on as usual.

I laugh as I think of all your new aunts and cousins looking you over and wondering if you'll fit, and then saying to one another as they go to bed: "She is lovely— isn't she?" I could tell 'em a thing or two if I had a whack at 'em.

And you'll soon have all your pretty things in place in your pretty home, and a lot more that I haven't seen. I'll see 'em all before many years—and you, too! Tell me, did Chud get you a dinner book? Keep your record of things: you'll enjoy it in later years. And you'll have a nice time this autumn—your new kinsfolk, your new friends and old and Boston and Cambridge. If you run across Mr. Mifflin, William Roscoe Thayer, James Ford Rhodes, President Eliot—these are my particular old friends whose names occur at the moment.

My love to you and Chud too,

Affectionately,

W. H. P.

The task of being "German Ambassador to Great Britain" was evidently not without its irritations.

To Arthur W. Page

September 15, 1915.

DEAR ARTHUR:

Yesterday was my German day. When the boy came up to my room, I told him I had some official calls to make.

---

[1] A messenger in the American Embassy.

"Therefore get out my oldest and worst suit." He looked much confused; and when I got up both my worst and best suits were laid out. Evidently he thought he must have misunderstood me. I asked your mother if she was ready to go down to breakfast. "Yes."—"Well, then I'll leave you." She grunted something and when we both got down she asked: "What *did* you say to me upstairs?" I replied: "I regard the incident as closed." She looked a sort of pitying look at me and a minute or two later asked: "What on earth is the matter with you? Can't you hear at all?" I replied: "No. Therefore let's talk." She gave it up, but looked at me again to make sure I was all there.

I stopped at the barber shop, badly needing a shave. The barber got his brush and razor ready. I said: "Cut my hair." He didn't talk for a few minutes, evidently engaged in deep thought.

When I got to my office, a case was brought to me of a runaway American who was caught trying to send news to Germany. "Very good," said I, "now let it be made evident that it shall appear therefore that his innocence having been duly established he shall be shot."

"What, sir?"

"That since it must be evident that his guilt is genuine therefore see that he be acquitted and then shot."

Laughlin and Bell and Stabler were seen in an earnest conference in the next room for nearly half an hour.

Shoecraft brought me a letter. "This is the most courteous complaint about the French passport bureau we have yet had. I thought you'd like to see this lady's letter. She says she knows you."

"Do not answer it, then."

He went off and conferred with the others.

Hodson spoke of the dog he sold to Frank. "Yes,"

said I, "since he was a very nice dog, therefore he was worthless."

"Sir?"

And he went off after looking back at me in a queer way.

The day went on in that fashion. When I came out to go to lunch, the stairs down led upward and I found myself, therefore, stepping out of the roof on to the sidewalk —the house upside down. Smith looked puzzled. "Home, sir?"

"No. Go the other way." After he had driven two or three blocks, I told him to turn again and go the other way—home!

Your mother said almost as soon as I got into the door —"What *was* the matter with you this morning?"

"Oh, nothing. You forget that I am the German Ambassador."

Now this whole narrative is a lie. Nothing in it occurred. If it were otherwise it wouldn't be German.

Affectionately,
W. H. P.

To Mrs. Charles G. Loring

London, 6 Grosvenor Square.
Sunday, September 19, 1915.

My dear Kitty:

You never had a finer autumnal day in the land of the free than this day has been in this old kingdom—fresh and fair; and so your mother said to herself and me: "Let's go out to the Laughlins' to lunch," and we went. There never was a prettier drive. We found out among other things that you pleased Mrs. Laughlin very much by your letter. Her garden changes every week or so, and it never was lovelier than it is now.—Then we came back home and dined alone. Well, since we can't have you and Chud and Frank, I don't care if we do dine alone sometimes for some time to come. Your mother's monstrous good company, and sometimes three is a crowd. And now is a good time to be alone. London never was so dull or deserted since I've known it, nor ever so depressed. The military (land) operations are not cheerful; the hospitals are all full; I see more wounded soldiers by far than at any previous time; the Zeppelins came somewhere to this island every night for a week— one of them, on the night of the big raid, was visible from our square for fifteen or twenty minutes—in general it is a dull and depressing time. I have thought that since you were determined to run off with a young fellow, you chose a pretty good time to go away. I'm afraid there'll be no more of what we call "fun" in this town as long as we stay here.

Worse yet: in spite of the Coalition Government and everybody's wish to get on smoothly and to do nothing but to push the war, since Parliament convened there's been a great row, which doesn't get less. The labour men give trouble; people blame the politicians: Lloyd George is saving the country, say some; Lloyd George ought to be hanged, say others. Down with Northcliffe! They seem likely to burn him at the stake—except those who contend that he has saved the nation. Some maintain that the cabinet is too big—twenty-two. More say that it has no leadership. If you favour conscription, you are a traitor: if you don't favour it, you are pro-German. It's the same sort of old quarrel they had before the war, only it is about more subjects. In fact, nobody seems very clearly to know what it's about. Meantime the Government is spending money at a rate that nobody ever dreamed of before. Three million pounds a day—some days five million. The Germans meantime are taking Russia; the Allies are not taking the Dardanelles; in France the old deadlock continues.   Boston at its worst must be far more cheerful than this.

Affectionately and with my love to Chud,

W. H. P.

To the President

London, September 26, 1915.

DEAR MR. PRESIDENT:

The suppression of facts about the military situation is more rigorous than ever since the military facts have become so discouraging.   The volume of pretty well authenticated news that I used to hear privately has become sensibly diminished.   Rumours that reach me by the back door, in all sorts of indirect ways, are not fewer, but fewer of them are credible.   There is great confusion, great fear, very great depression—far greater, I think, than England has felt, certainly since the Napoleonic scare and probably since the threat of the Armada.   Nobody, I think, supposes that England herself will be conquered: confidence in the navy is supreme.   But the fear of a practical defeat of the Allies on the continent is become general.   Russia may have to pay a huge indemnity, going far to reimburse Germany for the cost of the war; Belgium may be permanently held unless Germany receive an indemnity to evacuate, and her seaports may be held anyhow; the Germans may reach Constantinople before the Allies, and Germany may thus hold, when the war ends, an open way to the East; and France may have to pay a large sum to regain her northern territory now held by the Germans. These are not the convictions of men here, but they have distinctly become the fears; and many men's mind are beginning to adjust themselves to the possible end of the war, as a draw, with these results.   Of course such an end would be a real German victory and—another war as soon as enough men grow up to fight it.

When the more cheerful part of public opinion, especially when any member of the Government, affects to laugh at these fears, the people say: "Well, make known the facts that you base your hope on. Precisely how many men have volunteered? Is the voluntary system a success or has it reached its limit? Precisely what is the situation in the Dardanelles? Are the allied armies strong enough to make a big drive to break through the German line in France? Have they big guns and ammunition enough? What are the facts about the chance in the Dardanelles? What have we done with reference to the Balkan States?" Thus an angry and ominous political situation is arising. The censorship on war news apparently becomes severer, and the general fear spreads and deepens. The air, of course, becomes heavily charged with such rumours as these: that if the Government continue its policy of secrecy, Lloyd George will resign, seeing no hope of a real victory: that, if he do resign, his resignation will disrupt the Government—cause a sort cf earthquake; that the Government will probably fall and Lloyd George will be asked to form another one, since he is, as the public sees it, the most active and efficient man in political life; that, if all the Balkan States fail the Allies, Sir Edward Grey will be reckoned a failure and must resign; and you even now hear talk of Mr. Balfour's succeeding him.

It is impossible to say what basis there is for these and other such rumours, but they show the general very serious depression and dissatisfaction. Of that there is no doubt. Nor is there any doubt about grave differences in the Cabinet about conscription nor of grave fear in the public mind about the action of labour unions in hindering the utmost production of ammunition, nor of the increasing feeling that the Prime Minister doesn't lead the nation. Except Lloyd George and the Chancellor of the Exchequer[1] the Cabinet seems to suffer a sort of paralysis. Lord Kitchener's speech in the House of Lords, explaining the military situation, reads like a series of month-old bulletins and was a great disappointment. Mr. Asquith's corresponding speech in the House seemed to lack complete frankness. The nation feels that it is being kept in the dark, and all the military information that it gets is discouraging. Sir Edward Grey, as philosophic and enduring a man as I know, seems much more depressed than I have ever known him to be; Bryce is very very far from cheerful; Plunkett,[2] whom also you know, is in the dumps—it's hard to find a cheerful or a hopeful man.

The secrecy of official life has become so great and successful that prophecy of political changes must be mere guess work. But, unless good news come from the Dardanelles in particular, I have a feeling that Asquith may resign—be forced out by the gradual pressure of public opinion; that Lloyd George will become Prime Minister, and that (probably) Sir Edward Grey may resign. Yet I cannot take the prevailing military discouragement at its face value. The last half million men and the last million pounds will decide the contest, and the Allies will have these. This very depression strengthens the nation's resolution to a degree that they for the moment forget. The blockade and the armies in the field will wear Germany down—not absolutely conquer her, but wear her down—probably in another year.

In the meantime our prestige (if that be the right word), in British judgment, is gone. As they regard it, we have

[1]The Rt. Hon. Reginald McKenna.
[2]Sir Horace Plunkett.

permitted the Germans to kill our citizens, to carry on a worldwide underhand propaganda from our country (as well as in it), for which they have made no apology and no reparation but only vague assurances for the future now that their submarine fleet has been almost destroyed.   They think that we are credulous to the point of simplicity to accept any assurances that Bernstorff may give—in a word, that the peace-at-any-price sentiment so dominates American opinion and the American Government that we will submit to any indignity or insult—that we will learn the Germans' real character when it is too late to save our honour or dignity. There is no doubt of the definiteness or depth of this opinion.

And I am afraid that this feeling will show itself in our future dealings with this government.   The public opinion of the nation as well as the Government accepts their blockade as justified as well as necessary.   They will not yield on that point, and they will regard our protests as really inspired by German influence—thus far at least: that the German propaganda has organized and encouraged the commercial objection in the United States, and that this propaganda and the peace-at-any-price sentiment demand a stiff controversy with England to offset the stiff controversy with Germany; and, after all, they ask, what does a stiff controversy with the United States amount to?   I had no idea that English opinion could so quickly become practically indifferent as to what the United States thinks or does.   And as nearly as I can make it out, there is not a general wish that we should go to war.   The prevalent feeling is not a selfish wish for military help.   In fact they think that, by the making of munitions, by the taking of loans, and by the sale of food we can help them more than by military and naval action.

Their feeling is based on their disappointment at our submitting to what they regard as German dallying with us and to German insults. They believe that, if we had sent Bernstorff home when his government made its unsatisfactory reply to our first *Lusitania* note, Germany would at once have "come down"; opportunist Balkan States would have come to the help of the Allies; Holland and perhaps the Scandinavian States would have got some consideration at Berlin for their losses by torpedoes; that more attention would have been paid by Turkey to our protest against the wholesale massacre of the Armenians; and that a better settlement with Japan about Pacific islands and Pacific influence would have been possible for the English at the end of the war. Since, they argue, nobody is now afraid of the United States, her moral influence is impaired at every capital; and I now frequently hear the opinion that, if the war lasts another year and the Germans get less and less use of the United States as a base of general propaganda in all neutral countries, especially all American countries, they are likely themselves to declare war on us as a mere defiance of the whole world and with the hope of stirring up internal trouble for our government by the activity of the Germans and the Irish in the United States, which may hinder munitions and food and loans to the Allies.

I need not remark that the English judgment of the Germans is hardly judicial. But they reply to this that every nation has to learn the real, incredible character of the Prussian by its own unhappy experience. France had so to learn it, and England, Russia, and Belgium; and we (the United States), they say, fail to profit in time by the experience of these. After the Germans have used us to the utmost in peace, they will force us into war—or even flatly declare war on us when they think they can thus cause more embarrassment to the Allies, and when they conclude that the time is come to make sure that no great nation shall emerge from the war with a clear commercial advantage over the others; and in the meantime they will prove to the world by playing with us that a democracy is necessarily pacific and hence (in their view) contempt-ible. I felt warranted the other day to remark to Lord Bryce on the unfairness of much of the English judgment of us (he is very sad and a good deal depressed). "Yes," he said, "I have despaired of one people's ever really understanding another even when the two are as closely related and as friendly as the Americans and the Eng-lish."

You were kind enough to inquire about my health in your last note. If I could live up to the popular concep-tion here of my labours and responsibilities and delicate duties (which is most flattering and greatly exaggerated), I should be only a walking shadow of a man. But I am most inappreciately well. I imagine that in some year to come, I may enjoy a vacation, but I could not enjoy it now. Besides since civilization has gone backward several centuries, I suppose I've gone back with it to a time when men knew no such thing as a vacation. (Let's forgive House for his kindly, mistaken solicitude.) The truth is, I often feel that I do not know myself—body or soul, boots or breeches. This experience is making us all here different from the men we were—but in just what respects it is hard to tell. We are not within hearing of the guns (except the guns that shoot at Zeppelins when they come); but the war crowds itself in on us sensibly more and more. There are more wounded soldiers on the streets and in the parks. More and more families one knows lose their sons, more and more women their hus-bands. Death is so common that it seems a little thing.

Four persons have come to my house to-day (Sunday) in the hope that I may find their missing kinsmen, and two more have appealed to me on the telephone and two more still have sent me notes. Since I began this letter, Mrs. Page insisted on my going out on the edge of the city to see an old friend of many years who has just lost both his sons and whose prospective son-in-law is at home wounded. The first thing he said was: "Tell me, what is America going to do?" As we drove back, we made a call on a household whose nephew is "missing."—"Can't you possibly help us hear definitely about him?"

This sort of thing all day every day must have some effect on any man. Then—yesterday morning gave promise of a calm, clear day. I never know what sensational experience awaits me around the next corner. Then there was put on my desk the first page of a reputable weekly paper which was filled with an open letter to me written by the editor and signed. After the usual description of my multitudinous and delicate duties, I was called on to insist that my government should protest against Zeppelin raids on London because a bomb might kill me! Humour doesn't bubble much now on this side the world, for the censor had forbidden the publication of this open letter lest it should possibly cause American-German trouble! Then the American correspondents came in to verify a report that a news agency is said to have had that I was deluged with threatening letters!— More widows, more mothers looking for lost sons! . . . Once in a while—far less often than if I lived in a sane and normal world—I get a few hours off and go to a lonely golf club. Alas! there is seldom anybody there but now and then a pair of girls and now and then a pair of old fellows who have played golf for a century. Yet back in

London in the War Office I hear they indulge in dis-respectful hilarity at the poor game I play. Now how do they know? (You'd better look to your score with Grayson: the English have spies in America. A major-general in their spy-service department told Mrs. Page that they knew all about Archibald[1] before he got on the ship in New York.)

All this I send you not because it is of the slightest per-manent importance (except the English judgment of us) but because it will prove, if you need proof, that the world is gone mad. Everything depends on fighting power and on nothing else. A victory will save the Government. Even distinctly hopeful military news will. And English depression will vanish with a turn of the military tide. If it had been Bernstorff instead of Dumba—*that* would have affected even the English judgment of us. Tyrrell[2] remarked to me—did I write you? "Think of the freaks of sheer, blind Luck; a man of considerable ability like Dumba caught for taking a risk that an idiot would have avoided, and a fool like Bernstorff escaping!" Then he added: "I hope Bernstorff will be left. No other human being could serve the English as well as he is serving them." So, you see, even in his depression the English-man has some humour left—e. g., when that old sea dog Lord Fisher heard that Mr. Balfour was to become First Lord of the Admiralty, he cried out: "Damn it! he won't do: Arthur Balfour is too much of a gentleman." So John Bull is now, after all, rather pathetic—de-pressed as he has not been depressed for at least a hundred years. The nobility and the common man are doing their whole duty, dying on the Bosphorus or in France without

---

[1] It was Archibald's intercepted baggage that furnished the documents which caused Dumba's dismissal.

[2] Sir William Tyrrell, private secretary to Sir Edward Grey.

a murmur, or facing an insurrection in India; but the labour union man and the commercial class are holding back and hindering a victory. And there is no great national leader.

Sincerely yours,

WALTER H. PAGE.

CHAPTER XVII

CHRISTMAS IN ENGLAND, 1915

To Edward M. House

London, December 7, 1915.

MY DEAR HOUSE:

I hear you are stroking down the Tammany tiger—an easier job than I have with the British lion. You can find out exactly who your tiger is, you know the house he lives in, the liquor he drinks, the company he goes with. The British lion isn't so easy to find. At times in English history he has dwelt in Downing Street—not so now. So far as our struggle with him is concerned, he's all over the Kingdom; for he is public opinion. The governing crowd in usual times and on usual subjects can here overrun public opinion—can make it, turn it, down it, dodge it. But it isn't so now—as it affects us. Every mother's son of 'em has made up his mind that Germany must and shall be starved out, and even Sir Edward's scalp isn't safe when they suspect that he wishes to be lenient in that matter. They keep trying to drive him out, on two counts: (1) he lets goods out of Germany for the United States "and thereby handicaps the fleet"; and (2) he failed in the Balkans. Sir Edward is too much of a gentleman for this business of rough-riding over all neutral rights and for bribing those Balkan bandits.

I went to see him to-day about the *Hocking*, etc. He asked me: "Do *you know* that the ships of this line are really owned, in good faith, by Americans?"

"I'll answer your question," said I, "if I may then ask

103

you one.   No, I don't know of my own knowledge.   Now, *do you know* that they are *not* owned by Americans?"

He had to confess that he, of his own knowledge, didn't know.

"Then," I said, "for the relief of us both, I pray you hurry up your prize court."

When we'd got done quarrelling about ships and I started to go, he asked me how I liked Wordsworth's war poems.   "The best of all war poems," said he, "because they don't glorify war but have to do with its philosophy."   Then he told me that some friend of his had just got out a little volume of these war poems selected from Wordsworth; "and I'm going to send you a copy."

"Just in time," said I, "for I have a copy of 'The Life and Letters of John Hay'[1] that I'm sending to you."

He's coming to dine with me in a night or two: he'll do anything but discuss our Note with me.   And he's the only member of the Government who, I think, would like to meet our views; and he can't.   To use the language of Lowell about the campaign of Governor Kent—these British are hell-bent on starving the Germans out, and neutrals have mighty few rights till that job's done.

The worst of it is that the job won't be done for a very long time.   I've been making a sort of systematic round of the Cabinet to see what these fellows think about things in general at this stage of the game.   Bonar Law (the Colonies) tells me that the news from the Balkans is worse than the public or the newspapers know, and that still worse news will come.   Germany will have it all her own way in that quarter.

"And take Egypt and the canal?"

"I didn't say *that*," he replied.   But he showed that he fears even that.

[1]By William Roscoe Thayer, published in 1915.

Herbert C. Hoover, in 1914

principle it is the same fight that we have made, in our domestic field, during recent decades. Now the same fight has come on a far larger scale than men ever dreamed of before.

It isn't, therefore, for merely doctrinal reasons that we are concerned for the spread of democracy nor merely because a democracy is the only scheme of organization yet wrought out that keeps the door of opportunity open and invites all men to their fullest development. But we are interested in it because under no other system can the world be made an even reasonably safe place to live in. For autocracies (only) wage aggressive wars. Aggressive autocracies, especially military autocracies, must be softened down by peace (and they have never been so softened) or destroyed by war. The All-Highest doctrine of Germany today is the same as the Taxation-without-Representation of George III — only more virulent, stronger, and further-reaching. Only by its end can the German people recover and build up their character and take the permanent place in the world that they — thus changed — will be entitled to. They will either reduce Europe to the vassalage of a military autocracy, which may then overrun the whole world or drench it in blood, or they must through stages of Liberalism work their way towards some approach to a democracy; and there is no doubt which event is impending. The Liberal idea will win this struggle, and Europe will be out of danger of a

A facsimile page from the Ambassador's letter of November 24, 1916, resigning his Ambassadorship

I could go on with a dozen of 'em; but I sat down to write you a Christmas letter, and nothing else. The best news I have for you is not news at all, but I conceive it to be one of the best hopes of the future. In spite of Irishmen past, present, and to come; in spite of Germans, whose fuss will soon be over; in spite of lawyers, who (if left alone) would bankrupt empires as their clients and think they'd won a victory; I'm going to leave things here in a year and a half so that, if wise men wish to lay a plan for keeping the peace of the world, all they need to do will be to say first to Uncle Sam: "This fellow or that must understand that he can't break loose like a wild beast." If Uncle Sam agrees (and has a real navy himself), he'll wink at John Bull, and John will follow after. You see our blackleg tail-twisters have the whole thing backward. They say we truckle to the British. My plan is to lead the British—not for us to go to them but to have them come to us. We have three white men to every two white men in their whole Empire; and, when peace comes, we'll be fairly started on the road to become as rich as the war will leave them. There are four clubs in London which have no other purpose than this; and the best review[1] in the world exists chiefly for this purpose. All we need to do is to be courteous (we can do what we like if we do it courteously). Our manners, our politicians, and our newspapers are all that keep the English-speaking white man, under our lead, from ruling the world, without any treaty or entangling alliance whatsoever. If, when you went to Berlin to talk to your gentle and timid friend, the Emperor, about disarmament before the war—if about 200 American dreadnaughts and cruisers, with real grog on 'em, had come over to make a friendly call, in the North Sea, on the 300 English dread-

---

[1] The Ambassador had in mind *The Round Table.*

naughts and cruisers—just a friendly call, admirals on admirals—the "Star-Spangled Banner" and "God Save the King"—and if General Bell, from the Philippines, had happened in London just when Kitchener happened to be home from Egypt—*then, there wouldn't have been this war now.* Nothing need have been said—no treaty, no alliance, nothing. For then 100 or more British naval ships would have joined the Panama naval procession and any possible enemy would have seen that combined fleet clean across the Pacific.

Now this may all be a mere Christmas fancy—a mere yarn about what might have been—because we wouldn't have sent ships here in our old mood; the crew would have missed one Sunday School. But it's *this kind* of thing that does the trick. But this means the practice of courtesy, and we haven't acquired the habit. Two years or more ago the training ships from Annapolis with the cadets aboard anchored down the Thames and stayed several weeks and let the boys loose in England. They go on such a voyage every two years to some country, you know. The English didn't know that fact and they took the visit as a special compliment. Their old admirals were all greatly pleased, and I hear talk about that yet. We ought to have two or three of our rear-admirals here on their fleet now. Symington, of course, is a good fellow; but he's a mere commander and attaché—not an admiral—in other words, not any particular compliment or courtesy to the British Navy. (As soon as the war began, a Japanese admiral turned up here and he is here now.) We sent over two army captains as military observers. The Russians sent a brigadier-general. We ought to have sent General Wood. You see the difference? There was no courtesy in our method. It would be the easiest and prettiest job in the world to swallow

the whole British organization, lock, stock, and barrel—
King, Primate, Cabinet, Lords, and Commons, feathers
and all, and to make 'em follow our *courteous* lead anywhere. The President had them in this mood when the
war started and for a long time after—till the *Lusitania*
seemed to be forgotten and till the lawyers began to write
his Notes. He can get 'em back, after the war ends, by
several acts of courtesy—if we could get into the habit of
doing such things as sending generals and admirals as
compliments to them. The British Empire is ruled by a
wily use of courtesies and decorations. If I had the President himself to do the correspondence, if I had three or
four fine generals and admirals and a good bishop or
two, a thoroughbred senator or two and now and then a
Supreme Court Justice to come on proper errands and
be engineered here in the right way—wc could do or say
anything we liked and they'd do whatever we'd say. I'd
undertake to underwrite the whole English-speaking world
to keep peace, under our leadership. Instead whereof,
every move we now make is to *follow* them or to *drive*
them. The latter is impossible, and the former is unbe-
coming to us.

But to return to Christmas.—I could go on writing for
a week in this off-hand, slap-dash way, saying wise things
flippantly. But Christmas—that's the thing now. Christmas! What bloody irony it is on this side the world!
Still there will be many pleasant and touching things
done. An Englishman came in to see me the other day
and asked if I'd send $1,000 to Gerard[1] to use in making
the English prisoners in Germany as happy as possible
on Christmas Day—only I must never tell anybody who
did it. A lady came on the same errand—for the British

---

[1]James W. Gerard, American Ambassador to Germany, and, as such, in charge
of British interests in Germany.

prisoners in Turkey, and with a less but still a generous sum. The heroism, the generosity, the endurance and self-restraint and courtesy of these people would melt a pyramid to tears. Of course there are yellow dogs among 'em, here and there; but the genuine, thoroughbred English man or woman is the real thing—one of the realest things in this world. So polite are they that not a single English person has yet mentioned our Note to me—not one.

But every one I've met for two days has mentioned the sending of Von Papen and Boy-Ed[1] home—not that they expect us to get into the war, but because they regard this action as maintaining our self-respect.

Nor do they neglect other things because of the war. I went to the annual dinner of the Scottish Corporation the other night—an organization which for 251 years has looked after Scotchmen stranded in London; and they collected $20,000 then and there. There's a good deal of Christmas in 'em yet. One fellow in a little patriotic speech said that the Government is spending twenty-five million dollars a day to whip the Germans.—"Cheap work, very cheap work. We can spend twice that if necessary. Why, gentlemen, we haven't exhausted our pocket-change yet."

Somehow I keep getting away from Christmas. It doesn't stay put. It'll be a memorable one here for its sorrows and for its grim determination—an empty chair at every English table. But nowhere in the world will it be different except in the small neutral states here and in the lands on your side the world.

How many Christmases the war may last, nobody's wise enough to know. That depends absolutely on

---

[1]The German military and naval attachés, whose persistent and outrageous violation of American laws led to their dismissal by President Wilson.

Germany. The Allies announced their terms ten months ago, and nothing has yet happened to make them change them. That would leave the Germans with Germany and a secure peace—no obliteration or any other wild nonsense, but only a secure peace. Let 'em go back home, pay for the damage they've done, and then stay there. I do hope that the actual fighting will be ended by Christmas of next year. Of course it *may* end with dramatic suddenness at any time, this being the only way, perhaps, for the Kaiser to save his throne. Or it may go on for two or three years. My guess is that it'll end next year—a guess subject to revision, of course, by events that can't be foreseen.

But as I said before—to come back to Christmas. Mrs. Page and I send you and Mrs. House our affectionate good wishes and the hope that you keep very well and very happy in your happy, prosperous hemisphere. We do, I thank you. We haven't been better for years—never before so busy, never, I think, so free from care. We get plenty to eat (such as it is in this tasteless wet zone), at a high cost, of course; we have comfortable beds and shoes (we spend all our time in these two things, you know); we have good company, enough to do (!!), no grievances nor ailments, no ill-will, no disappointments, a keen interest in some big things—all the chips are blue, you know; we don't feel ready for halos, nor for other uncomfortable honours; we deserve less than we get and are content with what the gods send. This, I take it, is all that Martin[1] would call a comfortable mood for Christmas; and we are old enough and tough enough to have thick armour against trouble. When Worry knocks at the door, the butler tells him we're not at home.

And I see the most interesting work in the world cut

[1] E. S. Martin, Editor of *Life.*

out for me for the next twenty-five or thirty years—to get such courtesy into our dealings with these our kinsmen here, public and private—as will cause them to follow us in all the developments of democracy and—in keeping the peace of the world secure. I can't impress it on you strongly enough that the English-speaking folk have got to set the pace and keep this world in order. Nobody else is equal to the job. In all our dealings with the British, public and private, we allow it to be assumed that *they* lead: they don't. *We* lead. They'll follow, if we do really lead and are courteous to them. If we hold back, the Irishman rears up and says we are surrendering to the English! Suppose we go ahead and the English surrender to us, what can your Irishmen do then? Or your German? The British Navy is a pretty good sort of dog to have to trot under your wagon. If we are willing to have ten years of thoughtful good manners, I tell you Jellicoe will eat out of your hand.

Therefore, cheer up! It's not at all improbable that Ford[1] and his cargo of cranks, if they get across the ocean, may strike a German mine in the North Sea. Then they'll die happy, as martyrs; and the rest of us will live happy, and it'll be a Merry Christmas for everybody.

Our love to Mrs. House.

Always heartily yours,
W. H. P.

To Frank N. Doubleday and Others

London, Christmas, 1915.

DEAR D. P. & Co.

. . . Now, since we're talking about the war, let me deliver my opinion and leave the subject. They're

---

[1]Mr. Henry Ford at this time was getting together his famous peace ship, which was to sail to Europe "to get the boys out of the trenches by Christmas."

killing one another all right; you needn't have any doubt about that—so many thousand every day, whether there's any battle or not. When there's "nothing to report" from France, that means the regular 5,000 casualties that happen every day. There isn't any way of getting rid of men that has been forgotten or neglected. Women and children, too, of course, starve in Serbia and Poland and are massacred in Turkey. England, though she has by very much the largest army she ever had, has the smallest of all the big armies and yet I don't know a family that had men of fighting age which hasn't lost one or more members. And the worst is to come. But you never hear a complaint. Poor Mr. Dent,[1] for instance (two sons dead), says: "It's all right. England must be saved."

And this Kingdom alone, as you know, is spending twenty-five million dollars a day. The big loan placed in the United States[2] would last but twenty days! If this pace of slaughter and of spending go on long enough, there won't be any men or any money left on this side the world. Yet there will be both left, of course; for somehow things never quite go to the ultimate smash that seems to come. Read the history of the French Revolution. How did the French nation survive?

It will go on, unless some unexpected dramatic military event end it, for something like another year at least— many say for two years more, and some, three years more. It'll stop, of course, whenever Germany will propose terms that the Allies can consider—or something near such terms; and it won't stop before. By blockade pressure and by fighting, the Allies are gradually wearing the Germans out. We can see here the gradual pressure

---

[1] J. M. Dent, the London publisher.

[2] $500,000,000.

of events in that direction. My guess is that they won't go into a third winter.

Well, dear gentlemen, however you may feel about it, that's enough for me. My day—every day—is divided into these parts: (1) two to three hours listening to Americans or their agents here whose cargoes are stopped, to sorrowing American parents whose boys have run away and gone into the English Army, to nurses and doctors and shell makers who wish to go to France, to bereaved English men and women whose sons are "missing": can I have them found in Germany? (2) to answering letters about these same cheerful subjects; (3) to going over cases and documents prepared about all these sorts of troubles and forty other sorts, by the eight or ten secretaries of the Embassy, and a conference with every one of them; (4) the reading of two books of telegrams, one incoming, the other outgoing, and the preparation of a lot of answers; (5) going to the Foreign Office, not every day but often, to discuss more troubles there; (6) home to dinner at 8 o'clock—at home or somewhere else, and there is more talk about the war or about the political troubles. That for a regular daily routine for pretty nearly a year and a half! As I say, if anybody is keeping the war up for my entertainment, he now has my permission to stop. No time to read, no time to write, little time to think, little or no time to see the people you most wish to see, I often don't know the day of the week or of the month: it's a sort of life in the trenches, without the immediate physical danger. Then I have my cabinet meetings, my financial reports (money we spend for four governments: I had till recently about a million dollars subject to my check); then the commission for the relief of Belgium; then the Ambassadors and Ministers of the other neutral states— our task is worse than war!

Well, praise God for sleep. I get from seven to nine hours a night, unbroken; and I don't take Armageddon to bed with me.

I don't mind telling *you* (nobody else) that the more I see just how great statesmen work and manage great governments—the more I see of them at close range—whether in Washington or London or Berlin or Vienna or Constantinople (for these are *my* Capitals), the more I admire the methods of the Long Island farmers. Boys, I swear I could take our crowd and do a better job than many of these great men do. I have to spend a lot of time to correct their moves before the other fellow finds out the mistake. For instance I know I spent $2,000 in telegrams before I could make the German Government understand the British military age, and the British Government understand the German military age, for exchanging prisoners who had lost two legs or arms or both eyes; and I've had to send a man to Berlin to get a financial report from one man on one floor of a building there and to take it to another man on the floor above. Just yesterday I was reminded that I had made eighteen requests for the same information of the British Government, when the nineteenth request for it came from Washington; and I have now telegraphed that same thing nineteen times since the war began. Of course everybody's worked to death. But something else ails a lot of 'em all the way from Constantinople to London. Leaving out common gutter lying (and there's much of it) the sheer stupidity of governments is amazing. They are all so human, so mighty human! I wouldn't be a government for any earthly consideration. I'd rather be a brindled dog and trot under the wagon.

But it has been an inexpressibly interesting experience to find all this out for myself. There's a sort of weary satisfaction in feeling that you've seen too much of them to be fooled by 'em any more.   And, although most men now engaged in this game of government are mere common mortals with most of the common mortal weaknesses, now and then a really big man does stumble into the business. I have my doubts whether a really big man ever deliberately goes into it.   And most of the men who the crowd for the moment thinks are big men don't really turn out so.   It's a game like bull fighting.   The bull is likely to kill you—pretty sure to do so if you keep at the business long enough; but in the meantime you have some exciting experiences and the applause of the audience.   When you get killed, they forget you—immediately.   There are two rather big men in this Government, and you wouldn't guess in three rounds who they are. But in general the war hasn't so far developed very big men in any country.   Else we are yet too close to them to recognize their greatness.   Joffre seems to have great stuff in him; and (I assure you) you needn't ever laugh at a Frenchman again.   They are a great people.   As for the British, there was never such a race.   It's odd—I hear that it happens just now to be the fashion in the United States to say that the British are not doing their share.   There never was a greater slander.   They absolutely hold the Seven Seas.   They have caught about seventy submarines and some of them are now destroying German ships in the Baltic Sea.   They've sent to France by several times the largest army that any people ever sent over the sea.   They are financing most of their allies and they have turned this whole island into gun and shell factories. They made a great mistake at the Dardanelles and they are slower than death to change their set methods.   But no family in the land, from charcoal burners to dukes, hesitates one moment to send its sons into the army.

When the news comes of their death, they never whimper. When you come right down to hard facts, the courage and the endurance of the British and the French excel anything ever before seen on this planet. All the old stories of bravery from Homer down are outdone every day by these people. I see these British at close range, full-dress and undress; and I've got to know a lot of 'em as well as we can ever come to know anybody after we get grown. There is simply no end to the silly sides of their character. But, when the real trial comes, they don't flinch; and (except the thoroughbred American) there are no such men in the world.

A seven-foot Kansas lawyer (Kansas all over him) came to see me yesterday. He came here a month ago on some legal business. He told me yesterday that he had always despised Englishmen. He's seen a few with stud-horse clothes and white spats and monocles on who had gone through Kansas to shoot in the Rocky Mountains. He couldn't understand 'em and he didn't like 'em. "So infernally uppish," said he.

"Well, what do you think of 'em now?"

"The very best people in the world," said he. I think he has a notion of enlisting!

You're still publishing books, I hear. That's a good occupation. I'd like to be doing it myself. But I can't even get time to read 'em now.

But, as you know, nobody's writing anything but war books—from Kipling to Hall Caine. Poor Kipling!—his boy's dead. I have no doubt of it. I've had all the German hospitals and prison camps searched for him in vain. These writing men and women, by the way, are as true blue and as thoroughbred as any other class. I can never forget Maurice Hewlett's brave behaviour when he thought that his flying corps son had been killed by the

Germans or drowned at sea.   He's no prig, but a real man. And the women are as fine as the men.   .   .   .

To go back to books: Of course nobody can tell what effect the war will have on the writing of them, nor what sort of new writers may come up.   You may be sure that everything is stirred to its profoundest depths and will be stirred still more.   Some old stagers will be laid on the shelf; that's certain.   What sort of new ones will come? I asked H. G. Wells this question.   He has promised to think it out and tell me.   He has the power to guess some things very well.   I'll put that question to Conrad when I next see him.

Does anybody in the United States take the Prime Minister, Mr. Asquith, to be a great man?   His wife is a brilliant woman; and she has kept a diary ever since he became Prime Minister; and he now has passed the longest single term in English history.   Mr. Dent thinks he's the biggest man alive, and Dent has some mighty good instincts.

Talk about troubles!   Think of poor Northcliffe.   He thinks he's saved the nation from its miserable government, and the government now openly abuses him in the House of Commons.   Northcliffe puts on his brass knuckles and turns the *Times* building upside down and sets all the *Daily Mail* machine guns going, and has to go to bed to rest his nerves, while the row spreads and deepens.   The Government keeps hell in the prayerbook because without it they wouldn't know what to do with Northcliffe; and Northcliffe is just as sure that he has saved England as he is sure the Duke of Wellington did.

To come back to the war.   (We always do.)   Since I wrote the first part of this letter, I spent an evening with a member of the Cabinet and he told me so much bad military news, which they prevent the papers from publishing or even hearing, that to-night I almost share this man's opinion that the war will last till 1918. That isn't impossible. If that happens the offer that I heard a noble old buck make to a group of ladies the other night may be accepted. This old codger is about seventy-five, ruddy and saucy yet. "My dear ladies," said he, "if the war goes on and on we shall have no young men left. A double duty will fall on the old fellows. I shall be ready, when the need comes, to take four extra wives, and I daresay there are others of my generation who are as patriotic as I am."

All of which is only my long-winded, round-about diplomatic way of wishing you every one and every one of yours and all the folk in the office, their assigns, superiors, dependents, companions in labour—all, everyone and sundry, the happiest of Christmases; and when you take stock of your manifold blessings, don't forget to be thankful for the Atlantic Ocean. That's the best asset of safety that we have.

Affectionately yours,

W. H. P.

To Mrs. Charles G. Loring

6 Grosvenor Square,
London, December 7, 1915.

DEAR KITTY:

This is my Christmas letter to you and Chud—a poor thing, but the best I have to give you. At least it carries my love, dear, and my wishes that every Christmas under your own roof will be happier than the preceding one. Since your starting point is on the high level of your first Christmas in your own home—that's a good wish: isn't it?

I'm beginning to think a good deal of your mother and me. Here we are left alone by every one of you—in a foreign land; and, contrary to all predictions that any of you would have made about us four or five years ago, we're faring pretty well, thank you, and not on the edge of dying of loneliness at all. I tell you, I think we're pretty brave and hardy.

We're even capable of becoming cocky and saucy to every one of you. Be careful, then.

You see if you have a war to live with you don't necessarily need children: you'll have strife enough without 'em. We'll console ourselves with such reflections as these.

And the truth is—at least about me—that there isn't time to think of what you haven't got. Of course, I'm working, as always, to soften the relations between these two governments. So far, in spite of the pretty deep latent feeling on both sides—far worse than it ought to be and far worse than I wish it were—I'm working all the time to keep things as smooth as possible. Happily, nobody can prove it, but I believe it, that there is now and there has been all along more danger of a serious misunderstanding than anybody has known. The Germans have, of course, worked in 1000 ways to cause misunderstanding between England and the United States. Then, of course, there has been constant danger in the English bull-headed insularity which sees nothing but the Englishman's immediate need, and in the English slowness. Add to these causes the American ignorance of war and of European conditions. It has been a God's mercy for us that we have so far had a man like Sir Edward Grey in his post. And in my post, while there might well have been a better man, this much at least has been lucky—that I do have a consciousness of English history and of our common origin and some sense of the inevitable destiny of the great English-speaking race— so that, when we have come to sharp corners in the road, I have known that whatever happen we must travel in the right general direction—have known that no temporary difference must be allowed to assume a permanent quality. I have thought several times that we had passed the worst possible place, and then a still worse one would appear. It does look now as if we had faced most of the worst difficulties that can come, but I am not sure what Congress may do or provoke. If we outlast Congress, we shall be safe. Now to come through this enormous war even with no worse feeling than already exists between the two countries—that'll be a big thing to have done. But it's work like the work of the English fleet. Nobody can prove that Jellicoe has been a great admiral. Yet the fleet has done the whole job more successfully than if it had had sea-fights and lost a part of their ships.

Our Note has left a great deal of bad feeling—suppressed, but existent. A part of it was inevitable and (I'd say) even necessary. But we put in a lot of things that seem to me to be merely disputatious, and we didn't write it in the best form. It corresponds to what you once called *suburban:* do you remember? Not thoroughbred. But we'll get over even that, especially if the Administration and the courts continue to bring the Germans to book who are insulting our dignity and destroying our property and killing Americans. If we can satisfactorily settle the *Lusitania* trouble, the whole outlook will be very good.

Your mother and I are hearing much interesting political talk. We dined last night with Mr. Bonar Law. Sir Edward Carson was there. To-day we lunched with Lady P.—the other side, you see. There are fundamental differences continually arising. They thought a few weeks ago that they had the Prime Minister's scalp. He proved too nimble for them. Now one person after another says to you: "Kitchener doesn't deserve the reverence the people give him." More and more folks say he's hard to work with—is domineering and selfish. Nobody seems really to know him; and there are some signs that there may be a row about him.

We've heard nothing from Harold in quite a little while. We have, you know, three of our footmen in the war. Allen was wounded at Loos—a flesh, bullet-wound. He's about well now and is soon going back. Leslie is in the trenches and a postal card came from him the other day. The third one, Philip, is a prisoner in Germany. Your mother sent him a lot of things, but we've never heard whether he received them or not. The general strain—military, political, financial—gets greater. The streets are darker than ever. The number of wounded increases rapidly. More houses are turned into hospitals. The Manchesters', next door, is a hospital now. And everybody fears worse days are to come. But they have no nerves, these English. They grit their teeth, but they go on bravely, enduring everything. We run into experiences every day that melt you, and the heroic things we hear outnumber and outdo all the stories in all the books.

I keep forgetting Xmas, Kitty, and this is my Xmas letter. You needn't put it in your stocking, but you'd really better burn it up. It would be the ruination of the world if my frank comments got loose. It's for you and Chud only. You may fill your stocking full of the best wishes you ever received—enough to fill the polar bear skin. And I send you both my love.

W. H. P.

To Ralph W., Arthur W., and Frank C. Page[1]

London, Christmas, 1915.

DEAR BOYS: R. W. P., A. W. P., F. C. P.

A Merry Christmas to you! Good cheer, good company, good food, good fires, good golf. I suppose (though the Lord only knows) that I'll have to be here another Christmas; but another after that? Not on your life!

I think I'm as cheerful and hopeful as I ever was, but this experience here and the war have caused my general confidence in the orderly progress of civilization somewhat to readjust itself. I think that any man who looks over the world and who knows something of the history of human society—I mean any American who really believes in democracy and in human progress—is somewhat saddened to see the exceeding slowness of that progress. In the early days of our Republic hopeful Americans held the opinion that the other countries of the world would follow our example; that is to say, would educate the people, would give the masses a chance to become real men, would make their governments and institutions serve the people, would dispense with kings and gross privileges and become free. Well, they haven't done it. France is nominally a republic, but the masses of its people are far, far backward. Switzerland *is* a republic, but a very small one. Denmark is a very free state, in spite of its monarchical form of government. In South America they think they have republics, but they haven't the slightest idea of the real education and freedom of the people. Practically, therefore, the United States and the self-governing British colonies are the only really free countries of much importance in the whole world—

[1] The Ambassador's sons.

these and this Kingdom. Our example hasn't been followed. In Europe, Germany and Russia in particular have monarchs who are in absolute command. Thus on both sides the world, so far as government and the danger of war are concerned, there hasn't been very much real progress in five hundred years.

This is a little disappointing. And it means, of course, that we are likely to have periodical earthquakes like this present one till some radical change come. Republics have their faults, no doubt. But they have at least this virtue: that no country where the people really have the control of their government is likely to start out deliberately on any war of conquest—is not likely to run amuck—and will not regard its population as mere food for shell and powder.

Nor do I believe that our example of our government has, relatively to our strength and wealth and population, as much influence in the world as we had one hundred years ago. Our people have no foreign consciousness and I know that our government knows almost nothing about European affairs; nor do our people know. As regards foreign affairs our government lacks proper machinery. Take this as an illustration: The President wrote vigorous and proper notes about the *Lusitania* and took a firm stand with Germany. Germany has paid no attention to the *Lusitania* outrage. Yet (as I understand it) the people will not run the risk of war—or the Administration thinks they will not—and hence the President can do nothing to make his threat good. Therefore we stand in a ridiculous situation; and nobody cares how many notes we write. I don't know that the President could have done differently—unless, before he sent the *Lusitania* notes, he had called Congress together and submitted his notes to Congress. But, as the matter stands, the Germans are merely encouraged to blow up factories and practically to carry on war in the United States, because they know we can (or will) do nothing. Mere notes break nobody's skin.

We don't seem to have any machinery to bring any influence to bear on foreign governments or on foreign opinion; and, this being so, it is little wonder that the rest of the world does not follow our republican example.

And this sort of impotence in influence has curious effects at home. For example, the ship-purchase bill, as it was at the last session of Congress, was an economic crime. See what has happened: We have waked up to the fact that we must have a big navy. Well, a navy is of no far-fighting value unless we have auxiliary ships and a lot of 'em. Admiral Jellicoe has 3,000 ships under his command; and he couldn't keep his fleet on the job if he didn't have them. Most of them are commandeered merchant, passenger, and fishing ships. Now we haven't merchant, passenger, and fishing ships to commandeer. We've got to build and buy auxiliary ships to our navy. This, to my mind, makes the new ship-purchase bill, or something like it, necessary. Else our navy, when it comes to the scratch, will be of no fighting value, however big it be. It's the price we've got to pay for not having built up a merchant marine. And we haven't built up a merchant marine because we've had no foreign consciousness. While our Irishmen have been leading us to twist the Lion's tail, we've been depending almost wholly on English ships—and, in late years, on German ships. You can't cross the ocean yet in a decent American ship. You see, we've declared our independence; and, so far as individual development goes, we've worked it out. But the governmental machinery for maintaining it and for making it visible to the world—we've simply neglected to build it or to shape it. Hence the President's notes hurt nobody and accomplish nothing; nor could our navy put up a real fight, for lack of colliers and supply ships. It's the same way all around the horizon. And these are the reasons we haven't made our democracy impress the world more.

A democracy is not a quick-trigger war-engine and can't be made into one. When the quick-trigger engines get to work, they forget that a democracy does not consider fighting the first duty of man. You can bend your energies to peaceful pursuits or you can bend them to war. It's hard to do both at the same time. The Germans are the only people who have done both at the same time; and even they didn't get their navy big enough for their needs.

When the infernal thing's over—that'll be a glad day; and the European world won't really know what it has cost in men and money and loss of standards till it is over. . . .

Affectionately,

W. H. P.

To Walter H. Page, Jr.[1]

London, Christmas, 1915.

SIR:

For your first Christmas, I have the honour to send you my most affectionate greetings; and in wishing you all good health, I take the liberty humbly to indicate some of the favours of fortune that I am pleased to think I enjoy in common with you.

First—I hear with pleasure that you are quite well content with yourself—not because of a reasoned conviction of your own worth, which would be mere vanity and un-

---

[1] The Ambassador's infant grandson, son of Arthur W. Page.

worthy of you, but by reason of a philosophical disposition. It is too early for you to bother over problems of
self-improvement—as for me it is too late; wherefore we
are alike in the calm of our self-content. What others
may think or say about us is a subject of the smallest
concern to us. Therefore they generally speak well of
us; for there is little satisfaction in speaking ill of men
who care nothing for your opinion of them. Then, too,
we are content to be where we happen to be—a fact that
we did not order in the beginning and need not now
concern ourselves about. Consider the eternal coming
and going of folk. On every road many are travelling
one way and an equal number are travelling the other way.
It is obvious that, if they were all content to remain at
the places whence they set forth, the distribution of the
population would be the same. Why therefore move
hither and yon at the cost of much time and labour and
money, since nothing is accomplished thereby? We
spare ourselves by being content to remain where we are.
We thereby have the more time for reflection. Nor can
we help observing with a smile that all persons who have
good reasons to see us themselves make the necessary
journey after they discover that we remain fixed.

Again, people about us are continually doing this service and that for some other people—running errands,
mending fences, bearing messages, building, and tearing
down; and they all demand equal service in return. Thus
a large part of mankind keeps itself in constant motion
like bubbles of water racing around a pool at the foot of a
water-fall—or like rabbits hurrying into their warrens
and immediately hurrying out again. Whereas, while
these antics amuse and sadden us, we for the most part
remain where we are. Hence our wants are few; they
are generally most courteously supplied without our ask-

ing; or, if we happen to be momentarily forgotten, we can quickly secure anything in the neighbourhood by a little judicious squalling. Why, then, should we whirl as bubbles or scurry as rabbits? Our conquering self-possession gives a masterful charm to life that the victims of perpetual locomotion never seem to attain.

You have discovered, and my experience confirms yours, that a perpetual self-consciousness brings most of the misery of the world. Men see others who are richer than they; or more famous, or more fortunate—so they think; and they become envious. You have not reached the period of such empty vanity, and I have long passed it. Let us, therefore, make our mutual vows not to be disturbed by the good luck or the good graces of others, but to continue, instead, to contemplate the contented cat on the rug and the unenvious sky that hangs over all alike.

This mood will continue to keep our lives simple. Consider our diet. Could anything be simpler or better? We are not even tempted by the poisonous victuals wherewith mankind destroys itself. The very first sound law of life is to look to the belly; for it is what goes into a man that ruins him. By avoiding murderous food, we may hope to become centenarians. And why not? The golden streets will not be torn up and we need be in no indecent haste to travel even on them. The satisfactions of this life are just beginning for us; and we shall be wise to endure this world for as long a period as possible.

And sleep is good—long sleep and often; and your age and mine permit us to indulge in it without the sneers of the lark or the cock or the dawn.

I pray you, sir, therefore, accept my homage as the philosopher that you are and my assurance of that high

esteem indicated by my faithful imitation of your virtues.
I am,
  With the most distinguished consideration,
  With the sincerest esteem, and
  With the most affectionate good wishes,
                    Sir,
                      Your proud,
                        Humble,
                          Obedient
                            GRANDDADDY.

To Master Walter Hines Page,
  On Christmas, 1915.

CHAPTER XVIII

A PERPLEXED AMBASSADOR

THE beginning of the new year saw no improvement in German-American relations. Germany and Austria continued to violate the pledge given by Bernstorff after the sinking of the *Arabic*—if that shifty statement could be regarded as a "pledge." On November 7, 1915, the Austrians sank the *Ancona*, in the Mediterranean, drowning American citizens under conditions of particular atrocity, and submarine attacks on merchant ships, without the "warning" or attempt to save passengers and crew which Bernstorff had promised, took place nearly every day. On April 18, 1916, the *Sussex* was torpedoed in the English Channel, without warning and with loss of American life. This caused what seemed to be a real crisis; President Wilson sent what was practically an ultimatum to Germany, demanding that it "immediately declare and effect an abandonment of its present methods of warfare against passenger and freight carrying vessels," declaring that, unless it did so, the United States would sever diplomatic relations with the German Empire. In reply, Germany apparently backed down and gave the promise the President had demanded. However, it coupled this concession with an expression of its expectation that the United States would compel Great Britain to observe international law in the blockade. As this latter statement might be interpreted as a qualification of its surrender, the incident hardly ended satisfactorily.

128

To Arthur W. Page

Bournemouth
May 22, 1916.

DEAR ARTHUR:

I stick on the back of this sheet a letter that Sydney Brooks wrote from New York (May 1st) to the *Daily Mail*. He formulates a question that we have many times asked ourselves and that, in one way or other, comes into everybody's mind here. Of course the common fellow in Jonesville who has given most of his time and energy to earning a living for his wife and children has no foreign consciousness, whether his Jonesville be in the United States or in England or in France or in Zanzibar. The real question is, *Do* these fellows in Jonesville make up the United States? or has there been such a lack of prompt leadership as to make all the Jonesville people confused? It's hard for me to judge at this distance just how far the President has led and just how far he has waited and been pushed along. Suppose he had stood on the front steps every morning before breakfast for a month after the *Lusitania* went down and had called to the people in the same tone that he used in his note to Germany—had sounded a bugle call—would we have felt as we now feel? What would the men in Jonesville have done then? Would they have got their old guns down from over the doors? Or do they so want peace and so think that they can have peace always that they've lost their spine? Have they really been Bryanized, Fordized, Janeaddamsized, Sundayschooled, and Chautauquaed into supine creatures to whom the United States and the ideals of the Fathers mean nothing? Who think a German is as good as an Englishman? Who have no particular aims or aspirations for our country and for democracy? When T. R. was in the White House he surely was an active fellow. He called us to exercise ourselves every morning. He bawled "Patriotism" loudly. We surely thought we were awake during those strenuous years. Were we really awake or did we only look upon him and his antics as a sort of good show? All that time Bryan was peace-a-footing and prince-of-peacing. Now did he really have the minds of the people or did T. R.?

If we've really gone to sleep and if the United States stands for nothing but personal comfort and commercialism to our own people, what a job you and the patriotic men of your generation have cut out for you!

My own conviction (which I don't set great store by) is that our isolation and prosperity have not gone so far in softening us as it seems. They've gone a good way, no doubt; but I think that even the Jonesville people yet feel their Americanism. What they need is—leadership. Their Congressmen are poor, timid, pork-barrel creatures. Their governors are in training for the Senate. The Vice-President reads no official literature of the war, "because then I might have a conviction about it and that wouldn't be neutral." And so on. If the people had a *real* leadership, I believe they'd wake up even in Jonesville.

Well, let's let these things go for the moment. How's the Ambassador?[1] And the Ambassador's mother and sister? They're nice folks of whom and from whom I hear far too little. Give 'em my love. I don't want you to rear a fighting family. But these kids won't and mustn't grow up peace-cranks—not that anybody objects to peace, but I do despise and distrust a crank, a crank about anything. That's the lesson we've got to learn from these troubled times. First, let cranks alone—the other side of the street is good enough for them. Then,

---

[1] A playful reference to the Ambassador's infant grandson, Walter H. Page, **Jr.**

if they persist, I see nothing to do but to kill 'em, and that's troublesome and inconvenient.

But, as I was saying, bless the babies. I can't begin to tell you how very much I long to see them, to make their acquaintance, to chuckle 'em and punch 'em and see 'em laugh, and to see just what sort of kids they be.

I've written you how in my opinion there's no country in the world fit for a modern gentleman and man-of-char-acter to live in except (1) the United States and (2) this island. And this island is chiefly valuable for the breed of men—the right stock. They become more valuable to the world after they go away from home. But the right blood's here. This island's breed is the best there is. An Englishman or a Scotchman is the best ancestor in this world, many as his shortcomings are. Some English-man asked me one night in what, I thought, the English-man appeared at his best. I said, "As an ancestor to Americans!" And this is the fundamental reason why we (two peoples) belong close together. Reasons that flow from these are such as follows: (1) The race is the sea-mastering race and the navy-managing race and the ocean-carrying race; (2) the race is the literary race, (3) the exploring and settling and colonizing race, (4) the race to whom fair play appeals, and (5) that insists on individual development.

Your mother having read these two days 1,734 pages of memoirs of the Coke family, one of whose members wrote the great law commentaries, another carried pro-Ameri-can votes in Parliament in our Revolutionary times, re-fused peerages, defied kings and—begad! here they are now, living in the same great house and saying and doing what they darn please—we know this generation of 'em!—well, your mother having read these two big volumes about the old ones and told me 175 good stories out of these books, bless her soul! she's gone to sleep in a big chair on the other side of the table.   Well she may, she walked for two hours this morning over hills and cliffs and through pine woods and along the beach.   I guess I'd better wake her up and get her to go to bed—as the properer thing to do at this time o'night, viz. 11.   My golf this afternoon was too bad to confess.   But I must say that a 650 and a 730 yard hole argues the audacity of some fellow and the despair of many more.   Nature made a lot of obstructions there and Man made more.   It must be seven or eight miles around that course!   It's almost a three hour task to follow my slow ball around it.   I suggested we play with howitzers instead of clubs.   Good night!

W. H. P.

To Frank N. Doubleday and Others

Royal Bath and East Cliff Hotel,
Bournemouth, May 29, 1916.

DEAR D. P. & Co.:

I always have it in mind to write you letters; but there's no chance in my trenches in London; and, since I have not been out of London for nearly two years—since the war began—only an occasional half day and a night—till now—naturally I've concocted no letter.   I've been down here a week—a week of sunshine, praise God—and people are not after me every ten minutes, or Governments either; and my most admirable and efficient staff (now grown to one hundred people) permit few letters and telegrams to reach me.   There never was a little rest more grateful.   The quiet sea out my window shows no sign of crawling submarines; and, in general, it's as quiet and peaceful here as in Garden City itself.

I'm on the home-stretch now in all my thoughts and plans.   Three of my four years are gone, and the fourth will quickly pass. That's not only the limit of my leave, but it's quite enough for me. I shouldn't care to live through another such experience, if the chance should ever come to me. It has changed my whole life and my whole outlook on life; and, perhaps, you'd like to hear some inpressions that it has made upon me.

The first impression—perhaps the strongest—is a loss of permanent interest in Europe, especially all Europe outside of this Kingdom. I have never had the illusion that Europe had many things that we needed to learn. The chief lesson that it has had, in my judgment, is the lesson of the art of living—the comforts and the courtesies of life, the refinements and the pleasures of conversation and of courteous conduct. The upper classes have this to teach us; and we need and can learn much from them. But this seems to me all—or practically all. What we care most for are individual character, individual development, and a fair chance for every human being. Character, of course, the English have—immense character, colossal character. But even they have not the dimmest conception of what we mean by a fair chance for every human being—not the slightest. In one thousand years they *may* learn it from us. Now on the continent, the only important Nation that has any character worth mentioning is the French. Of course the little nations— some of them—have character, such as Holland, Switzerland, Sweden, etc. But these are all. The others are simply rotten. In giving a free chance to every human creature, we've nothing to learn from anybody. In character, I bow down to the English and Scotch; I respect the Frenchman highly and admire his good taste. But, for our needs and from our point of view, the English can teach us only two great lessons—character and the art of living (if you are rich).

The idea that we were brought up on, therefore, that Europe is the home of civilization in general—nonsense! It's a periodical slaughter-pen, with all the vices that this implies. I'd as lief live in the Chicago stock-yards. There they kill beeves and pigs. Here they kill men and (incidentally) women and children. I should no more think of encouraging or being happy over a child of mine becoming a European of any Nation than I should be happy over his fall from Grace in any other way.

Our form of government and our scheme of society— God knows they need improving—are yet so immeasurably superior, as systems, to anything on this side the world that no comparison need be made.

My first strong impression, then, is not that Europe is "effete"—that isn't it. It is mediæval—far back toward the Dark Ages, much of it yet uncivilized, held back by *inertia* when not held back by worse things. The caste system is a constant burden almost as heavy as war itself and often quite as cruel.

The next impression I have is, that, during the thousand years that will be required for Europe to attain real (modern) civilization, wars will come as wars have always come in the past. The different countries and peoples and governments will not and cannot learn the lesson of federation and coöperation so long as a large mass of their people have no voice and no knowledge except of their particular business. Compare the miles of railway in proportion to population with the same proportion in the United States—or the telephones, or the use of the mails, or of bank checks; or make any other practical measure you like. Every time, you'll come back to the discouraging fact that the masses in Europe are driven as cattle. So long as this is true, of course, they'll be driven periodically into wars. So many countries, so many races, so many languages all within so small an area as Europe positively invite deadly differences. If railroads had been invented before each people had developed its own separate language, Europe could somehow have been coördinated, linked up, federated, made to look at life somewhat in the same way. As it is, wars will be bred here periodically for about another thousand years. The devil of this state of things is that they may not always be able to keep their wars at home.

For me, then, except England and the smaller exceptions that I have mentioned, Europe will cut no big figure in my life. In all the humanities, we are a thousand years ahead of any people here. So also in the adaptabilities and the conveniences of life, in its versatilities and in its enjoyments. Most folk are stolid and sad or dull on this side of the world. Else how could they take their kings and silly ceremonies seriously?

Now to more immediate and definite impressions. I have for a year had the conviction that we ought to get into the war—into the economic war—for the following among many reasons.

1. That's the only way to shorten it. We could cause Germany's credit (such as she has) instantly to collapse, and we could hasten her hard times at home which would induce a surrender.

2. That's the only way we can have any real or important influence in adjusting whatever arrangements can be made to secure peace.

3. That's the best way we can inspire complete respect for us in the minds of other nations and thereby, perhaps, save ourselves from some wars in the future.

4. That's the best way we can assert our own character—our Americanism, and forever get rid of all kinds of hyphens.

5. That's the only way we shall ever get a real and sensible preparedness, which will be of enormous educational value even if no military use should ever be made of our preparation.

6. That's the only way American consciousness will ever get back to the self-sacrificing and patriotic point of view of the Fathers of the Republic.

7. That's the best way to emancipate ourselves from cranks.

8. That's the only way we'll ever awaken in our whole people a foreign consciousness that will enable us to assert our natural influence in the world—political, financial, social, commercial—the best way to make the rest of the world our customers and friends and followers.

All the foregoing I have fired at the Great White Chief for a year by telegraph and by mail; and I have never fired it anywhere else till now. Be very quiet, then.

No man with whom I have talked or whose writings I have read seems to me to have an adequate conception of the colossal changes that the war is bringing and will bring. Of course, I do not mean to imply that I have any adequate conception. Nobody can yet grasp it. The loss of (say) ten million men from production of work or wares or children; what a changed world that fact alone will make! The presence in all Europe of (perhaps) fifteen or twenty million more women than men will upset the whole balance of society as regards the sexes. The loss of most of the accumulated capital of Europe and the vast burdens of debt for the future to pay will change the financial relations of the whole world. From these two great losses—men and money—God knows the many kinds of changes that will come. Women are doing and will continue to do many kinds of work hitherto done by men.

Of course there are some great gains. Many a flabby or abject fellow will come out of the war a real man: he'll be nobody's slave thereafter. The criminal luxury of the rich will not assert itself again for a time. The unparalleled addition to the world's heroic deeds will be to the good of mankind, as the unparalleled suffering has eclipsed all records. The survivors will be in an heroic mood for the rest of their lives. In general, life will start on a new plane and a lot of old stupid habits and old party quarrels and class prejudices will disappear. To get Europe going again will call for new resolution and a new sort of effort. Nobody can yet see what far-reaching effects it will have on government.

If I could make the English and Scotch over, I could greatly improve them. I'd cut out the Englishman's arrogance and key him up to a quicker gait. Lord! he's a slow beast. But he's worked out the germ and the beginning of all real freedom, and he has character. He knows how to conserve and to use wealth. He's a great John Bull, after all. And as for commanding the sea, for war or trade, you may properly bow down to him and pay him homage. The war will, I think, quicken him up. It will lessen his arrogance—to *us*, at least. I think it will make him stronger and humbler. And, whatever his virtues and his faults, he's the only Great Power we can go hand in hand with. . . .

These kinds of things have been going on now nearly two years, and not till these ten days down here have I had time or chance or a free mind to think them over; and now there's nothing in particular to think—nothing but just to go on, doing these 40,000 things (and they take a new turn every day) the best I can, without the slightest regard to consequences. I've long ago passed the place where, having acted squarely according to my best judgment, I can afford to pay the slightest attention to what anybody thinks. I see men thrown on the scrap heap every day. Many of them deserve it, but a good many do not. In the abnormal state of mind that everybody has, there are inevitable innocent misunderstandings, which are as fatal as criminal mistakes. The diplomatic service is peculiarly exposed to misunderstandings: and, take the whole diplomatic service of all nations as shown up by this great strain, it hasn't stood the test very well. I haven't the respect for it that I had when I started. Yet, God knows, I have a keen sympathy for it. I've seen some of 'em displaced; some of 'em lie down; some of 'em die.

As I've got closer and closer to big men, as a rule they shrink up. They are very much like the rest of us— many of 'em more so. Human nature is stripped in these times of most of its disguises, and men have to stand and be judged as a rule by their real qualities. Among all the men in high place here, Sir Edward Grey stands out in my mind bigger, not smaller, than he stood in the beginning. He's a square, honourable gentleman, if there is one in this world. And it is he, of course, with whom I have had all my troubles. It's been a truly great experience to work and to quarrel with such a man. We've kept the best friendship—a constantly ripening one. There are others like him—only smaller.

Yet they are all in turn set upon by the press or public opinion and hounded like criminals. They try (somebody tries) to drive 'em out of office every once in a while. If there's anything I'm afraid of, it's the newspapers. The correspondents are as thick as flies in summer—all hunting sensations—especially the yellow American press. I play the game with these fellows always squarely, sometimes I fear indiscreetly. But what is discretion? That's the hardest question of all. We have regular meetings. I tell 'em everything I can—always on the condition that I'm kept out of the papers. If they'll never mention me, I'll do everything possible for them. Absolute silence of the newspapers (as far as I can affect it) is the first rule of safety. So far as I know, we've done fairly well; but always in proportion to silence. I don't want any publicity. I don't want any glory. I don't want any office. I don't want nothin'—but to do this job squarely, to get out of this scrape, to go off somewhere in the sunshine and to see if I can slip back into my old self and see the world sane again. Yet I'm immensely proud that I have had the chance to do some good—to keep our record straight—as far as I can, and to be of what service I can to these heroic people.

Out of it all, one conviction and one purpose grows and becomes clearer. The world isn't yet half-organized. In the United States we've lived in a good deal of a fool's paradise. The world isn't half so safe a place as we supposed. Until steamships and telegraphs brought the nations all close together, of course we could enjoy our isolation. We can't do so any longer. One mad fool in Berlin has turned the whole earth topsy-turvy. We'd forgotten what our forefathers learned—the deadly dangers of real monarchs and of castes and classes. There are a lot of 'em left in the world yet. We've grown rich and—weak; we've let cranks and old women shape our ideas. We've let our politicians remain provincial and ignorant.

And believe me, dear D. P. & Co. with affectionate greeting to every one of you and to every one of yours, collectively and singly,

Yours heartily,

W. H. P.

Memorandum written after attending the service at St. Paul's in memory of Lord Kitchener.[1]

American Embassy, London.

There were two Kitcheners, as every informed person knows—(1) the popular hero and (2) the Cabinet Minister with whom it was impossible for his associates to get along. He made his administrative career as an autocrat dealing with dependent and inferior peoples. This experience fixed his habits and made it impossible for him to do team work or to delegate work or even to inform his associates of what he had done or was doing. While, therefore, his name raised a great army, he was in many ways a hindrance in the Cabinet. First one thing and then another was taken out of his hands—ordnance, munitions, war plans. When he went to Gallipoli, some persons predicted that he would never come back. There was a hot meeting of the Cabinet at which he was asked to go to Russia, to make a sort of return visit for the visit that important Russians had made here, and to link up Russia's military plans with the plans of the Western Allies. He is said to have remarked that he was going only because he had been ordered to go. There was a hope and a feeling again that he might not come back till after the war.

Now just how much truth there is in all this, one has to guess; but undoubtedly a good deal. He did much in raising the army, but his name did more. What an extraordinary situation! The great hero of the Nation an impossible man to work with. The Cabinet could not tell the truth about him: the people would not believe it and would make the Cabinet suffer. Moreover, such a row would have given comfort to the enemy. Kitchener,

---

[1] Drowned on the *Hampshire*, June 5, 1916, off the coast of Scotland.

on his part, could not afford to have an open quarrel. The only solution was to induce him to go away for a long time. Both sides saw that. Such thoughts were in everybody's mind while the impressive funeral service was said and sung in St. Paul's. The Great Hero, who had failed, was celebrated of course as a Great Hero—quite truly and yet far from true. For him his death came at a lucky time: his work was done.

There is even a rumour, which I don't for a moment believe, that he is alive on the Orkney Islands and prefers to disappear there till the war ends. This is fantastic, and it was doubtless suggested by the story that he did disappear for several years while he was a young officer.

I could not help noticing, when I saw all the Cabinet together at the Cathedral, how much older many of them look than they looked two years ago. Sir Edward Grey, Mr. Asquith, Mr. Balfour, who is really an old man, Lloyd George—each of these seems ten years older. And so does the King. The men in responsible places who are not broken by the war will be bent. General French, since his retirement to command of the forces in England, seems much older. So common is this quick aging that Lady Jellicoe, who went to Scotland to see her husband after the big naval battle, wrote to Mrs. Page in a sort of rhapsody and with evident surprise that the Admiral really did not seem older! The weight of this thing is so prodigious that it is changing all men who have to do with it. Men and women (who do not wear mourning) mention the death of their sons in a way that a stranger might mistake for indifference. And it has a curious effect on marriages. Apparently every young fellow who gets a week's leave from the trenches comes home and marries and, of course, goes straight back—especially the young officers.   You see weddings all day as you pass the favourite churches; and already the land is full of young widows.

To Edwin A. Alderman[1]

Embassy of the U. S. A., London,
June 22, 1916.

MY DEAR ED ALDERMAN:

I shall not forget how good you were to take time to write me a word about the meeting of the Board—*the* Board: there's no other one in that class—at Hampton,[2] and I did most heartily appreciate the knowledge that you all remembered me.   Alas! it's a long, long time ago when we all met—so long ago that to me it seems a part of a former incarnation.   These three years—especially these two years of the war—have changed my whole outlook on life and foreshortened all that came before.   I know I shall never link back to many things (and alas! too, to many people) that once seemed important and surely were interesting.   Life in these trenches (five warring or quarrelling governments mining and sapping under me and shooting over me)—two years of universal ambassadorship in this hell are enough—enough I say, even for a man who doesn't run away from responsibilities or weary of toil.   And God knows how it has changed me and is changing me: I sometimes wonder, as a merely intellectual and quite impersonal curiosity.

Strangely enough I keep pretty well—very well, in fact. Perhaps I've learned how to live more wisely than I knew in the old days; perhaps again, I owe it to my old grandfather who lived (and enjoyed) ninety-four years.   I

---

[1]President of the University of Virginia.

[2]Hampton Institute, at Hampton, Va.

have walked ten miles to-day and I sit down as the clock strikes eleven (P. M.) to write this letter.

You will recall more clearly than I certain horrible, catastrophic, universal-ruin passages in Revelation—monsters swallowing the universe, blood and fire and clouds and an eternal crash, rolling ruin enveloping all things—well, all that's come. There are, perhaps, ten million men dead of this war and, perhaps, one hundred million persons to whom death would be a blessing. Add to these as many millions more whose views of life are so distorted that blank idiocy would be a better mental outlook, and you'll get a hint (and only a hint) of what the continent has already become—a bankrupt slaughter-house inhabited by unmated women. We have talked of "problems" in our day. We never had a problem; for the worst task we ever saw was a mere blithe pastime compared with what these women and the few men that will remain here must face. The hills about Verdun are not blown to pieces worse than the whole social structure and intellectual and spiritual life of Europe. I wonder that anybody is sane.

Now we have swung into a period and a state of mind wherein all this seems normal. A lady said to me at a dinner party (think of a dinner party at all!), "Oh, how I shall miss the war when it ends! Life without it will surely be dull and tame. What can we talk about? Will the old subjects ever interest us again?" I said, "Let's you and me try and see." So we talked about books—not war books—old country houses that we both knew, gardens and gold and what not; and in fifteen minutes we swung back to the war before we were aware.

I get out of it, as the days rush by, certain fundamental convictions, which seem to me not only true—true beyond any possible cavil—truer than any other political things are true—and far more important than any other contemporary facts whatsoever in any branch of endeavour, but better worth while than anything else that men now living may try to further:

1.   The cure for democracy is more democracy.   The danger to the world lies in autocrats and autocracies and privileged classes; and these things have everywhere been dangerous and always will be.   There's no security in any part of the world where people cannot think of a government without a king, and there never will be.   You cannot conceive of a democracy that will unprovoked set out on a career of conquest.   If all our religious missionary zeal and cash could be turned into convincing Europe of this simple and obvious fact, the longest step would be taken for human advancement that has been taken since 1776.   If Carnegie, or, after he is gone, his Peace People could see this, his Trust might possibly do some good.

2.   As the world stands, the United States and Great Britain must work together and stand together to keep the predatory nations in order.   A League to Enforce Peace and the President's idea of disentangling alliances are all in the right direction, but vague and general and cumbersome, a sort of bastard children of Neutrality. *The* thing, the *only* thing is—a perfect understanding between the English-speaking peoples.   That's necessary, and that's all that's necessary.   We must boldly take the lead in that.   I frankly tell my friends here that the English have got to throw away their damned arrogance and their insularity and that we Americans have got to throw away our provincial ignorance ("What is abroad to us?"), hang our Irish agitators and shoot our hyphenates and bring up our children with reverence for English history and in the awe of English literature.   This is the only job now in the world worth the whole zeal and

energy of all first-class, thoroughbred English-speaking men. *We* must lead. We are natural leaders. The English must be driven to lead. Item: We must get their lads into our universities, ours into theirs. They don't know how to do it, except the little driblet of Rhodes men. Think this out, remembering what fools we've been about exchange professors with Germany! How much good could Fons Smith[1] do in a thousand years, on such an errand as he went on to Berlin? And the English don't know *how* to do it. They are childish (in some things) beyond belief. An Oxford or Cambridge man never thinks of going back to his university except about twice a lifetime when his college formally asks him to come and dine. Then he dines as docilely as a scared Freshman. I am a D. C. L. of Oxford. I know a lot of their faculty. They are hospitality itself. But I've never yet found out one important fact about the university. They never tell me. I've been down at Cambridge time and again and stayed with the Master of one of the colleges. I can no more get at what they do and how they do it than I could get at the real meaning of a service in a Buddhist Temple. I have spent a good deal of time with Lord Rayleigh, who is the Chancellor of Cambridge University. He never goes there. If he were to enter the town, all the men in the university would have to stop their work, get on their parade-day gowns, line-up by precedent and rank and go to meet him and go through days of ceremony and incantations. I think the old man has been there once in five years. Now this mediævalism must go—or be modified. You fellers who have universities must work a real alliance—a big job here. But to go on.

[1] C. Alphonso Smith, Professor of English, U. S. Naval Academy; Roosevelt Professor at Berlin, 1910–11.

The best informed English opinion is ripe for a complete working understanding with us. We've got to work up our end—get rid of our ignorance of foreign affairs, our shirt-sleeve, complaining kind of diplomacy, our sport of twisting the lion's tail and such things and fall to and bring the English out. It's the *one* race in this world that's got the guts.

Hear this in confirmation: I suppose 1,000 English women have been to see me—as a last hope—to ask me to have inquiries made in Germany about their "missing" sons or husbands, generally sons. They are of every class and rank and kind, from marchioness to scrub-woman. Every one tells her story with the same dignity of grief, the same marvellous self-restraint, the same courtesy and deference and sorrowful pride. Not one has whimpered—but one. And it turned out that she was a Belgian. It's the breed. Spartan mothers were theatrical and pinchbeck compared to these women.

I know a lady of title, very well to do, who for a year got up at 5:30 and drove herself in her own automobile from her home in London to Woolwich where she worked all day long in a shell factory as a volunteer and got home at 8 o'clock at night. At the end of a year they wanted her to work in a London place where they keep the records of the Woolwich work. "Think of it," said she, as she shook her enormous diamond ear-rings as I sat next to her at dinner one Sunday night not long ago, "think of it—what an easy time I now have. I don't have to start till half-past seven and I get home at half-past six!"

I could fill forty pages with stories like these. This very Sunday I went to see a bedridden old lady who sent me word that she had something to tell me. Here it was: An English flying man's machine got out of order and he had to descend in German territory. The Germans captured him and his machine. They ordered him to take two of their flying men in his machine to show them a particular place in the English lines. He declined. "Very well, we'll shoot you, then." At last he consented. The three started. The Englishman quietly strapped himself in. There were no straps for the two Germans. The Englishman looped-the-loop. The Germans fell out. The Englishman flew back home. "My son has been to see me from France. He told me that. He knows the man"—thus said the old lady and thanked me for coming to hear it! She didn't know that the story has been printed.

But the real question is, "How are you?" Do you keep strong? Able, without weariness, to keep up your good work? I heartily hope so, old man. Take good care of yourself—very.

My love to Mrs. Alderman. Please don't quote me—yet. I have to be very silent publicly about everything. After March 4th, I shall again be free.

Yours always faithfully,
W. H. P.

CHAPTER XIX

WASHINGTON IN THE SUMMER OF 1916

I

IN JULY Page received a cablegram summoning him to Washington. This message did not explain why his presence was desired, nor on this point was Page ever definitely enlightened, though there were more or less vague statements that a "change of atmosphere" might better enable the Ambassador to understand the problems which were then engrossing the State Department.

The President had now only a single aim in view. From the date of the so-called *Sussex* "pledge," May 4, 1916, until the resumption of submarine warfare on February 1, 1917, Mr. Wilson devoted all his energies to bringing the warring powers together and establishing peace. More than one motive was inspiring the President in this determination. That this policy accorded with his own idealistic tendencies is true, and that he aspired to a position in history as the great "peace maker" is probably the fact, but he had also more immediate and practical purposes in mind. Above all, Mr. Wilson was bent on keeping the United States out of the war; he knew that there was only one certain way of preserving peace in this country, and that was by bringing the war itself to an end. "An early peace is all that can prevent the Germans from driving us at last into the war," Page wrote at about this time; and this single sentence gives the key to the President's activities for the succeeding nine months. The negotiations over the *Sussex* had taught

148

Mr. Wilson this truth. He understood that the pledge which the German Government had made was only a conditional one; that the submarine campaign had been suspended only for the purpose of giving the United States a breathing spell during which it could persuade Great Britain and France to make peace.

"I repeat my proposal," Bernstorff cabled his government on April 26,[1] "to suspend the submarine war at least for the period of negotiations. This would remove all danger of a breach [with the United States] and also enable Wilson to continue his labours in his great plan of bringing about a peace based upon the freedom of the seas—i. e., that for the future trade shall be free from all interference in time of war. According to the assurances which Wilson, through House, has given me, he would in that case take in hand measures directly against England. He is, however, of the opinion that it would be easier to bring about peace than to cause England to abandon the blockade. This last could only be brought about by war and it is well known that the means of war are lacking here. A prohibition of exports as a weapon against the blockade is not possible as the prevailing prosperity would suffer by it.

"The inquiries made by House have led Wilson to believe that our enemies would not be unwilling to consider peace. In view of the present condition of affairs, I repeat that there is only one possible course, namely, that Your Excellency [Von Jagow] empower me to declare that we will enter into negotiations with the United States touching the conduct of the submarine war while the negotiations are proceeding. This would give us the advantage that the submarine war, being over Mr.

---

[1]This is quoted from a hitherto unpublished despatch of Bernstorff's to Berlin which is found among Page's papers.

Wilson's head, like the sword of Damocles, would compel him at once to take in hand the task of mediation."

This dispatch seems sufficiently to explain all the happenings of the summer and winter of 1916–1917. It was sent to Berlin on April 26th; the German Government gave the *Sussex* "pledge" on May 4th, eight days afterward. In this reply Germany declared that she would now expect Mr. Wilson to bring pressure upon Great Britain to secure a mitigation or suspension of the British blockade, and to this Mr. Wilson promptly and energetically replied that he regarded the German promise as an unconditional one and that the Government of the United States "cannot for a moment entertain, much less discuss, a suggestion that respect by German naval authorities for the rights of citizens of the United States upon the high seas should in any way or in the slightest degree be made contingent upon the conduct of any other government affecting the rights of neutrals and non-combatants. Responsibility in such matters is single not joint; absolute not relative."

This reply gave satisfaction to both the United States and the countries of the Allies, and Page himself regarded it as a master stroke. "The more I think of it," he wrote on May 17th, "the better the strategy of the President appears, in his latest (and last) note to Germany. They laid a trap for him and he caught them in their own trap. The Germans had tried to 'put it up' to the President to commit the first unfriendly act. He now 'puts it up' to them. And this is at last bound to end the controversy if they sink another ship unlawfully. The French see this clearly and so do the best English, and it has produced a most favourable impression. The future? The German angling for peace will prove futile. They'll have another fit of fury. Whether they will again become reckless or commit 'mistakes' with their submarines will depend partly on their fury, partly on their fear to make a breach with the United States, but mainly on the state of their submarine fleet.   How many have the English caught and destroyed?   That's the main question, after all.   The English view may not be fair to them.   But nobody here believes that they will long abstain from the luxury of crime."

It is thus apparent that when the Germans practically demanded, as a price of their abstention from indiscriminate submarine warfare, that Mr. Wilson should move against Great Britain in the matter of the blockade, they realized the futility of any such step, and that what they really expected to obtain was the presidential mediation for peace.   President Wilson at once began to move in this direction.   On May 27th, three weeks after the *Sussex* "pledge," he made an address in Washington before the League to Enforce Peace, which was intended to lay the basis for his approaching negotiations.   It was in this speech that he made the statement that the United States was "not concerned with the causes and the objects" of the war.   "The obscure fountains from which its stupendous flood has burst forth we are not interested to search for or to explain."   This was another of those unfortunate sentences which made the President such an unsympathetic figure in the estimation of the Allies and seemed to indicate to them that he had no appreciation of the nature of the struggle.   Though this attitude of non-partisanship, of equal balance between the accusations of the Allies and Germany, was intended to make the President acceptable as a mediator, the practical result was exactly the reverse, for Allied statesmen turned from Wilson as soon as those sentences appeared in print. The fact that this same oration specified the "freedom of the seas" as one of the foundation rocks of the proposed new settlement only accentuated this unfavourable attitude.

This then was clearly the "atmosphere" which prevailed in Washington at the time that Page was summoned home. But Page's letters of this period indicate how little sympathy he entertained for such negotiations. "It is quite apparent," he had recently written to Colonel House, "that nobody in Washington understands the war. Come over and find out." Extracts from a letter which he wrote to his brother, Mr. Henry A. Page, of Aberdeen, North Carolina, are especially interesting when placed side by side with the President's statements of this particular time. These passages show that a two years' close observation of the Prussians in action had not changed Page's opinion of their motives or of their methods; in 1916, as in 1914, Page could see in this struggle nothing but a colossal buccaneering expedition on the part of Germany. "As I look at it," he wrote, "our dilly-dallying is likely to get us into war. The Germans want somebody to rob—to pay their great military bills. They've robbed Belgium and are still robbing it of every penny they can lay their hands on. They robbed Poland and Serbia—two very poor countries which didn't have much. They set out to rob France and have so far been stopped from getting to Paris. If they got to Paris there wouldn't be thirty cents' worth of movable property there in a week, and they'd levy fines of millions of francs a day. Their military scheme and teaching and open purpose is to make somebody pay for their vast military outlay of the last forty years. They must do that or go bankrupt. Now it looks as if they would go bankrupt. But in a little while they may be able to bombard New York and demand billions of dollars to refrain from destroying the city. That's the richest place left to spoil.

"Now they say that—quite openly and quite frankly. Now if we keep 'neutral' to a highwayman—what do we get for our pains? That's the mistake we are making. If we had sent Bernstorff home the day after the *Lusitania* was sunk and recalled Gerard and begun to train an army we'd have had no more trouble with them. But since they have found out that they can keep us discussing things forever and a day, they will keep us discussing things till they are ready. We are very simple; and we'll get shot for it yet. . . .

"The prestige and fear of the United States has gone down, down, down—disappeared; and we are regarded as 'discussors,' incapable of action, scared to death of war. That's all the invitation that robbers, whose chief business is war, want—all the invitation they need. These devils are out for robbery—and you don't seem to believe it in the United States: that's the queer thing. This neutrality business makes us an easy mark. As soon as they took a town in Belgium, they asked for all the money in the town, all the food, all the movable property; and they've levied a tax every month since on every town and made the town government borrow the money to pay it. If a child in a town makes a disrespectful remark, they fine the town an extra $1,000. They haven't got enough so far to keep them going flush; and they won't unless they get Paris—which they can't do now. If they got London, they'd be rich; they wouldn't leave a shilling and they'd make all the rich English get all the money they own abroad. This is the reason that Frenchmen and Englishmen prefer to be killed by the 100,000. In the country over which their army has passed a crow would die of starvation and no human being has ten cents of real money.   The Belgian Commission is spending more than 100 million dollars a year to keep the Belgians alive—only because they are robbed every day.   They have a rich country and could support themselves but for these robbers.   That's the meaning of the whole thing.   And yet we treat them as if they were honourable people.   It's only a question of time and of power when they will attack us, or the Canal, or South America.   Everybody on this side the world knows that.   And they are 'yielding' to keep us out of this war so that England will not help us when they (the Germans) get ready to attack America.

"There is the strangest infatuation in the United States with Peace—the strangest illusion about our safety without preparation."

Several letters to Colonel House show the state of the British mind on the subject of the President's peace proposals:

To Edward M. House

Royal Bath and East Cliff Hotel,
Bournemouth,
23 May, 1916.

DEAR HOUSE:

The motor trip that the Houses, the Wallaces, and the Pages took about a year ago was the last trip (three days) that I had had out of London; and I'd got pretty tired. The *China* case having been settled (and settled as we wanted it), I thought it a good time to try to get away for a week.   So here Mrs. Page and I are—very much to my benefit.   I've spent a beautiful week out of doors, on this seashore; and I have only about ten per cent. of the fatal diseases that I had a week ago.   That is to say, I'm as sound as a dollar and feel like a fighting cock.

Sir Edward was fine about the *China*[1] case. He never disputed the principle of the inviolability of American ships on the high seas; but the Admiralty maintained that some of these men are officers in the German Army and are now receiving officers' pay. I think that that is probably true. Nevertheless, the Admiralty had bungled the case badly and Sir Edward simply rode over them. They have a fine quarrel among themselves and we got all we wanted and asked for.

Of course, I can't make out the Germans but I am afraid some huge deviltry is yet coming. When the English say that the Germans must give up their militarism, I doubt if the Germans yet know what they mean. They talk about conquered territory—Belgium, Poland, and the rest. It hasn't entered their heads that they've got to give up their armies and their military system. When this does get into their heads, if it ever do, I think they may so swell with rage at this "insult" that they may break loose in one last desperate effort, ignoring the United States, defying the universe, running amuck. Of course it would be foolhardy to predict this, but the fear of it keeps coming into my mind. The fear is the more persistent because, if the worst comes to them, the military caste and perhaps the dynasty itself will prefer to die in one last terrific onslaught rather than to make a peace on terms which will require the practical extinction of their supreme power. This, I conceive, is the really great danger that yet awaits the world—if the Allies hold together till defeat and famine drive the Germans to the utmost desperation.

In the meantime, the Allies still holding together as

---

[1]The *China* case was a kind of *Trent* case reversed. In 1861 the American ship *San Jacinto* stopped the British vessel *Trent* and took off Mason and Slidell, Confederate commissioners to Great Britain. Similarly a British ship, in 1916, stopped an American ship, the *China*, and removed several German subjects. As the British quickly saw the analogy, and made suitable amends, the old excitement over the *Trent* was not duplicated in the recent war.

they are, there's no peace yet in the British and French minds. They're after the militarism of Prussia—not territory or other gains; and they seem likely to get it, as much by the blockade as by victories on land. Do you remember how in the Franco-Prussian War, Bismarck refused to deal with the French Emperor? He demanded that representatives of the French people should deal with him. He got what he asked for and that was the last of the French Emperor. Neither the French nor the English have forgotten that. You will recall that the Germans starved Paris into submission. Neither the French nor the English have forgotten that. These two leaves out of the Germans' own book of forty-five years ago—these two and no more—*may* be forced on the Germans themselves. They are both quite legitimate, too. You can read a recollection of both these events between the lines of the interviews that Sir Edward and Mr. Balfour recently gave to American newspapers.

There is nothing but admiration here for the strategy of the President's last note to Germany. That was the cleverest play made by anybody since the war began—clever beyond praise. Now he's "got 'em." But nobody here doubts that they will say, sooner or later, that the United States, not having forced the breaking of the British blockade, has not kept its bargain—that's what they'll *say*—and it is in order again to run amuck. This is what the English think—provided the Germans have enough submarines left to keep up real damage. By that time, too, it will be clear to the Germans that the President can't bring peace so long as only one side wishes peace. The Germans seem to have counted much on the Irish uprising, which came to pass at all only because of the customary English stupid bungling; and the net result has been only to put the mass of the Irish on their mettle to show that they are not Sinn Feiners. The final upshot will be to strengthen the British Army. God surely is good to this bungling British Government. Wind and wave and the will of High Heaven seem to work for them. I begin to understand their stupidity and their arrogance. If your enemies are such fools in psychological tactics and Heaven is with you, why take the trouble to be alert? And why be modest? Whatever the reason, these English are now more cocky and confident than they've been before since the war began. They are beginning to see results. The only question seems to be to hold the Allies together, and they seem to be doing that. In fact, the battle of Verdun has cemented them. They now have visible proof that the German Army is on the wane. And they have trustworthy evidence that the blockade is telling severely on the Germans. Nobody, I think, expects to thrash 'em to a frazzle; but the almost universal opinion here is that the hold of militarism will be shaken loose. And the German High Canal Navy—what's to become of that? Von Tirpitz is down and out, but there are thousands of Germans, I hear, who complain of their naval inactivity. But God only knows the future— I don't. I think that I do well if I keep track of the present. . . .

My kindest regards to Mrs. House,

Yours very heartily,
W. H. P.

To Edward M. House

London, 25 May, 1916.

DEAR HOUSE:

No utterance by anybody has so stirred the people of this kingdom for many months as Sir Edward Grey's impromptu speech last night in the House of Commons about Peace, when he called the German Chancellor a first-class liar. I sent you to-day a clipping from one of the morning papers. Every paper I pick up compliments Sir Edward. Everyone says, "We must fight to a finish." The more sensational press intimates that any Englishman who uses the word "peace" ought to be shot. You have never seen such a rally as that which has taken place in response to Sir Edward's cry. In the first place, as you know, he is the most gentle of all the Cabinet, the last man to get on a "war-rampage," the least belligerent and rambunctious of the whole lot. When he felt moved to say that there can be no peace till the German military despotism is broken, everybody from one end of the Kingdom to the other seems to have thrown up his hat and applauded. Except the half-dozen peace-cranks in the House (Bryan sort of men) you can't find a man, woman, child, or dog that isn't fired with the determination to see the war through. The continued talk about peace which is reported directly and indirectly from Germany—coming from Switzerland, from Rome, from Washington—has made the English and the French very angry: no, "angry" isn't quite the right word. It has made them very determined. They feel insulted by the impudence of the Germans, who, since they know they are bound to lose, seem to be turning heaven and earth to induce neutrals to take their view of peace. People are asking here, "If they are victorious, why doesn't their fleet come out of the canal and take the seas, and again open their commerce? Why do they whimper about the blockade when they will not even risk a warship to break it?" You'll recall how the talk here used to be that the English wouldn't wake up. You wouldn't know 'em now. Your bulldog has got his grip and even thunder doesn't disturb him.

Incidentally, all the old criticism of Sir Edward Grey seems to have been forgotten. You hear nothing but praise of him now. I am told that he spoke his impromptu speech last night with great fire and at once left the House. His speech has caused a greater stir than the Irish rebellion, showing that every Englishman feels that Sir Edward said precisely what every man feels.

The Germans have apparently overdone and overworked their premature peace efforts and have made things worse for them. They've overplayed their hand.

In fact, I see no end of the war. The Allies are not going to quit prematurely. They won't even discuss the subject yet with one another, and the Germans, by their peace-talk of the sort that they inspire, simply postpone the day when the Allies will take the subject up.

All the while, too, the Allies work closer and closer together. They'll soon be doing even their diplomatic work with neutrals, as a unit—England and France as one nation, and (on great subjects) Russia and Italy also with them.

I've talked lately not only with Sir Edward but with nearly half the other members of the Cabinet, and they are all keyed up to the same tune. The press of both parties, too, are (for once) wholly agreed: Liberal and Conservative papers alike hold the same war-creed.

Sincerely yours,
WALTER H. PAGE.

Before leaving for Washington Page discussed the situation personally with Sir Edward Grey and Lord Bryce. He has left memoranda of both interviews.

Notes of a Private and Informal Conversation with Sir Edward Grey, at his residence, on July 27, 1916, when I called to say good-bye before sailing on leave to the United States

. . . Sir Edward Grey went on to say quite frankly that two thoughts expressed in a speech by the President some months ago had had a very serious influence on British opinion.   One thought was that the causes or objects of the war were of no concern to him, and the other was his (at least implied) endorsement of "the freedom of the seas," which the President did not define.

Concerning the first thought, he understood of course that a neutral President could not say that he favoured one side or the other: everybody understood that and nobody expected him to take sides.   But when the President said that the objects of the war did not concern him, that was taken by British public opinion as meaning a condemnation of the British cause, and it produced deep feeling.

Concerning the "freedom of the seas," he believed that the first use of the phrase was made by Colonel House (on his return from one of his visits to Berlin),[1] but the public now regarded it as a German invention and it meant to the British mind a policy which would render British supremacy at sea of little value in time of war; and public opinion resented this.   He knew perfectly well that at a convenient time new rules must be made governing the conduct of war at sea and on the land, too.   But the German idea of "the freedom of the seas" ("freedom" was needed on land also) is repulsive to the British mind.

He mentioned these things because they had produced

---

[1] See Chapter XIII, page 434.

in many minds an unwillingness, he feared, to use the good offices of the President whenever any mediatorial service might be done by a neutral. The tendency of these remarks was certainly in that direction. Yet Sir Edward carefully abstained from expressing such an unwillingness on his own part, and the inference from his tone and manner, as well as from his habitual attitude, is that he feels no unwillingness to use the President's good office, if occasion should arise.

I asked what he meant by "mediatorial"—the President's offering his services or good offices on his own initiative? He said—No, not that. But the Germans might express to the President their willingness or even their definite wish to have an armistice, on certain terms, to discuss conditions of peace coupled with an intimation that he might sound the Allies. He did not expect the President to act on his own initiative, but at the request or at least at the suggestion of the German Government, he might conceivably sound the Allies—especially, he added, "since I am informed that the notion is wide-spread in America that the war will end inconclusively—as a draw." He smiled and remarked, as an aside, that he didn't think that this notion was held by any considerable group of people in any other country, certainly not in Great Britain.

In further talk on this subject he said that none of the Allies could mention peace or discuss peace till France should express such a wish; for it is the very vitals cf France that have received and are receiving the shock of such an assault as was never before launched against any nation. Unless France was ready to quit, none of France's Allies could mention peace, and France showed no mood to quit. Least of all could the English make or receive any such suggestion at least till her new great army had done its best; for until lately the severest fighting had not been done by the British, whose army had practically been held in reserve. There had for a long time been a perfect understanding between Joffre and Haig—that the English would wait to begin their offensive till the moment arrived when it best suited the French.

The impression that I got from this part of the conversation was that Sir Edward hoped that I might convey to the President (as, of course, he could not) Sir Edward's idea of the effect of these parts of the President's speech on feeling in England toward him. Nowhere in the conversation did he make any request of me. Any one, overhearing it, might have supposed it to be a conversation between two men, with no object beyond expressing their views. But, of course, he hoped and meant that I should, in my own way, make known to the President what he said. He did not say that the President's good offices, when the time should come, would be unwelcome to him or to his government; and he meant, I am sure, to convey only the fear that by these assertions the President had planted an objection to his good offices in a large section of British opinion.

Among the conditions of peace that Sir Edward himself personally would like to see imposed (he had not yet discussed the subject with any of his colleagues in the Government) was this: that the German Government should agree to submit to an impartial (neutral) commission or court the question, Who began the war and who is responsible for it? The German Chancellor and other high German officials have put it about and continue to put it about that England is responsible, and doubtless the German people at least believe it. All the governments concerned must (this is his idea) submit to the tribunal all its documents and other evidence bearing on the subject; and of course the finding of the tribunal must be published.

Then he talked a good deal about the idea that lies behind the League for Enforcing Peace—in a sympathetic mood. He went on to point out how such a league—with force behind it—would at any one of three stages have prevented this war—(1) When England proposed a conference to France, Germany, Italy, and Russia, all agreed to it but Germany. Germany alone prevented a discussion. If the League to Enforce Peace had included England, France, Italy, and Russia—there would have been no war; for Germany would have seen at once that they would all be against her. (2) Later, when the Czar sent the Kaiser a personal telegram proposing to submit their differences to some tribunal, a League to Enforce Peace would have prevented war. And (3) when the question of the invasion of Belgium came up, every signatory to the treaty guaranteeing Belgium's integrity gave assurance of keeping the treaty—but Germany, and Germany gave an evasive answer. A league would again have prevented a war—or put all the military force of all its members against Germany.

Throughout the conversation, which lasted about an hour, Sir Edward said more than once, as he has often said to me, that he hoped we should be able to keep the friction between our governments at the minimum. He would regard it as the greatest calamity if the ill-feeling that various events have stirred up in sections of public opinion on each side should increase or should become permanent. His constant wish and effort were to lessen and if possible to remove all misunderstandings.

Lord Bryce was one of the Englishmen with whom Page was especially inclined to discuss pending problems.

Notes on a conversation with Lord Bryce,
July 31, 1916

Lord Bryce spoke of the President's declaration that we were not concerned with the causes or objects of the war and he said that that remark had caused much talk—all, as he thought, on a misunderstanding of Mr. Wilson's meaning. "He meant, I take it, only that he did not propose at that time to discuss the causes or the objects of the war; and it is a pity that his sentence was capable of being interpreted to mean something else; and the sentence was published and discussed here apart from its context—a most unfair proceeding. I can imagine that the President and his friends may be much annoyed by this improper interpretation."

I remarked that the body of the speech in which this remark occurred might have been written in Downing Street, so friendly was it to the Allies.

"Quite, quite," said he.

This was at dinner, Lady Bryce and Mrs. Page and he and I only being present.

When he and I went into the library he talked more than an hour.

"And what about this blacklist?" he asked.   I told him.   He had been in France for a week and did not know just what had been done.   He said that that seemed to him a mistake. "The Government doesn't know America—neither does the British public.   Neither does the American Government (*no* American government) know the British.   Hence your government writes too many notes—all governments are likely to write too many notes. Everybody gets tired of seeing them and they lose their effect."

He mentioned the blockade and said that it had become quite effective—wonderfully effective, in fact; and he implied that he did not see why we now failed to recognize it. Our refusal to recognize it had caused and doubtless is now causing such ill-feeling as exists in England.

Then he talked long about peace and how it would probably be arranged. He judged, from letters that he receives from the United States as well as from Americans who come over here, that there was an expectation in America that the President would be called in at the peace settlement and that some persons even expected him to offer mediation. He did not see how that could be. He knew no precedent for such a proceeding. The President might, of course, on the definite request of either side, make a definite inquiry of the other side; but such a course would be, in effect, merely the transmission of an inquiry.

But after peace was made and the time came to set up a League for Enforcing Peace, or some such machinery, of course the United States would be and would have to be a party to that if it were to succeed. He reminded me that a little group of men here, of whom he was one, early in the war sketched substantially the same plan that the American League to Enforce Peace has worked out. It had not seemed advisable to have any general public discussion of it in England till the war should end: nobody had time now to give to it.

As he knew no precedent for belligerents to call in a third party when they met to end a war, so he knew no precedent for any outside government to protest against the invasion of a country by a Power that had signed a treaty to guarantee the integrity of the invaded country—no precedent, that is to say, for the United States to protest against the invasion of Belgium. "That precedent," I said, "was found in Hysteria."

Lord Bryce, who had just returned from a visit to the British headquarters in France, hardly dared hope for the end of the war till next year; and the intervening time between now and the end would be a time, he feared, of renewed atrocities and increasing hatred. He cited the killing of Captain Fryatt of the *Brussels* and the forcible deportation of young women from Lille and other towns in the provinces of France occupied by the Germans.

The most definite idea that he had touching American-British relations was the fear that the anti-British feeling in the United States would become stronger and would outlast the war. "It is organized," he said. "The disaffected Germans and the disaffected Irish are interested in keeping it up." He asked what effect I thought the Presidential campaign would have on this feeling. He seemed to have a fear that somehow the campaign would give an occasion for stirring it up even more.

"Good-bye. Give my regards to all my American friends; and I'm proud to say there are a good many of them."

One episode that was greatly stirring both Great Britain and the United States at this time was the trial of Sir Roger Casement, the Irish leader who had left Wilhelmshaven for Ireland in a German submarine and who had been captured at Tralee in the act of landing arms and munitions for an Irish insurrection. Casement's subsequent trial and conviction on a charge of high treason had inspired a movement in his favour from Irish-Americans, the final outcome of which was that the Senate, in early August, passed a resolution asking the British Government for clemency and stipulating that this resolution should be presented to the Foreign Office. Page was then on the ocean bound for the United States and the delicate task of presenting this document to Sir Edward Grey fell upon Mr. Laughlin, who was now Chargé d'affaires. Mr. Laughlin is a diplomat of great experience, but this responsibility at first seemed to be something of a poser even for him. He had received explicit instructions from Washington to present this resolution, and the one thing above all which a diplomatic officer must do is to carry out the orders of his government, but Mr. Laughlin well knew that, should he present this paper in the usual manner, the Foreign Secretary might decline to receive it; he might regard it as an interference with matters that exclusively concerned the sovereign state. Mr. Laughlin, however, has a technique all his own, and, in accordance with this, he asked for an interview with Sir Edward Grey to discuss a matter of routine business. However, the Chargé d'affaires carried the Casement resolution tucked away in an inside pocket when he made his call.

Like Mr. Page, Mr. Laughlin was on the friendliest terms with Sir Edward Grey, and, after the particular piece of business had been transacted, the two men, as usual, fell into casual conversation. Casement then loomed large in the daily press, and the activities of the American Senate had likewise caused some commotion in London. In round-about fashion Mr. Laughlin was able to lead Sir Edward to make some reference to the Casement case.

"I see the Senate has passed a resolution asking clemency," said the Foreign Secretary—exactly the remark which the American wished to elicit.

"Yes," was the reply. "By the way, I happen to have a copy of the resolution with me. May I give it to you?"

"Yes, I should like to have it."

The Foreign Secretary read it over with deliberation.

"This is a very interesting document," he said, when he

had finished. "Would you have any objection if I showed it to the Prime Minister?"

Of course that was precisely what Mr. Laughlin did wish, and he replied that this was the desire of his government. The purpose of his visit had been accomplished, and he was able to cable Washington that its instructions had been carried out and that the Casement resolution had been presented to the British Government. Simultaneously with his communication, however, he reported also that the execution of Roger Casement had taken place. In fact, it was being carried out at the time of the interview. This incident lends point to Page's memorandum of the last interview which he had before leaving England.

August 1st. I lunched with Mr. Asquith. One does not usually bring away much from his conversations, and he did not say much to-day worth recording. But he showed a very eager interest in the Presidential campaign, and he confessed that he felt some anxiety about the anti-British feeling in the United States. This led him to tell me that he could not in good conscience interfere with Casement's execution, in spite of the shoals of telegrams that he was receiving from the United States. This man, said he, visited Irish prisoners in German camps and tried to seduce them to take up arms against Great Britain— their own country. When they refused, the Germans removed them to the worst places in their Empire and, as a result, some of them died. Then Casement came to Ireland in a German man-of-war (a submarine) accompanied by a ship loaded with guns. "In all good conscience to my country and to my responsibilities I cannot interfere." He hoped that thoughtful opinion in the United States would see this whole matter in a fair and just way.

I asked him about anti-American feeling in Great Brit-

ain.   He said: "Do not let that unduly disturb you.   At
bottom we understand you.   At bottom the two people
surely understand one another and have unbreakable
bonds of sympathy.   No serious breach is conceivable."
He went on quite earnestly: "Mr. Page, after any policy
or plan is thought out on its merits my next thought always is how it may affect our relations with the United
States.   That is always a fundamental consideration."

I ventured to say that if he would keep our relations
smooth on the surface, I'd guarantee their stability at the
bottom.   It's the surface that rolls high at times, and the
danger is there.   Keep the surface smooth and the bottom
will take care of itself.

Then he asked about Mexico, as he usually has when
I have talked with him.   I gave him as good a report as I
could, reminding him of the great change in the attitude of
all Latin-America caused by the President's patient policy
with Mexico.   When he said, "Mexico is a bad problem,"
I couldn't resist the impulse to reply: "When Mexico
troubles you, think of—Ireland.   As there are persons in
England who concern themselves with Mexico, so there
are persons in the United States who concern themselves
about Ireland.   Ireland and Mexico have each given
trouble for two centuries.   Yet these people talk about
them as if they could remove all trouble in a month."

"Quite true," he said, and smiled himself into silence.
Then he talked about more or less frivolous subjects; and,
as always, he asked about Mr. Bryan and Mr. Roosevelt,
"alike now, I suppose, in their present obscure plight."
I told him I was going from his house to the House of
Lords to see Sir Edward Grey metamorphosed into Viscount Grey of Fallodon.

"The very stupidest of the many stupid ceremonies that
we have," said he—very truly.

He spoke of my "onerous duties" and so on and so on—tut, tut! talk that gets nowhere. But he did say, quite sincerely, I think, that my frankness called forth frankness and avoided misunderstanding; for he has said that to other people about me.

Such is the Prime Minister of Great Britain in this supreme crisis in English history, a remarkable man, of an abnormally quick mind, pretty nearly a great man, but now a spent force, at once nimble and weary. History may call him Great. If it do, he will owe this judgment to the war, with the conduct of which his name will be forever associated.

II

Mr. and Mrs. Page's homecoming was a tragedy. They sailed from Liverpool on August 3rd, and reached New York on the evening of August 11th. But sad news awaited them upon the dock. About two months previously their youngest son, Frank, had been married to Miss Katherine Sefton, of Auburn, N. Y., and the young couple had settled down in Garden City, Long Island. That was the summer when the epidemic of infantile paralysis swept over the larger part of the United States. The young bride was stricken; the case was unusually rapid and unusually severe; at the moment of the Pages' arrival, they were informed that there was practically no hope; and Mrs. Frank Page died at two o'clock on the afternoon of the following day. The Pages had always been a particularly united and happy family; this was the first time that they had suffered from any domestic sorrow of this kind, and the Ambassador was so affected that it was with difficulty that he could summon himself for the task that lay ahead.

In a few days, however, he left for Washington. He has

himself described his experience at the Capital in words that must inevitably take their place in history.   To appreciate properly the picture which Page gives, it must be remembered that the city and the officialdom which he portrays are the same city and the same men who six months afterward declared war on Germany.   When Page reached Washington, the Presidential campaign was in full swing, with Mr. Wilson as the Democratic candidate and Mr. Charles E. Hughes as the Republican.   But another crisis was absorbing the nation's attention: the railway unions, comprising practically all the 2,000,000 railway employees in the United States, were threatening to strike—ostensibly for an eight-hour day, in reality for higher wages.

Mr. Page's memorandum of his visit to Washington in August, 1916

The President was very courteous to me, in his way. He invited me to luncheon the day after I arrived.   Present: the President, Mrs. Wilson, Miss Bones, Tom Bolling, his brother-in-law, and I.   The conversation was general and in the main jocular.   Not a word about England, not a word about a foreign policy or foreign relations.

He explained that the threatened railway strike engaged his whole mind.   I asked to have a talk with him when his mind should be free.   Would I not go off and rest and come back?—I preferred to do my minor errands with the Department, but I should hold myself at his convenience and at his command.

Two weeks passed.   Another invitation to lunch. Sharp, the Ambassador to France, had arrived.   He, too, was invited.   Present: the President, Mrs. Wilson, Mrs.

Wallace, the Misses Smith of New Orleans, Miss Bones, Sharp, and I.   Not one word about foreign affairs.

After luncheon, the whole party drove to the Capitol, where the President addressed Congress on the strike, proposing legislation to prevent it and to forestall similar strikes.   It is a simple ceremony and somewhat impressive.   The Senators occupy the front seats in the House, the Speaker presides and the President of the Senate sits on his right.   An escorting committee is sent out to bring the President in.   He walks to the clerk's or reader's desk below the presiding officer's, turns and shakes hands with them both and then proceeds to read his speech, very clearly and audibly.   Some passages were applauded. When he had done, he again shook hands with the presiding officer and went out, preceded and followed by the White House escort.   I sat in the Presidential (or diplomatic?) gallery with the White House party, higgledy-piggledy.

The speech ended, the President drove to the White House with his escort in his car.   The crowds in the corridors and about the doors waited and crowded to see Mrs. Wilson, quite respectful but without order or discipline. We had to push our way through them.   Now and then a policeman at a distance would yell loudly, "Make way there!"

When we reached the White House, I asked the doorman if the President had arrived.

"Yes."

"Does he expect me to go in and say good-bye?"

"No."

Thus he had no idea of talking with me now, if ever. Not at lunch nor after did he suggest a conversation about American-British affairs or say anything about my seeing him again.

This threatened strike does hold his whole mind—

bothers him greatly.   It seems doubtful if he can avert a general strike.   The Republicans are trying "to put him in a political hole," and they say he, too, is playing politics. Whoever be to blame for it, it is true that politics is in the game.   Nobody seems to foresee who will make capital out of it.   Surely I can't.

There's no social sense at the White House.   The President has at his table family connections only—and they say few or no distinguished men and women are invited, except the regular notables at the set dinners—the diplomatic, the judiciary, and the like.   His table is his private family affair—nothing more.   It is very hard to understand why so intellectual a man doesn't have notable men about him.   It's the college professor's village habit, I dare say.   But it's a great misfortune.   This is one way in which Mr. Wilson shuts out the world and lives too much alone, feeding only on knowledge and subjects that he has already acquired and not getting new views or fresh suggestions from men and women.

He sees almost nobody except members of Congress for whom he sends for special conferences, and he usually sees these in his office.   The railroad presidents and men he met in formal conference—no social touch.

A member of his Cabinet told me that Mr. Wilson had shown confidence in him, given him a wide range of action in his own Department and that he relies on his judgment.   This Cabinet member of course attends the routine state dinners and receptions, as a matter of required duty.   But as for any social recognition of his existence—he had never received a hint or nod.   Nor does any member of the Cabinet (except, no doubt, Mr. McAdoo, his son-in-law).   There is no social sense nor reason in this.   In fact, it works to a very decided disadvantage to the President and to the Nation.

By the way, that a notable man in our educational life could form such a habit does not speak well for our educational life.

What an unspeakably lamentable loss of opportunity! This is the more remarkable and lamentable because the President is a charming personality, an uncommonly good talker, a man who could easily make personal friends of all the world. He does his own thinking, untouched by other men's ideas. He receives nothing from the outside. His domestic life is spent with his own, nobody else, except House occasionally. His contact with his own Cabinet is a business man's contact with his business associates and kind—at his office.

He declined to see Cameron Forbes[1] on his return from the Philippines.

The sadness of this mistake!

Another result is—the President doesn't hear the frank truth about the men about him. He gives nobody a chance to tell him. Hence he has several heavy encumbrances in his official family.

The influence of this lone-hand way of playing the game extends very far. The members of the Cabinet do not seem to have the habit of frankness with one another. Each lives and works in a water-tight compartment. I sat at luncheon (at a hotel) with Lansing, Secretary of State; Lane, Secretary of the Interior; Gregory, Attorney-General; Baker, Secretary of War; Daniels, Secretary of the Navy; and Sharp, Ambassador to France; and all the talk was jocular or semi-jocular, and personal—mere cheap chaff. Not a question was asked either of the Ambassador to France or of the Ambassador to Great Britain about the war or about our foreign relations. The

---

[1] Mr. Forbes had been Governor-General of the Philippines from 1909 to 1913. His work had been extraordinarily successful.

war wasn't mentioned. Sharp and I might have come from Bungtown and Jonesville and not from France and England. We were not encouraged to talk—the local personal joke held the time and conversation. This astounding fact must be the result of this lone-hand, watertight compartment method and—of the neutrality suppression of men. The Vice-President confessed to his neighbour at a Gridiron dinner that he had read none of the White Papers, or Orange Papers, etc., of the belligerent governments—confessed this with pride—lest he should form an opinion and cease to be neutral! Miss X, a member of the President's household, said to Mrs. Y, the day we lunched there, that she had made a remark privately to Sharp showing her admiration of the French.

"Was that a violation of neutrality?" she asked in all seriousness.

I can see it in no other way but this: the President suppressed free thought and free speech when he insisted upon personal neutrality. He held back the deliberate and spontaneous thought and speech of the people except the pro-Germans, who saw their chance and improved it! The mass of the American people found themselves forbidden to think or talk, and this forbidding had a sufficient effect to make them take refuge in indifference. It's the President's job. He's our leader. He'll attend to this matter. We must not embarrass him. On this easy cushion of non-responsibility the great masses fell back at their intellectual and moral ease—softened, isolated, lulled.

That wasn't leadership in a democracy. Right here is the President's vast failure. From it there is now no escape unless the Germans commit more submarine crimes. They have kept the United States for their own exploiting after the war. They have thus had a real triumph of us.

I have talked in Washington with few men who showed any clear conception of the difference between the Germans and the British. To the minds of these people and high Government officials, German and English are alike foreign nations who are now foolishly engaged in war. Two of the men who look upon the thing differently are Houston[1] and Logan Waller Page.[2] In fact, there is no realization of the war in Washington. Secretary Houston has a proper perspective of the situation. He would have done precisely what I recommended—paved the way for claims and let the English take their course. "International law" is no strict code and it's all shot to pieces anyhow.

The Secretary [of State] betrayed not the slightest curiosity about our relations with Great Britain. I saw him several times—(1) in his office; (2) at his house; (3) at the French Ambassador's; (4) at Wallace's; (5) at his office; (6) at Crozier's[3]—this during my first stay in Washington. The only remark he made was that I'd find a different atmosphere in Washington from the atmosphere in London. Truly. All the rest of his talk was about "cases." Would I see Senator Owen? Would I see Congressman Sherley? Would I take up this "case" and that? His mind ran on "cases."

Well, at Y's, when I was almost in despair, I rammed down him a sort of general statement of the situation as I saw it; at least, I made a start. But soon he stopped me and ran off at a tangent on some historical statement I had made, showing that his mind was not at all on the real subject, the large subject. When I returned to Washington, and he had read my interviews with Grey, Asquith,

---

[1]Secretary of Agriculture.

[2]In charge of government road building, a distant relative of the Ambassador.

[3]Major General William Crozier, U. S. A., Chief of Ordnance.

and Bryce,[1] and my own statement, he still said nothing, but he ceased to talk of "cases." At my final interview he said that he had had difficulty in preventing Congress from making the retaliatory resolution mandatory. He had tried to keep it back till the very end of the session, etc.

This does not quite correspond with what the President told me—that the State Department asked for this retaliatory resolution.

I made specific suggestions in my statement to the President and to Lansing. They have (yet) said nothing about them. I fancy they will not. I have found nowhere any policy—only "cases."

I proposed to Baker and Daniels that they send a General and an Admiral as attachés to London. They both agreed. Daniels later told me that Baker mentioned it to the President and he "stepped on the suggestion with both feet." I did not bring it up. In the Franco-Prussian War of 1870, both General McClellan (or Sheridan?[2]) and General Forsythe were sent to the German Army. Our military ideas have shrunk since then!

I find at this date (a month before the Presidential election), the greatest tangle and uncertainty of political opinion that I have ever observed in our country. The President, in spite of his unparalleled leadership and authority in domestic policy, is by no means certain of election. He has the open hostility of the Germans—all very well, if he had got the fruits of a real hostility to them; but they have, in many ways, directed his foreign policy. He has lost the silent confidence of many men upon whose conscience this great question weighs heavily. If he be defeated he will owe his defeat to the loss of con-

[1]See Chapter XIX, pages 160–164.

[2]It was General Sheridan.

fidence in his leadership on this great subject. His opponent has put forth no clear-cut opinion. He plays a silent game on the German "issue." Yet he will command the support of many patriotic men merely as a lack of confidence in the President.

Nor do I see any end of the results of this fundamental error. In the economic and political readjustment of the world we shall be "out of the game," in any event—unless we are yet forced into the war by Hughes's election or by the renewal of the indiscriminate use of submarines by the Germans.

There is a great lesson in this lamentable failure of the President really to lead the Nation. The United States stands for democracy and free opinion as it stands for nothing else and as no other nation stands for it. Now when democracy and free opinion are at stake as they have not before been, we take a "neutral" stand—we throw away our very birthright. We may talk of "humanity" all we like: we have missed the largest chance that ever came to help the large cause that brought us into being as a Nation. . . .

And the people, sitting on the comfortable seats of neutrality upon which the President has pushed them back, are grateful for Peace, not having taken the trouble to think out what Peace has cost us and cost the world —except so many as have felt the uncomfortable stirrings of the national conscience.

There is not a man in our State Department or in our Government who has ever met any prominent statesmen in any European Government—except the third Assistant Secretary of State, who has no authority in forming policies; there is not a man who knows the atmosphere of Europe. Yet when I proposed that one of the under Secretaries should go to England on a visit of a few weeks for observation, the objection arose that such a visit would not be "neutral."

III

The extraordinary feature of this experience was that Page had been officially summoned home, presumably to discuss the European situation, and that neither the President nor the State Department apparently had the slightest interest in his visit.

"The President," Page wrote to Mr. Laughlin, "dominates the whole show in a most extraordinary way.   The men about him (and he sees them only on 'business') are very nearly all very, very small fry, or worse—the narrowest twopenny lot I've ever come across.   He has no real companions.   Nobody talks to him freely and frankly.   I've never known quite such a condition in American life."   Perhaps the President had no desire to discuss inconvenient matters with his Ambassador to Great Britain, but Page was certainly determined to have an interview with the President.   "I'm not going back to London," he wrote Mr. Laughlin, "till the President has said something to me or at least till I have said something to him.   I am now going down to Garden City and New York till the President send for me; or, if he do not send for me, I'm going to his house and sit on his front steps till he come out!"   Page had brought from England one of the medals which the Germans had struck in honour of the *Lusitania* sinking, and one reason why he particularly wished to see the President alone was to show him this memento.

Another reason was that in early September Page had received important news from London concerning the move which Germany was making for peace and the attitude of Great Britain in this matter.   The several plans which

Germany had had under consideration had now taken the form of a definite determination to ask for an armistice before winter set in.   A letter from Mr. Laughlin, Chargé d'affaires in Page's absence, tells the story.

From Irwin Laughlin

Embassy of the United States of America.
London, August 30, 1916.

DEAR MR. PAGE:

For some little time past I have heard persistent rumours, which indeed are more than rumours, since they have come from important sources, of an approaching movement by Germany toward an early armistice.   They have been so circumstantial and so closely connected—in prospect—with the President, that I have examined them with particular attention and I shall try to give you the results, and my conclusions, with the recommendation that you take the matter up directly with the President and the Secretary of State.   I have been a little at a loss to decide how to communicate what I have learned to the Government in Washington, for the present conditions make it impossible to set down what I want to say in an official despatch, but the fortunate accident of your being in the United States gives me the safe opportunity I want, and so I send my information to you, and by the pouch, as time is of less importance than secrecy.

There seems to be no doubt that Germany is casting about for an opportunity to effect an armistice, if possible before the winter closes in.   She hopes it may result in peace—a peace more or less favourable to her, of course— but even if such a result should fail of accomplishment she would have gained a breathing space; have secured an opportunity to improve her strategic position in a military sense, perhaps by shortening her line in Flanders; have stiffened the resistance of her people; and probably have influenced a certain body of neutral opinion not only in her favour but against her antagonists.

I shall not try to mention the various sources from which the threads that compose this fabric have been drawn, but I finally fastened on X of the Admiralty as a man with whom I could talk profitably and confidentially, and he told me positively that his information showed that Germany was looking in the direction I have indicated, and that she would soon approach the President on the subject—even if she had not already taken the first steps toward preparing her advance to him.

I asked X if he thought it well for me to broach the subject to Lord Grey and he suggested that I first consult Y, which I did.   The latter seemed very wary at the outset, but he warmed up at last and in the course of the conversation told me he had reliable information that when Bethmann-Hollweg went to Munich just before the beginning of the allied offensive in the west in June he told the King of Bavaria that he was confident the Allies would be obliged to begin overtures for peace next October; adding that if they didn't Germany would have to do so. The King, it appears, asked him how Germany could approach the Allies if it proved to be advisable and he replied: "Through our good friend Wilson."

I asked Y if the King of Spain's good offices would not be enlisted jointly with those of the President in attempting to arrange an armistice, but he thought not, and said that the King of Spain was very well aware that the Allies would not consider anything short of definite peace proposals from Germany and that His Majesty knew the moment for them had not arrived.   I then finally asked him point blank if he thought the Germans would approach the President for an armistice, and, if so, when.

He said he was inclined to think they might do so perhaps about October.   On my asking him if he was disposed to let me communicate his opinion privately to the Government in Washington he replied after some hesitation that he had no objection, but he quickly added that I must make it clear at the same time that the British Government would not listen to any such proposals.

These conversations took place during the course of last week, and on Sunday—the 27th—I invited the Spanish Ambassador to luncheon at Tangley when I was able to get him to confirm what Y had said of his Sovereign's attitude and opinions.

I may mention for what it is worth that on Hoover's last trip to Germany he was told by Bullock, of the Philadelphia *Ledger*, that Zimmermann of the Berlin Foreign Office had told him that the Germans had intended in June to take steps for an armistice which were prevented by the preparations for the allied offensive in the west.

Y was very emphatic in what he said of the attitude of his government and the British people toward continuing the war to an absolutely conclusive end, and I was much impressed.   He said among other things that the execution of Captain Fryatt had had a markedly perceptible effect in hardening British public opinion against Germany and fixing the determination to fight to a relentless finish. This corresponds exactly with my own observations.

I leave this letter entirely in your hands.   You will know what use to make of it.   It is meant as an official communication in everything but the usual form from which I have departed for reasons I need not explain further.

I look forward eagerly to your return,

Very sincerely yours,

IRWIN LAUGHLIN.

Page waited five weeks before he succeeded in obtaining his interview with Mr. Wilson.

To the President

The New Willard, Washington, D. C.
Thursday, September 21, 1916.

DEAR MR. PRESIDENT:

While I am waiting for a convenient time to come when you will see me for a conference and report, I send you notes on conversations with Lord Grey and Lord Bryce.[1]   They are, in effect, though of course not in form, messages to you.

The situation between our government and Great Britain seems to me most alarming; and (let me add) easily removable, if I can get the ear of anybody in authority.   But I find here only an atmosphere of suspicion— unwarranted by facts and easily dissipated by straight and simple friendly methods.   I am sure of this.

I have, besides, a most important and confidential message for you from the British Government which they prefer should be orally delivered.

And I have written out a statement of my own study of the situation and of certain proposals which, I think, if they commend themselves to you, will go far to remove this dangerous tension.   I hope to go over them with you at your convenience.

Yours faithfully,
WALTER H. PAGE.

The situation was alarming for more reasons than the determination of Germany to force the peace issue.   The State Department was especially irritated at this time

---

[1]See Chapter XIX, pages 160 and 164.

over the blockade. Among the "trade advisers" there was a conviction, which all Page's explanations had not destroyed, that Great Britain was using the blockade as a means of destroying American commerce and securing America's customers for herself. Great Britain's regulations on the blacklist and "bunker coal" had intensified this feeling. In both these latter questions Page regarded the British actions as tactless and unjust; he had had many sharp discussions at the Foreign Office concerning them, but had not made much headway in his efforts to obtain their abandonment. The purpose of the "blacklist" was to strike at neutral firms with German affiliations which were trading with Germany. The Trading with the Enemy Act provided that such firms could not trade with Great Britain; that British vessels must refuse to accept their cargoes, and that any neutral ship which accepted such cargoes would be denied bunker coal at British ports. Under this law the Ministry of Blockade issued a "blacklist" of more than 1,000 proscribed exporting houses in the United States. So great was the indignation against this boycott in the United States that Congress, in early September, had passed a retaliatory act; this gave the President the authority at any time to place an embargo upon the exports to the United States of countries which discriminated against American firms and also to deny clearance to ships which refused to accept American cargoes. The two countries indeed seemed to be hastening toward a crisis.

Page's urgent letter to Mr. Wilson brought a telegram from Mr. Tumulty inviting the Ambassador to spend the next evening and night with the President at Shadow Lawn, the seaside house on the New Jersey coast in which Mr. Wilson was spending the summer. Mr. Wilson received his old friend with great courtesy and listened

quietly and with apparent interest to all that he had to say.
The written statement to which Page refers in his letter
told the story of Anglo-American relations from the time
of the Panama tolls repeal up to the time of Page's visit
to Shadow Lawn. Quotations have already been made
from it in preceding chapters, and the ideas which it
contains have abundantly appeared in letters already
printed. The document was an eloquent plea for American coöperation with the Allies—for the dismissal of
Bernstorff, for the adoption of a manly attitude toward
Germany, and for the vindication of a high type of Americanism.

Page showed the President the *Lusitania* medal, but
that did not especially impress him. "The President said to me," wrote Page in reference to this visit,
"that when the war began he and all the men he met
were in hearty sympathy with the Allies; but that now
the sentiment toward England had greatly changed.
He saw no one who was not vexed and irritated by the
arbitrary English course. That is, I fear, true—that
he sees no one but has a complaint. So does the Secretary of State, and the Trade Bureau and all the rest
in Washington. But in Boston, in New York, and in
the South and in Auburn, N. Y., I saw no one whose
sympathy with the Allies had undergone any fundamental change. I saw men who felt vexed at such an
act as the blacklist, but that was merely vexation, not
a fundamental change of feeling. Of course, there
came to see me men who had 'cases.' Now these are
the only kind of men, I fear, whom the Government at
Washington sees—these and the members of Congress
whom the Germans have scared or have 'put up' to
scare the Government—who are 'twisting the lion's tail,'
in a word."

"The President said," wrote Page immediately after coming from Shadow Lawn, "'Tell those gentlemen for me'—and then followed a homily to the effect that a damage done to any American citizen is a damage to him, etc. He described the war as a result of many causes, some of long origin. He spoke of England's having the earth and of Germany wanting it. Of course, he said, the German system is directly opposed to everything American. But I do not gather that he thought that this carried any very great moral reprehensibility.

"He said that he wouldn't do anything with the retaliatory act till after election lest it might seem that he was playing politics. But he hinted that if there were continued provocation afterward (in case he were elected) he would. He added that one of the worst provocations was the long English delay in answering our Notes. Was this delay due to fear or shame? He evidently felt that such a delay showed contempt. He spoke of the Bryan treaty.[1] But on no question had the British 'locked horns' with us—on no question had they come to a clear issue so that the matter might be referred to the Commission."

Page delivered his oral message about the German determination to obtain an armistice. This was to the effect that Great Britain would not grant it. Page intimated that Britain would be offended if the President proposed it.

"If an armistice, no," answered Mr. Wilson. "That's a military matter and is none of my business. But if they propose an armistice looking toward peace—yes, I shall be glad."

---

[1]The treaty between the United States and Great Britain, adopted through the urgency of Mr. Bryan, providing for the arbitration of disputes between the two countries.

The experience was an exceedingly trying one for both men. The discussion showed how far apart were the President and his Ambassador on practically every issue connected with the crisis. Naturally the President's reference to the causes of the war—that there were many causes, some of them of long persistence, and that Great Britain's domination of the "earth" was one of them— conflicted with the judgment of a man who attributed the origin of the struggle to German aggression. The President's statement that American sympathy for the Allies had now changed to irritation, and the tolerant attitude toward Germany which Mr. Wilson displayed, affected Page with the profoundest discouragement. The President's intimation that he would advance Germany's request for an armistice, if it looked toward peace—this in reply to Page's message that Great Britain would not receive such a proposal in a kindly spirit— seemed to lay the basis of further misunderstandings. The interview was a disheartening one for Page. Many people whom the Ambassador met in the course of this visit still retain memories of his fervour in what had now become with him a sacred cause. With many friends and officials he discussed the European situation almost like a man inspired. The present writer recalls two long conversations with Page at this time: the recollection of his brilliant verbal portraiture, his description of the determination of Englishmen, his admiration for the heroic sacrifice of Englishwomen, remain as about the most vivid memories of a life-time. And now the Ambassador had brought this same eloquence to the President's ear at Shadow Lawn. It was in this interview that Page had hoped to show Mr. Wilson the real merits of the situation, and persuade him to adopt the course to which the national honour and safety pointed; he talked long and eloquently, paint-

ing the whole European tragedy with that intensity and
readiness of utterance and that moral conviction which
had so moved all others with whom he had come into contact during this memorable visit to the United States; but
Mr. Wilson was utterly cold, utterly unresponsive, interested only in ending the war.   The talk lasted for a whole
morning; its nature may be assumed from the many letters
already printed; but Page's voice, when it attempted to fire
the conscience of the President, proved as ineffective as
his pen.   However, there was nothing rasping or conten-
tious about the interview.   The two men discussed everything with the utmost calmness and without the slightest indications of ill-nature.   Both men had in mind
their long association, both inevitably recalled the hopes
with which they had begun their official relationship
three years before, at that time neither having the
faintest intimation of the tremendous problems that were
to draw them asunder.   Mr. Wilson at this meeting
did not impress his Ambassador as a perverse character,
but as an extremely pathetic one.   Page came away
with no vexation or anger, but with a real feeling for a
much suffering and a much perplexed statesman.   The
fact that the President's life was so solitary, and that
he seemed to be so completely out of touch with men and
with the living thoughts of the world, appealed strongly
to Page's sympathies.   "I think he is the loneliest man
I have ever known," Page remarked to his son Frank
after coming away from this visit.

Page felt this at the time, for, as he rose to say good-bye
to the President, he put his hand upon his shoulder.
At this Mr. Wilson's eyes filled with tears and he gave
Page an affectionate good-bye.   The two men never met
again.

CHAPTER XX

"PEACE WITHOUT VICTORY"

O F ONE thing I am sure," Page wrote to his wife from Washington, while waiting to see President Wilson. "We wish to come home March 4th at midnight and to go about our proper business. There's nothing here that I would for the world be mixed up with. As soon as I can escape with dignity I shall make my bow and exit. . . . But I am not unhappy or hopeless for the long run. They'll find out the truth some day, paying, I fear, a heavy penalty for delay. But the visit here has confirmed me in our previous conclusions—that if we can carry the load until March 4th, midnight, we shall be grateful that we have pulled through."

Soon after President Wilson's reëlection, therefore, Page sent his resignation to Washington. The above quotation shows that he intended this to be more than a "courtesy resignation," a term traditionally applied to the kind of leave-takings which Ambassadors usually send on the formation of a new administration, or at the beginning of a new Presidential term, for the purpose of giving the President the opportunity of reorganizing his official family. Page believed that his work in London had been finished, that he had done everything in his power to make Mr. Wilson see the situation in its true light and that he had not succeeded. He therefore wished to give up his post and come home. This explains the fact that his resignation did not consist of the half dozen perfunctory lines which most diplomatic officers find sufficient on such an occasion, but took the form of a review of the reasons why the United States should align itself on the side of the Allies.

To the President

London, November 24, 1916.

DEAR MR. PRESIDENT:

We have all known for many years that the rich and populous and organized states in which the big cities are do not constitute the political United States. But, I confess, I hardly expected so soon to see this fact proclaimed at the ballot-box. To me that's the surprise of the election. And your popular majority as well as your clear majority in the Electoral College is a great personal triumph for you. And you have remade the ancient and demoralized Democratic party. Four years ago it consisted of a protest and of the wreck wrought by Mr. Bryan's long captaincy. This rebirth, with a popular majority, is an historical achievement—of your own.

You have relaid the foundation and reset the pillars of a party that may enjoy a long supremacy for domestic reasons. Now, if you will permit me to say so, from my somewhat distant view (four years make a long period of absence) the big party task is to build up a clearer and more positive foreign policy. We are in the world and we've got to choose what active part we shall play in it—I fear rather quickly. I have the conviction, as you know, that this whole round globe now hangs as a ripe apple for our plucking, if we use the right ladder while the chance lasts. I do not mean that we want or could get the apple for ourselves, but that we can see to it that it is put to proper uses. What we have to do, in my judgment, is to go back to our political fathers for our clue. If my long-time memory be good, they were sure that their establishment of a great free Republic would soon be imitated by European peoples—that democracies would take the place of autocracies in all so-called civilized countries; for that was the form that the fight took in their day against organized Privilege. But for one reason or another—in our life-time partly because we chose so completely to isolate ourselves—the democratic idea took root in Europe with disappointing slowness. It is, for instance, now perhaps for the first time, in a thoroughgoing way, within sight in this Kingdom. The dream of the American Fathers, therefore, is not yet come true. They fought against organized Privilege exerted from over the sea. In principle it is the same fight that we have made, in our domestic field, during recent decades. Now the same fight has come on a far larger scale than men ever dreamed of before.

It isn't, therefore, for merely doctrinal reasons that we are concerned for the spread of democracy nor merely because a democracy is the only scheme of organization yet wrought out that keeps the door of opportunity open and invites all men to their fullest development. But we are interested in it because under no other system can the world be made an even reasonably safe place to live in. For only autocracies wage aggressive wars. Aggressive autocracies, especially military autocracies, must be softened down by peace (and they have never been so softened) or destroyed by war. The All-Highest doctrine of Germany to-day is the same as the Taxation-without-Representation of George III—only more virulent, stronger, and farther-reaching. Only by its end can the German people recover and build up their character and take the permanent place in the world that they—thus changed—will be entitled to. They will either reduce Europe to the vassalage of a military autocracy, which may then overrun the whole world or drench it in blood, or they must through stages of Liberalism work their way toward some approach to a democracy; and there is no doubt which event is impending. The Liberal idea will win this struggle, and Europe will be out of danger of a general assault on free institutions till some other autocracy which has a military caste try the same Napoleonic game. The defeat of Germany, therefore, will make for the spread of the doctrine of our Fathers and our doctrine yet.

An interesting book might be made of concrete evidences of the natural antipathy that the present German autocracy has for successful democracy and hence for us. A new instance has just come to me. My son, Arthur, who succeeded to most of my activities at home, has been over here for a month and he has just come from a visit to France. In Paris he had a long conversation with Delcassé, who told him that the Kaiser himself once made a proposal to him to join in producing "the complete isolation" of the United States. What the Kaiser meant was that if the great Powers of Europe would hold off, he would put the Monroe Doctrine to the test and smash it.

The great tide of the world will, by reason of the war, now flow toward democracy—at present, alas! a tide of blood. For a century democracies and Liberal governments have kept themselves too much isolated, trusting prematurely and too simply to international law and treaties and Hague conventions. These things have never been respected, except as springes to catch woodcock, where the Divine Right held sway. The outgrowing or the overthrow of the Divine Right is a condition precedent to the effectiveness of international law and treaties.

It has seemed to me, looking at the subject only with reference to our country's duty and safety, that somehow and at some early time our championship of democracy must lead us to redeclare our faith and to show that we believe in our historic creed. Then we may escape falling away from the Liberal forces of the Old World and escape the suspicion of indifference to the great scheme of government which was set up by our fathers' giving their blood for it. I see no other way for us to take the best and biggest opportunity that has ever come to prove true to our faith as well as to secure our own safety and the safety of the world. Only some sort of active and open identification with the Allies can put us in effective protest against the assassins of the Armenians and the assassins of Belgium, Poland, and Serbia, and in a friendly attitude to the German people themselves, as distinguished from their military rulers. This is the attitude surely that our fathers would have wished us to take—and would have expected us to take—and that our children will be proud of us for taking; for it is our proper historic attitude, whether looked at from the past or looked back at from the future. There can be no historic approval of neutrality for years, while the world is bleeding to death.

The complete severance of relations, diplomatic at first and later possibly economic as well, with the Turks and the Germans, would probably not cost us a man in battle nor any considerable treasure; for the moral effect of withdrawing even our formal approval of their conduct—at least our passive acquiescence—would be—that the Germans would see that practically all the Liberal world stands against their system, and the war would end before we should need to or could put an army in the field. The Liberal Germans are themselves beginning to see that it is not they, but the German system, that is the object of attack because it is *the* dangerous thing in the world. Maximilian Harden presents this view in his

Berlin paper. He says in effect that Germany must get rid of its predatory feudalism. That was all that was the matter with George III.

Among the practical results of such action by us would, I believe, be the following:

1. The early ending of the war and the saving of, perhaps, millions of lives and of incalculable treasure;

2. The establishment in Germany of some form of more liberal government;

3. A league to enforce peace, ready-made, under our guidance—i.e., the Allies and ourselves;

4. The sympathetic coöperation and the moral force of every Allied Government in dealing with Mexico:

5. The acceptance—and even documentary approval— of every Allied Government of the Monroe Doctrine;

6. The warding off and no doubt the final prevention of danger from Japan, and, most of all, the impressive and memorable spectacle of our Great Democracy thus putting an end to this colossal crime, merely from the impulse and necessity to keep our own ideals and to lead the world right on. We should do for Europe on a large scale essentially what we did for Cuba on a small scale and thereby usher in a new era in human history.

I write thus freely, Mr. President, because at no time can I write in any other way and because I am sure that all these things can quickly be brought to pass under your strong leadership. The United States would stand, as no other nation has ever stood in the world—predominant and unselfish—on the highest ideals ever reached in human government. It is a vision as splendid as the Holy Grael. Nor have I a shadow of doubt of the eager and faithful following of our people, who would thereby reëstablish once for all our weakened nationality. We are made of the stuff that our Fathers were made of.

And I write this now for the additional reason that I am within sight of the early end of my service here. When you called me I answered, not only because you did me great honour and laid a definite patriotic duty on me, but because also of my personal loyalty to you and my pride in helping forward the great principles in which we both believe. But I understood then (and I am sure the subject lay in your mind in the same way) that my service would be for four years at the most. I made all my arrangements, professional and domestic, on this supposition. I shall, therefore, be ready to lay down my work here on March 4th or as soon thereafter as meets your pleasure.

I am more than proud of the confidence that you have shown in me. To it I am indebted for the opportunity I have had to give such public service to my country as I could, as well as for the most profitable experience of my life. A proper and sympathetic understanding between the two English-speaking worlds seems to me the most important duty of far-seeing men in either country. It has taken such a profound hold on me that I shall, in whatever way I can, work for its complete realization as long as I can work for anything.

I am, Mr. President, most faithfully and gratefully yours,

WALTER H. PAGE.

This letter was written at a time when President Wilson was exerting his best energies to bring about peace. The Presidential campaign had caused him to postpone these efforts, for he believed that neither Germany nor Great Britain could take seriously the activities of a President whose own political position was insecure. At the time Page's letter was received, the President was thinking only of a peace based upon a stalemate; it was then his apparent conviction that both sides to the struggle were about equally in the wrong and that a decisive victory of either would not be a good thing for the world. Yet it is interesting to compare this letter with the famous speech which the President made six months afterward when he asked Congress to declare the existence of a state of war with Germany. Practically all the important reasons which Mr. Wilson then advanced for this declaration are found in Page's letter of the preceding November. That autocracies are a constant menace to world peace, that the United States owes it to its democratic tradition to take up arms against the enemy of free government, that in doing this, it was not making war upon the German people, but upon its imperialistic masters—these were the arguments which Page laid before the President in his letter of resignation, and these were the leading ideas in Mr. Wilson's address of April 2nd. There are even sentences in Page's communication which seem to foreshadow Mr. Wilson's assertion that "The world must be made safe for democracy." This letter in itself sufficiently makes it clear that Page's correspondence, irritating in its later phases as it may have been, strongly influenced Mr. Wilson in his final determination on war.

On one point, indeed, Colonel House afterward called the Ambassador to account. When America was preparing to raise armies by the millions and to spend its treasure by the billions, he reminded Page of his statement that the severance of diplomatic relations "would probably not cost us a man in battle nor any considerable treasure." Page's statement in this November letter merely reiterated a conviction which for more than a year he had been forcing upon the President and Colonel House—that the dismissal of Bernstorff would not necessarily imply war with Germany, but that it would in itself be enough to bring the war to an end. On this point Page never changed his mind, as is evident from the letter which he wrote to Colonel House when this matter was called to his attention:

To Edward M. House

London, June 29, 1917.

MY DEAR HOUSE:

I never put any particular value on my own prophecies nor on anybody else's. I have therefore no pride as a prophet. Yet I do think that I hit it off accurately a year or a year and a half ago when I said that we could then have ended the war without any appreciable cost. And these are my reasons:

If we had then come in and absolutely prevented supplies from reaching Germany, as we are now about to do, the war would then have been much sooner ended than it can now be ended:

(1) Our supplies enabled her to go on.

(2) She got time in this way to build her great submarine fleet. She went at it the day she promised the President to reform.

(3) She got time and strength to overrun Rumania whence she got food and oil; and continues to get it.

(4) During this time Russia fell down as a military force and gave her more time, more armies for France and more supplies. Russian guns have been sold to the Germans.

If a year and a half ago we had starved her out, it would have been over before any of these things happened. This delay is what will cost us billions and billions and men and men.

And it cost us one thing more. During the neutrality

period we were as eager to get goods to the little neutral states which were in large measure undoubtedly bound to Germany as we are now eager to keep them out.   Grey, who was and is our best friend, and who was unwilling to quarrel with us more than he was obliged to, was thrown out of office and his career ended because the blockade, owing to his consideration for us, was not tight enough. Our delay caused his fall.

But most of all, it gave the Germans time (and to some extent material) to build their present fleet of submarines. They were at work on them all the while and according to the best opinion here they continue to build them faster than the British destroy them; and the submarines are destroying more merchant ships than all the shipbuilding docks of all the world are now turning out.   This is the most serious aspect of the war—by far the most serious.   I am trying to get our Government to send over hundreds of improvised destroyers—armed tugs, yachts, etc., etc.   Admiral Sims and the British Admiralty have fears that unless such help come the full fruits of the war may never be gathered by the Allies—that some sort of a compromise peace may have to be made.

It is, therefore, true that the year and a half we waited after the *Lusitania* will prove to be the most costly year and a half in our history; and for once at least my old prophecy was quite a good guess.   But that water has flowed over the dam and it is worth mentioning now only because you challenged me.   .   .   .

That part of Page's letter which refers to his retirement had a curious history.   It was practically a resignation and therefore called for an immediate reply, but **Mr.** Wilson did not even acknowledge its receipt.   For two months the Ambassador was left in the dark as to the attitude of Washington. Finally, in the latter part of January, 1917, Page wrote urgently to Mr. Lansing, asking him to bring the matter to the President's attention. On February 5, 1917, Mr. Lansing's reply was received. "The President," he said, "under extreme pressure of the present situation, has been unable to consider your communication in regard to your resignation. He desires me to inform you that he hopes that, at the present time, you will not press to be relieved from service; that he realizes that he is asking you to make a personal sacrifice, but he believes that you will appreciate the importance, in the crisis which has developed, that no change should be made. I hardly need to add my personal hope that you will put aside any thought of resigning your post for the present."

At this time, of course, any idea of retiring was out of the question. The President had dismissed Bernstorff and there was every likelihood that the country would soon be at war. Page would have regarded his retirement at this crisis as little less than the desertion of his post. Moreover, since Mr. Wilson had adopted the policy which the Ambassador had been urging for nearly two years, and had sent Bernstorff home, any logical excuse that may have existed for his resignation existed no longer. Mr. Wilson had now adopted a course which Page could enthusiastically support.

"I am happy to serve here at any sacrifice"—such was his reply to Mr. Lansing—"until after the end of the war, and I am making my arrangements to stay for this period."

The months that intervened between the Presidential election and the declaration of war were especially difficult for the American Embassy in London. Page had informed the President, in the course of his interview of September 22nd, how unfavourably Great Britain regarded his efforts in the direction of peace; he had in fact delivered a message from the Foreign Office that any Presidential attempt to "mediate" would be rejected by the Allies. Yet his earnest representation on this point had produced no effect upon Mr. Wilson. The pressure which Germany was bringing to bear upon Washington was apparently irresistible. Count Bernstorff's memoirs, with their accompanying documents, have revealed the intensity of the German efforts during this period; the most startling fact revealed by the German Ambassador is that the Kaiser, on October 9th, notified the President, almost in so many words, that, unless he promptly moved in the direction of peace, the German Government "would be forced to regain the freedom of action which it has reserved to itself in the note of May 4th last."[1]   It is unlikely that the annals of diplomacy contain many documents so cool and insolent as this one. It was a notification from the Kaiser to the President that the so-called "*Sussex* pledge" was not regarded as an unconditional one by the Imperial Government; that it was given merely to furnish Mr. Wilson an opportunity to bring the war to an end; and that unless the Presidential attempt to accomplish this were successful, there would be a resumption of the indiscriminate submarine campaign. The curious developments of the next two months are now a familiar story.   Possibly because the British Government had notified him, through Page, that his proffer of mediation would be unacceptable, Mr. Wilson moved cautiously and slowly, and Germany became impatient. The successful campaign against Rumania, resulting in the capture of Bucharest on December 6th, and the new vista which it opened to Germany of large food supplies, strengthened the Teutonic purpose.   Perhaps Germany,

---

[1]"My Three Years in America," by Count Bernstorff, p. 294.

with her characteristic lack of finesse, imagined that her own open efforts would lend emphasis to Mr. Wilson's pacific exertions. At any rate, on December 12th, just as Mr. Wilson was preparing to launch his own campaign for mediation, Germany herself approached her enemies with a proposal for a peace conference. A few days afterward Page, as the representative of Germany, called at the Foreign Office to deliver the large white envelope which contained the Kaiser's "peace proposal." In delivering this to Lord Robert Cecil, who was acting as Foreign Secretary in the temporary absence of Mr. Balfour, Page emphasized the fact that the American Government entirely disassociated itself from its contents and that he was acting merely in his capacity of "German Ambassador." Two communications from Lord Robert to Sir Cecil Spring Rice, British Ambassador at Washington, tell the story and also reveal that it was almost impossible for Page, even when engaged in an official proceeding, to conceal his contempt for the whole enterprise:

Lord R. Cecil to Sir C. Spring Rice

Foreign Office,
December 18, 1916.

SIR:

The American Ambassador came to see me this morning and presented to me the German note containing what is called in it the "offer of peace." He explained that he did so on instructions of his Government as representing the German Government, and not in any way as representing their own opinions. He also explained that the note must be regarded as coming from the four Central Powers, and as being addressed to all the Entente Powers who were represented by the United States.

He then read to me a telegram from his Government,

but declined to leave me a copy of it. The first part of the telegram explained that the Government of the United States would deeply appreciate a confidential intimation of the response to be made to the German note and that they would themselves have certain representations to make to the Entente Powers, to which they urgently begged the closest consideration. The telegram went on to explain that the Government of the United States had had it in mind for some time past to make such representations on behalf of neutral nations and humanity, and that it must not be thought that they were prompted by the Governments of the Central Powers. They wished us to understand that the note of the Central Powers created a good opportunity for making the American representations, but was not the cause of such representations being made.

I replied that I could of course say nothing to him on such an important matter without consulting my colleagues.

I am, etc.,

ROBERT CECIL.

Lord R. Cecil to Sir C. Spring Rice

Foreign Office,
19 December, 1916.

SIR:

The American Ambassador came to see me this afternoon.

I asked him whether he could tell me why his government were anxious to have confidential information as to the nature of our response to the German peace note.

He replied that he did not know, but he imagined it was to enable them to frame the representations of which he had spoken to me.

I then told him that we had asked the French to draft a reply, and that it would then be considered by the Allies, and in all probability an identic note would be presented in answer to the German note. I thought it probable that we should express our view that it was impossible to deal with the German offer, since it contained no specific proposals.

He said that he quite understood this, and that we should in fact reply that it was an offer "to buy a pig in a poke" which we were not prepared to accept. He added that he thought his Government would fully anticipate a reply in this sense, and he himself obviously approved it.

Then, speaking quite seriously, he said that he had heard people in London treating the German offer with derision, but that no doubt the belligerent governments would treat it seriously.

I said that it was certainly a serious thing, and no doubt would be treated seriously.

I asked him if he knew what would be contained in the proposed representations from his government.

He said that he did not; but as he understood that they were to be made to all the belligerents, he did not think that they could be much more than a pious aspiration for peace; since that was the only thing that was equally applicable to the Germans and to us.

As he was leaving he suggested that the German note might be published in our press.

> I am, etc.,
>
> ROBERT CECIL.

This so-called German "peace proposal" began with the statement that the war "had been forced" upon Germany, contained the usual reference to the military might of the Central Powers, and declared that the Fatherland was fighting for "the honour and liberty of national evolution." It is therefore not surprising that Lord Robert received it somewhat sardonically, especially as the communication contained no specific proposals, but merely a vague suggestion of "negotiations." But another spectacular performance now drove the German manœuvre out of everybody's mind. That President Wilson resented this German interference with his own plans is well known; he did not drop them, however, but on December 18th, he sent his long-contemplated peace communication to all the warring Powers. His appeal took the form of asking that they state the objects for which they were fighting, the Presidential belief evidently being that, if they did this, a common meeting ground might possibly be found. The suggestion that the Allied war aims were not public property, despite the fact that British statesmen had been broadly proclaiming them for three years, caused a momentary irritation in England, but this was not a serious matter, especially as the British Cabinet quickly saw that this request gave them a position of advantage over Germany, which had always refused to make public the terms on which it would end the war. The main substance in this Presidential approach, therefore, would have produced no ill-feeling; as usual, it was a few parenthetical phrases— phrases which were not essential to the main argument— which set the allied countries seething with indignation. The President, this section of his note ran, "takes the liberty of calling attention to the fact that the objects which the statesmen of the belligerents on both sides have in mind in this war, are virtually the same, as stated in general terms to their own people and to the world. Each side desires to make the rights and privileges of weak peoples and small states as secure against aggression and

denial in the future as the rights and privileges of the
great and powerful states now at war." This idea was
elaborated in several sentences of a similar strain, the
general purport of the whole passage being that there was
little to choose between the combatants, inasmuch as both
were apparently fighting for about the same things. Mr.
Wilson's purpose in this paragraph is not obscure; he was
making his long expected appearance as a mediator, and
he evidently believed that it was essential to this rôle that
he should not seem to be prejudiced in favour of either
side, but should hold the balance impartially between
them.

It is true that a minute reading indicates that Mr.
Wilson was merely quoting, or attempting to paraphrase,
the statements of the leaders of both sides, but there is such
a thing as quoting with approval, and no explanation
could convince the British public that the ruler of the
greatest neutral nation had not declared that the Allies
and the Central Powers stood morally upon the same level.
The popular indignation which this caused in Great
Britain was so intense that it alarmed the British authorities. The publication of this note in the British press was
withheld for several hours, in order to give the Government an opportunity to control the expression of editorial
opinion; otherwise it was feared that this would be so unrestrained in its bitterness that relations with the United
States might be imperilled. The messages which the London correspondents were permitted to send to the United
States were carefully censored for the same reason. The
dispatch sent by the Associated Press was the product of
a long struggle between the Foreign Office and its London
correspondent. The representatives spent half an hour
considering whether the American correspondents could
cable their country that the note had been received in

England with "surprise and irritation." After much discussion it was decided that "irritation" could not be used, and the message of the Associated Press, after undergoing this careful editing by the Foreign Office, was a weak and ridiculous description of the high state of excitement which prevailed in Great Britain. The fact that the British Foreign Office should have given all this trouble over the expressions sent to American newspapers and should even have spent half an hour debating whether a particular word should be used, almost pathetically illustrates the great care taken by the British Government not to influence American opinion against the Allies.

The Government took the same precautions with its own press in England. When the note was finally released the Foreign Office explicitly directed the London newspapers to comment with the utmost caution and in no case to question the President's sincerity. Most of them acquiesced in these instructions by maintaining silence. There was only one London newspaper, the *Westminster Gazette*, which made even a faint-hearted attempt to explain away the President's statement. From the first day of the war the British people had declared that President Wilson did not understand the issues at stake; and they now declared that this note confirmed their worst forebodings. The comments of the man-in-the-street were unprintable, but more serious than these was the impression which Mr. Wilson's dubious remarks made upon those Englishmen who had always been especially friendly to the United States and who had even defended the President in previous crises. Lord Bryce, who had accepted philosophically the Presidential statement that the United States was not "concerned with the causes" of the war, could not regard so indulgently this latest judgment of Great Britain and Germany. "Bryce came to see me in a state of great depression," wrote Page. "He has sent Mr. Wilson a personal letter on this matter." Northcliffe commanded his newspapers, the *Times* and the *Daily Mail*, to discuss the note in a judicial spirit, but he himself told Mr. Page that "everybody is as angry as hell." When someone attempted to discuss the Wilson note with Mr. Asquith, he brushed the subject away with a despairing gesture. "Don't talk to me about it," he said. "It is most disheartening." But the one man in England who was perhaps the most affected was King George. A man who had attended luncheon at Buckingham Palace on December 21st gave Page a description of the royal distress. The King, expressing his surprise and dismay that Mr. Wilson should think that Englishmen were fighting for the same things in this war as the Germans, broke down.

The world only now understands the dreadful prospect which was opening before Europe at the moment when this Presidential note added a new cause for general despondency. Rumania had collapsed, the first inkling of the Russian revolution had been obtained, the British well knew that the submarine warfare was to be resumed, and British finances were also in a desperate plight. More and more it was becoming evident to the British statesmen that they needed the intervention of the United States. This is the reason why they could not destroy the chances of American help by taking official offense even at what Page, in a communication to the Secretary of State, did not hesitate to call President Wilson's "insulting words"; and hence their determination to silence the press and to give no outward expression of what they felt. Page's interview with Lord Robert Cecil on December 26th, while the

Presidential communication was lying on his desk, discloses the real emotions of Englishmen. Apparently Page's frank cables concerning the reception of this paragraph had caused a certain interest in the State Department; at least the Ambassador was instructed to call at the Foreign Office and explain that the interpretation which had been commonly put upon the President's words was not the one which he had intended. At the same time Page was instructed to request the British Foreign Office, in case its reply were "favourable," not to publish it, but to communicate it secretly to the American Government. The purpose of this request is a little obscure; possibly it was the President's plan to use such a favourable reply to force Germany likewise to display an acquiescent mood. The object of Page's call was to present this disclaimer.

Lord Robert Cecil, the son of the late Lord Salisbury, —that same Lord Salisbury whose combats with Secretary Blaine and Secretary Olney form piquant chapters in British-American history—is one of the most able and respected of British statesmen. In his earlier life Lord Salisbury had been somewhat overbearing in his attitude toward the United States; in his later years, however, perhaps owing to the influence of his nephew, Mr. Balfour, his manner had changed. In his attitude toward the United States Lord Robert Cecil reflected only the later phases of his father's career. To this country and to its peaceful ideals he had always been extremely sympathetic, and to Page especially he had never manifested anything but cordiality. Yet it was evident, as Page came into his office this morning, that to Lord Robert, as to every member of the Government, the President's note, with its equivocal phrases, had been a terrible shock. His manner was extremely courteous, as always, but he made no attempt to conceal his feelings. Ordinarily Lord Robert did not wear his emotions on the surface; but he took occasion on this visit to tell Page how greatly the President's communication had grieved him.

"The President," he said, "has seemed to pass judgment on the allied cause by putting it on the same level as the German. I am deeply hurt."

Page conveyed Mr. Lansing's message that no such inference was justified. But this was not reassuring.

"Moreover," Lord Robert added, "there is one sentence in the note—that in which the President says that the position of neutrals is becoming intolerable—that seems almost a veiled threat."

Page hastened to assure Lord Robert that no threat was intended.

Lord Robert's manner became increasingly serious.

"There is nothing that the American Government or any other human power can do," he remarked slowly and solemnly, "which will bring this war to a close before the Allies have spent their utmost force to secure a victory. A failure to secure such a victory will leave the world at the mercy of the most arrogant and the bloodiest tyranny that has ever been organized. It is far better to die in an effort to defeat that tyranny than to perish under its success."

On any occasion Lord Robert is an impressive or at least a striking and unusual figure; he is tall, lank, and ungainly, almost Lincolnesque in the carelessness of his apparel and the exceeding awkwardness of his postures and manners. His angular features, sharp nose, pale face, and dark hair suggest the strain of ascetism, almost of fanaticism, which runs in the present generation of his family. And the deep sincerity and power of his words on this occasion made an impression which Page never forgot; they transformed the British statesman into an eloquent, almost an heroic figure.   If we are to understand the full tragedy of this moment we must remember that, incredible as it now seems, there was a fear in British officialdom that the United States might not only not pursue a course favourable to the Allies, but that it might even throw its support to Germany.   The fear, of course, was baseless; any suggestion of such a policy in the United States would have destroyed any official who had brought it forward; but Lord Robert knew and Page knew that there were insidious influences at work at that time, both in the United States and in Great Britain, which looked in this direction.   A group of Americans, whom Page used to re- fer to as "peace spies," were associated with English pacifists, for the purpose of bringing about peace on al- most any terms.   These "peace spies" had worked out a programme all their own.   The purpose was to compel Great Britain to accept the German terms for ending the war.   Unless she did accept them, then it was intended that the American Government should place an embargo on the shipment of foodstuffs and munitions to the Allies. There is little question that the United States, by taking such action, could have ended the war almost instan- taneously.   Should the food of her people and the great quantities of munitions which were coming from this country be suddenly cut off, there is little likelihood that Great Britain could have long survived.   The possibility that an embargo might shut out these supplies had hung over the heads of British statesmen ever since the war be- gan; they knew that the possession of this mighty power made the United States the potential dictator of events; and the fear that it might be used had never ceased to influence their thoughts or their actions.   Even while this interview was taking place, certain anti-British forces in the United States, such as Senator Hoke Smith of Georgia, were urging action of this kind.

"I have always been almost a Pacifist," Lord Robert continued. "No man has ever hated war worse than I. No man has ever had a more earnest faith that war can be abolished. But European civilization has been murderously assaulted and there is nothing now to do but to defeat this desperate enemy or to perish in the effort. I had hoped that the United States understood what is at stake."

Lord Robert went on:

"I will go so far as to say that if the United States will come into the war it will decide which will win, freedom or organized tyranny. If the United States shall help the Germans, civilization will perish and it will be necessary to build it up slowly again—if indeed it will ever appear again. If the United States will help the Allies, civilization will triumph."[1]

As to the proposal that the British terms should be conveyed confidentially to Mr. Wilson, Lord Robert said that that would be a difficult thing to do. The President's note had been published, and it therefore seemed necessary that the reply should also be given to the press. This was the procedure that was ultimately adopted.

Startling as was the sensation caused by the President's December note, it was mild compared with that which was now to come. Page naturally sent prompt reports of all these conversations to the President and likewise kept him completely informed as to the state of public feeling, but his best exertions apparently did not immediately affect the Wilson policy. The overwhelming fact is that

---

[1] This narrative is based upon memoranda made by Page.

the President's mind was fixed on a determination to compel the warring powers to make peace and in this way to keep the United States out of the conflict. Even the disturbance caused by his note of December 18th did not make him pause in this peace campaign. To that note the British sent a manly and definite reply, drafted by Mr. Balfour, giving in detail precisely the terms upon which the Allies would compose their differences with the Central Powers. The Germans sent a reply consisting of ten or a dozen lines, which did not give their terms, but merely asked again for a conference. Events were now moving with the utmost rapidity. On January 9th, a council of German military chieftains was held at Pless; in this it was decided to resume unrestricted submarine warfare. On January 16th the Zimmermann-Mexico telegram was intercepted; this informed Bernstorff, among other things, that this decision had been made. On January 16th, at nine o'clock in the morning, the American Embassy in London began receiving a long cipher despatch from Washington. The preamble announced that the despatch contained a copy of an address which the President proposed to deliver before the Senate "in a few days." Page was directed to have copies of the address "secretly prepared" and to hand them to the British Foreign Office and to newspapers of the type of the *Nation*, the *Daily News*, and the *Manchester Guardian*— all three newspapers well known for their Pacifist tendencies. As the speech approached its end, this sentence appeared: "It must be a peace without victory." The words greatly puzzled the secretary in charge, for they seemed almost meaningless. Suspecting that an error had been made in transmission, the secretary directed the code room to cable Washington for a verification of the cipher groups. Very soon the answer was received; there had been no mistake; the Presidential words were precisely those which had been first received: "Peace without victory." The slips were then taken to Page, who read the document, especially these fateful syllables, with a consternation which he made no effort to conceal. He immediately wrote a cable to President Wilson, telling him of the deplorable effect this sentence would produce and imploring him to cut it out of his speech—with what success the world now knows.

An astonishing feature of this episode is that Page had recently explained to the Foreign Office, in obedience to instructions from Washington, that Mr. Wilson's December note should not be interpreted as placing the Allies and the Central Powers on the same moral level. Now Mr. Wilson, in this "peace without victory" phrase, had repeated practically the same idea in another form. On the day the speech was received at the Embassy, about a week before it was delivered in the Senate, Page made the following memorandum:

The President's address to the Senate, which was received to-day (January 16th),[1] shows that he thinks he can play peace-maker. He does not at all understand, (or, if he do, so much the worse for him) that the Entente Powers, especially Great Britain and France, cannot make "peace without victory." If they do, they will become vassals of Germany. In a word, the President does not know the Germans; and he is, unconsciously, under their influence in his thought. His speech plays into their hands.

This address will give great offense in England, since it puts each side in the war on the same moral level.

I immediately saw the grave danger to our relations with

---

[1] It was delivered and published on January 22nd.

Great Britain by the Peace-without-Victory plan; and I telegraphed the President, venturing to advise him to omit that phrase—with no result.

Afterward Page added this to the above:

Compare this Senate speech with his speech in April calling for war: Just when and how did the President come to see the true nature of the German?   What made him change from Peace-Maker to War-Maker?   The Zimmermann telegram, or the February U-boat renewal of warfare?   Had he been so credulous as to believe the German promise?   This promise had been continuously and repeatedly broken.

Or was it the pressure of public opinion, the growing impatience of the people that pushed him in?

This distressing peace-move—utterly out of touch with the facts of the origin of the war or of its conduct or of the mood and necessities of Great Britain—a remote, academic deliverance, while Great Britain and France were fighting for their very lives—made a profoundly dejected feeling; and it made my place and work more uncomfortable than ever.   "Peace without victory" brought us to the very depths of European disfavour.

CHAPTER XXI

THE UNITED STATES AT WAR

I

THE United States broke off diplomatic relations with Germany on February 3, 1917. The occasion was a memorable one in the American Embassy in London, not unrelieved by a touch of the ridiculous. **All day** long a nervous and rather weary company had waited in the Ambassador's room for the decisive word from Washington. Mr. and Mrs. Page, Mr. and Mrs. Laughlin, Mr. Shoecraft, the Ambassador's secretary, sat there hour after hour, hardly speaking to one another in their tense excitement, waiting for the news that would inform them that Bernstorff's course had been run and that their country had taken its decision on the side of the Allies. Finally, at nine o'clock in the evening, the front door bell rang. Mr. Shoecraft excitedly left the room; half way downstairs he met Admiral William Reginald Hall, the head of the British Naval Intelligence, who was hurrying up to the Ambassador. Admiral Hall, as he spied Mr. Shoecraft, stopped abruptly and uttered just two words:

"Thank God!"

He then went into the Ambassador's room and read a secret code message which he had just received from Captain Gaunt, the British naval attaché at Washington. It was as follows:

"Bernstorff has just been given his passports. I shall probably get drunk to-night!"

It was in this way that Page first learned that the long tension had passed.

Page well understood that the dismissal of Bernstorff at that time meant war with the Central Empires. Had this dismissal taken place in 1915, after the sinking of the *Lusitania*, or in 1916, after the sinking of the *Sussex*, Page believed that a simple break in relations would in itself have brought the war to an early end. But by February, 1917, things had gone too far. For Germany had now decided to stake everything upon the chance of winning a quick victory with the submarine. Our policy had persuaded the Kaiser's advisers that America would not intervene; and the likelihood of rapidly starving Great Britain was so great—indeed the Germans had reduced the situation to a mathematical calculation of success—that an American declaration of war seemed to Berlin to be a matter of no particular importance. The American Ambassador in London regarded Bernstorff's dismissal much more seriously. It justified the interpretations of events which he had been sending to Mr. Wilson, Colonel House, and others for nearly three years. If Page had been inclined to take satisfaction in the fulfilment of his own prophecies, Germany's disregard of her promises and the American declaration of war would have seemed an ample justification of his course as ambassador.

But Page had little time for such vain communings. "All that water," as he now wrote, "has flowed over the dam." Occasionally his mind would revert to the dreadful period of "neutrality," but in the main his activities, mental and physical, were devoted to the future. A letter addressed to his son Arthur shows how quickly and how sympathetically he was adjusting himself to the new prospect. His mind was now occupied with ships, food, armies, warfare on submarines, and the approaching

Walter H. Page, at the time of America's entry into the war,
April, 1917

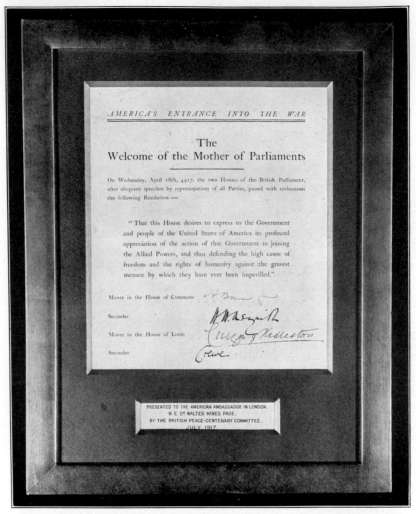

Resolution passed by the two Houses of Parliament, April 18, 1917,
on America's entry into the war

resettlement of the world. How completely he foresaw the part that the United States must play in the actual waging of hostilities, and to what an extent he himself was responsible for the policies that ultimately prevailed, appears in this letter:

To Arthur W. Page

25 March, 1917, London.

DEAR ARTHUR:

It's very hard, not to say impossible, to write in these swiftly moving days. Anything written to-day is out of date to-morrow—even if it be not wrong to start with. The impression becomes stronger here every day that we shall go into the war "with both feet"—that the people have pushed the President over in spite of his vision of the Great Peacemaker, and that, being pushed over, his idea now will be to show how he led them into a glorious war in defense of democracy. That's my reading of the situation, and I hope I am not wrong. At any rate, ever since the call of Congress for April 2nd, I have been telegraphing tons of information and plans that can be of use only if we go to war. Habitually they never acknowledge the receipt of anything at Washington. I don't know, therefore, whether they like these pieces of information or not. I have my staff of twenty-five good men getting all sorts of warlike information; and I have just organized twenty-five or thirty more—the best business Americans in London—who are also at work. I am trying to get the Government at Washington to send over a committee of conference—a General, an Admiral, a Reserve Board man, etc., etc. If they do half the things that I recommend we'll be in at the final lickin' big, and will save our souls yet.

There's lots of human nature in this world. A note is

now sometimes heard here in undertone (Northcliffe strikes it)—that they don't want the Americans in the war. This means that if we come in just as the Allies finish the job we'll get credit, in part, for the victory, which we did little to win! But that's a minor note. The great mass of people do want us in, quick, hard, and strong—our money and our guns and our ships.

A gift of a billion dollars[1] to France will fix Franco-American history all right for several centuries. Push it through. Such a gift could come to this Kingdom also but for the British stupidity about the Irish for three hundred years. A big loan to Great Britain at a low rate of interest will do the work here.

My mind keeps constantly on the effect of the war and especially of our action on our own country. Of course that is the most important end of the thing for us. I hope that—

1. It will break up and tear away our isolation;

2. It will unhorse our cranks and soft-brains.

3. It will make us less promiscuously hospitable to every kind of immigrant;

4. It will reëstablish in our minds and conscience and policy our true historic genesis, background, kindred, and destiny—i. e., kill the Irish and the German influence.

5. It will revive our real manhood—put the molly-coddles in disgrace, as idiots and dandies are;

6. It will make our politics frank and manly by restoring our true nationality;

7. It will make us again a great sea-faring people. It is this that has given Great Britain its long lead in the world;

8. Break up our feminized education—make a boy a

---

[1]At this time the proposal of such a gift found much popular favour. However, the plan was not carried through.

vigorous animal and make our education rest on a wholesome physical basis;

9. Bring men of a higher type into our political life.

We need waking up and shaking up and invigorating as much as the Germans need taking down.

There is no danger of "militarism" in any harmful sense among any English race or in any democracy.

By George! all these things open an interesting outlook and series of tasks—don't they?

My staff and I are asking everybody what the Americans can best do to help the cause along. The views are not startling, but they are interesting.

Jellicoe: More ships, merchant ships, any kind of ships, and take over the patrol of the American side of the Atlantic and release the British cruisers there.

Balfour: American credits in the United States big enough to keep up the rate of exchange.

Bonar Law: Same thing.

The military men: An expeditionary force, no matter how small, for the effect of the American Flag in Europe. If one regiment marched through London and Paris and took the Flag to the front, that would be worth the winning of a battle.

Think of the vast increase of territory and power Great Britain will have—her colonies drawn closer than ever, the German colonies, or most of them, taken over by her, Bagdad hers—what a way Germany chose to lessen the British Empire! And these gains of territory will be made, as most of her gains have been, not by any prearranged, set plan, but as by-products of action for some other purpose. The only people who have made a deliberate plan to conquer the earth—now living—are the Germans. And from first to last the additions to the British Empire have been made because she has been a first-class maritime power.

And that's the way she has made her trade and her money, too.

On top of this the President speculates about the danger of the white man losing his supremacy because a few million men get killed! The truth is every country that is playing a big part in the war was overpopulated. There will be a considerable productive loss because the killed men were, as a rule, the best men; but the white man's control of the world hasn't depended on any few million of males. This speculation is far up in the clouds. If Russia and Germany really be liberated from social and political and industrial autocracy, this liberation will bring into play far more power than all the men killed in the war could have had under the pre-war régime. I observe this with every year of my observation—there's no substitute for common-sense.

The big results of the war will, after all, be the freedom and the stimulation of men in these weary Old-World lands—in Russia, Germany itself, and in England. In five or ten years (or sooner, alas!) the dead will be forgotten.

If you wish to make a picture of the world as it will be when the war ends, you must conjure up such scenes as these—human bones along the Russian highways where the great retreat took place and all that such a sight denotes; Poland literally starved; Serbia, blasted and burned and starved; Armenia butchered; the horrible tragedy of Gallipoli, where the best soldiers in the world were sacrificed to politicians' policies; Austria and Germany starved and whipped but liberalized—perhaps no king in either country; Belgium—belgiumized; northern France the same and worse; more productive Frenchmen killed in proportion to the population perhaps than any other country will have lost; Great Britain—most of her best men gone or maimed; colossal debts; several Teutonic countries bankrupt; every atrocity conceivable committed somewhere—a hell-swept great continent having endured more suffering in three years than in the preceding three hundred. Then, ten years later, most of this suffering a mere memory; governments reorganized and liberalized; men made more efficient by this strenuous three years' work; the fields got back their bloom, and life going on much as it did before—with this chief difference—some kings have gone and many privileges have been abolished. The lessons are two—(1) that no government can successfully set out and conquer the world; and (2) that the hold that privilege holders acquire costs more to dislodge than any one could ever have guessed. That's the sum of it. Kings and privilege mongers, of course, have held the parts of the world separate from one another. They fatten on provincialism, which is mistaken for patriotism. As they lose their grip, human sympathy has its natural play between nations, and civilization has a chance. With any Emperor of Germany left the war will have been half in vain.

If we (the U. S. A.) cultivate the manly qualities and throw off our cranks and read our own history and be true to our traditions and blood and get some political vigour; then if we emancipate ourselves from the isolation theory and from the landlubber theory—get into the world and build ships, ships, ships, ships, and run them to the ends of the seas, we can dominate the world in trade and in political thought.

You know I have moments when it occurs to me that perhaps I'd better give whatever working years I may have to telling this story—the story of the larger meaning of the war. There's no bigger theme—never was one so big.

Affectionately,

W. H. P.

On April 1st, the day before President Wilson made his great address before Congress requesting that body to declare the existence of a state of war with Germany, Page committed to paper a few paragraphs which summed up his final judgment of President Wilson's foreign policy for the preceding two and a half years.

Embassy of the United States of America,
April 1, 1917.

In these last days, before the United States is forced into war—by the people's insistence—the preceding course of events becomes even clearer than it was before; and it has been as clear all the time as the nose on a man's face.

The President began by refusing to understand the meaning of the war.   To him it seemed a quarrel to settle economic rivalries between Germany and England.   He said to me last September[1] that there were many causes why Germany went to war.   He showed a great degree of toleration for Germany; and he was, during the whole morning that I talked with him, complaining of England. The controversies we had with England were, of course, mere by-products of the conflict.   But to him they seemed as important as the controversy we had with Germany.   In the beginning he had made—as far as it was possible—neutrality a positive quality of mind.   He would not move from that position.

That was his first error of judgment.   And by insisting on this he soothed the people—sat them down in comfortable chairs and said, "Now stay there."   He really suppressed speech and thought.

The second error he made was in thinking that he could

---

[1] At the meeting of Page and the President at Shadow Lawn, September 22, 1916.   See Chapter XIX.

play a great part as peacemaker—come and give a blessing to these erring children. This was strong in his hopes and ambitions. There was a condescension in this attitude that was offensive.

He shut himself up with these two ideas and engaged in what he called "thought." The air currents of the world never ventilated his mind.

This inactive position he has kept as long as public sentiment permitted. He seems no longer to regard himself nor to speak as a leader—only as the mouthpiece of public opinion after opinion has run over him.

He has not breathed a spirit into the people: he has encouraged them to supineness. He is *not* a leader, but rather a stubborn phrasemaker.

And now events and the aroused people seem to have brought the President to the necessary point of action; and even now he may act timidly.

"One thing pleases me," Page wrote to his son Arthur, "I never lost faith in the American people. It is now clear that I was right in feeling that they would have gladly come in any time after the *Lusitania* crime, Middle West in the front, and that the German hasn't made any real impression on the American nation. He was made a bug-a-boo and worked for all he was worth by Bernstorff; and that's the whole story. We are as Anglo-Saxon as we ever were. If Hughes had had sense and courage enough to say: 'I'm for war, war to save our honour and to save democracy,' he would now be President. If Wilson had said that, Hughes would have carried no important states in the Union. The suppressed people would have risen to either of them. That's God's truth as I believe it. The real United States is made up of you and Frank and the Page boys at Aberdeen and of the 10,000,000 other young fellows who are ready to do the job and who instinctively see the whole truth of the situation. But of course what the people would not have done under certain conditions—that water also has flowed over the dam; and I mention it only because I have resolutely kept my faith in the people and there has been nothing in recent events that has shaken it."

Two letters which Page wrote on this same April 1st are interesting in that they outline almost completely the war policy that was finally carried out:

To Frank N. Doubleday

Embassy of the United States of America,
April 1, 1917.

DEAR EFFENDI:

Here's the programme:

(1) Our navy in immediate action in whatever way a conference with the British shows we can best help.

(2) A small expeditionary force to France immediately—as large as we can quickly make ready, if only 10,000 men—as proof that we are ready to do some fighting.

(3) A large expeditionary force as soon as the men can be organized and equipped. They can be trained into an effective army in France in about one fourth of the time that they could be trained anywhere else.

(4) A large loan to the Allies at a low rate of interest.

(5) Ships, ships, ships—troop ships, food ships, munition ships, auxiliary ships to the navy, wooden ships, steel ships, little ships, big ships, ships, ships, ships without number or end.

(6) A clear-cut expression of the moral issue involved

in the war. Every social and political ideal that we stand for is at stake. If we value democracy in the world, this is the chance to further it or—to bring it into utter disrepute. After Russia must come Germany and Austria; and then the King-business will pretty nearly be put out of commission.

(7) We must go to war in dead earnest. We must sign the Allies' agreement not to make a separate peace, and we must stay in to the end. Then the end will be very greatly hastened.

It's been four years ago to-day since I was first asked to come here. God knows I've done my poor best to save our country and to help. It'll be four years in the middle of May since I sailed. I shall still do my best. I'll not be able to start back by May 15th, but I have a feeling, if we do our whole duty in the United States, that the end may not be very many months off. And how long off it may be may depend to a considerable degree on our action.

We are faring very well on army rations. None of us will live to see another time when so many big things are at stake nor another time when our country can play so large or important a part in saving the world. Hold up your end. I'm doing my best here.

I think of you engaged in the peaceful work of instructing the people, and I think of the garden and crocuses and the smell of early spring in the air and the earth and— push on; I'll be with you before we grow much older or get much grayer; and a great and prosperous and peaceful time will lie before us. Pity me and hold up your end for real American participation. Get together? Yes; but the way to get together is to get in!

Affectionately,
W. H. P.

To David F. Houston[1]

Embassy of the United States of America,
April 1, 1917.

DEAR HOUSTON:

The Administration can save itself from becoming a black blot on American history only by vigorous action— acts such as these:

Putting our navy to work—vigorous work—wherever and however is wisest. I have received the Government's promise to send an Admiral here at once for a conference. We must work out with the British Navy a programme whereby we can best help; and we must carry it without hesitancy or delay.

Sending over an expeditionary military force immediately—a small one, but as large as we can, as an earnest of a larger one to come. This immediate small one will have a good moral effect; and we need all the moral reinstatement that we can get in the estimation of the world; our moral stock is lower than, I fear, any of you at home can possibly realize. As for a larger expeditionary force later—even that ought to be sent quite early. It can and must spend some time in training in France, whatever its training beforehand may have been. All the military men agree that soldiers in France back of the line can be trained in at least half the time that they can be trained anywhere else. The officers at once take their turn in the trenches, and the progress that they and their men make in close proximity to the fighting is one of the remarkable discoveries of the war. The British Army was so trained and all the colonial forces. Two or three or four hundred thousand Americans could be sent over as soon almost as they are organized and equipped—provided transports

[1]Secretary of Agriculture in President Wilson's Cabinet.

and a continuous supply of food and munition ships can be got. They can be trained into fighting men—into an effective army—in about one third of the time that would be required at home.

I suppose, of course, we shall make at once a large loan to the Allies at a low rate of interest. That is most important, but that alone will not save us. We must also *fight*.

All the ships we can get—build, requisition, or confiscate—are needed immediately

Navy, army, money, ships—these are the first things, but by no means all. We must make some expression of a conviction that there is a moral question of right and wrong involved in this war—a question of humanity, a question of democracy. So far we have (officially) spoken only of the wrongs done to our ships and citizens. Deep wrongs have been done to all our moral ideas, to our ideals. We have sunk very low in European opinion because we do not seem to know even yet that a German victory would be less desirable than (say) a Zulu victory of the world.

We must go in with the Allies, not begin a mere single fight against submarines. We must sign the pact of London—not make a separate peace.

We mustn't longer spin dreams about peace, nor leagues to enforce peace, nor the Freedom of the Seas. These things are mere intellectual diversions of minds out of contact with realities. Every political and social ideal we have is at stake. If we make them secure, we'll save Europe from destruction and save ourselves, too.

I pray for vigour and decision and clear-cut resolute action.

(1) The Navy—full strength, no "grapejuice" action.

(2) An immediate expeditionary force.

(3)   A larger expeditionary force very soon.

(4)   A large loan at a low interest.

(5)   Ships, ships, ships.

(6)   A clear-cut expression of the moral issue.   Thus (and only thus) can we swing into a new era, with a world born again.

Yours in strictest confidence,

W. H. P.

A memorandum, written on April 3rd, the day after President Wilson advised Congress to declare a state of war with Germany:

The Day

When I went to see Mr. Balfour to-day he shook my hand warmly and said: "It's a great day for the world." And so has everybody said, in one way or another, that I have met to-day.

The President's speech did not appear in the morning papers—only a very brief summary in one or two of them; but the meaning of it was clear.   The fact that the House of Representatives organized itself in one day and that the President addressed Congress on the evening of that day told the story.   The noon papers had the President's speech in full; and everybody applauds.

My "Cabinet" meeting this morning was unusually interesting; and the whole group has never before been so delighted.   I spoke of the suggestive, constructive work we have already done in making reports on various war preparations and activities of this kingdom.   "Now we have greater need than ever, every man to do constructive work—to think of plans to serve.   We are in this excellent strategical position in the capital of the greatest belligerent—a position which I thank my stars, the President, and all the powers that be for giving us. We can each strive to justify our existence."

Few visitors called; but enthusiastic letters have begun to come in.

Nearly the whole afternoon was spent with Mr. Balfour and Lord Robert Cecil. Mr. Balfour had a long list of subjects. Could we help in (1)—(2)—(3)?— Every once in a while he stopped his enumeration of subjects long enough to tell me how the action of the United States had moved him.

To Lord Robert I said: "I pray you, give the Black List a decent burial: It's dead now, but through no act of yours. It insulted every American because you did not see that it was insulting: that's the discouraging fact to me." He thanked me earnestly. He'll think about that.

II

These jottings give only a faint impression of the change which the American action wrought in Page. The strain which he had undergone for twenty-nine months had been intense; it had had the most unfortunate effect upon his health; and the sudden lifting might have produced that reaction for the worse which is not unusual after critical experiences of this kind. But the gratification which Page felt in the fact that the American spirit had justified his confidence gave him almost a certain exuberance of contentment. Londoners who saw him at that time describe him as acting like a man from whose shoulders a tremendous weight had suddenly been removed. For more than two years Page had been compelled, officially at least, to assume a "neutrality" with which he had never had the slightest sympathy, but the necessity for this mask now no longer existed. A well-known Englishman happened to meet Page leaving his house in Grosvenor Square the day after the Declaration of War. He stopped and shook the Ambassador's hand.

"Thank God," the Englishman said, "that there is one hypocrite less in London to-day."

"What do you mean?" asked Page.

"I mean you. Pretending all this time that you were neutral! That isn't necessary any longer."

"You are right!" the Ambassador answered as he walked on with a laugh and a wave of the hand.

A few days after the Washington Declaration, the American Luncheon Club held a feast in honour of the event. This organization had a membership of representative American business men in London, but its behaviour during the war had not been based upon Mr. Wilson's idea of neutrality. Indeed its tables had so constantly rung with denunciations of the *Lusitania* notes that all members of the American Embassy, from Page down, had found it necessary to refrain from attending its proceedings. When Page arose to address his compatriots on this occasion, therefore, he began with the significant words, "I am glad to be back with you *again*," and the mingled laughter and cheers with which this remark was received indicated that his hearers had caught the point.

The change took place not only in Page, but in London and the whole of Great Britain. An England that had been saying harsh things of the United States for nearly two years now suddenly changed its attitude. Both houses of Parliament held commemorative sessions in honour of America's participation; in the Commons Mr. Lloyd George, Mr. Asquith, and other leaders welcomed their new allies, and in the Upper Chamber Lord Curzon, Lord

Bryce, the Archbishop of Canterbury, and others similarly voiced their admiration. The Stars and Stripes almost instantaneously broke out on private dwellings, shops, hotels, and theatres; street hucksters did a thriving business selling rosettes of the American colours, which even the most stodgy Englishmen did not disdain to wear in their buttonholes; wherever there was a band or an orchestra, the Star Spangled Banner acquired a sudden popularity; and the day even came when the American and the British flags flew side by side over the Houses of Parliament—the first occasion in history that any other than the British standard had received this honour. The editorial outgivings of the British press on America's entrance form a literature all their own. The theatres and the music halls, which had found in "notes" and "nootrality" an endless theme of entertainment for their patrons, now sounded Americanism as their most popular refrain. Churches and cathedrals gave special services in honour of American intervention, and the King and the President began to figure side by the side in the prayer book. The estimation in which President Wilson was held changed overnight. All the phrases that had so grieved Englishmen were instantaneously forgotten. The President's address before Congress was praised as one of the most eloquent and statesmanlike utterances in history. Special editions of this heartening document had a rapid sale; it was read in school houses, churches, and at public gatherings, and it became a most influential force in uplifting the hopes of the Allies and inspiring them to renewed activities. Americans everywhere, in the streets, at dinner tables, and in general social intercourse, could feel the new atmosphere of respect and admiration which had suddenly become their country's portion. The first American troops that passed through London—a company of engineers, an especially fine body of men—aroused a popular enthusiasm which was almost unprecedented in a capital not celebrated for its emotional displays.   Page himself records one particularly touching indication of the feeling for Americans which was now universal.   "The increasing number of Americans who come through England," he wrote, "most of them on their way to France, but some of them also to serve in England, give much pleasure to the British public—nurses, doctors, railway engineers, sawmill units, etc.   The sight of every American uniform pleases London.   The other morning a group of American nurses gathered with the usual crowd in front of Buckingham Palace while the Guards band played inside the gates.   Man after man as they passed them and saw their uniforms lifted their hats."

The Ambassador's mail likewise underwent a complete transformation.   His correspondence of the preceding two years, enormous in its extent, had contained much that would have disturbed a man who could easily get excited over trifles, but this aspect of his work never caused Page the slightest unhappiness.   Almost every crank in England who disliked the American policy had seemed to feel it his duty to express his opinions to the American Ambassador.   These letters, at times sorrowful, at others abusive, even occasionally threatening, varying in their style from cultivated English to the grossest illiteracy, now written in red ink to emphasize their bitterness, now printed in large block letters to preserve their anonymity, aroused in Page only a temporary amusement. But the letters that began to pour in upon him after our Declaration, many of them from the highest placed men and women in the Kingdom, brought out more vividly than anything else the changed position of his country. Sonnets and verses rained upon the Embassy, most of

The Rt. Hon. David Lloyd George, Chancellor of
the Exchequer, 1908–1915, Minister of Munitions,
1915–1916, Prime Minister of Great Britain, 1916-1922

The Rt. Hon. Arthur James Balfour (now the Earl of Balfour)
Secretary of State for Foreign Affairs, 1916–1919

them pretty bad as poetry, but all of them commendable for their admiring and friendly spirit. Of all these letters those that came from the steadfast friends of America perhaps gave Page the greatest satisfaction. "You will have been pleased at the universal tribute paid to the spirit as well as to the lofty and impressive terms of the President's speech," wrote Lord Bryce. "Nothing finer in our time, few things so fine." But probably the letter which gave Page the greatest pleasure was that which came from the statesman whose courtesy and broad outlook had eased the Ambassador's task in the old neutrality days. In 1916, Sir Edward Grey—now become Viscount Grey of Fallodon—had resigned office, forced out, Page says in one of his letters, mainly because he had refused to push the blockade to a point where it might produce a break with the United States. He had spent the larger part of the time since that event at his country place in Northumberland, along the streams and the forests which had always given him his greatest pleasure, attempting to recover something of the health that he had lost in the ten years which he had spent as head of the British Foreign Office and bearing with characteristic cheerfulness and fortitude the tragedy of a gradually failing eyesight. The American Declaration of War now came to Lord Grey as the complete justification of his policy. The mainspring of that policy, as already explained, had been a determination to keep the friendship of the United States, and so shape events that the support of this country would ultimately be cast on the side of the Allies. And now the great occasion for which he had prepared had come, and in Grey's mind this signified more than a help to England in soldiers and ships; it meant bringing together the two branches of a common race for the promotion of common ideals.

From Viscount Grey of Fallodon

Rosehall Post Office,
Sutherland,
April 8, 1917.

DEAR MR. PAGE:

This is a line that needs no answer to express my congratulations on President Wilson's address. I can't express adequately all that I feel. Great gratitude and great hope are in my heart. I hope now that some great and abiding good to the world will yet be wrought out of all this welter of evil. Recent events in Russia, too, stimulate this hope: they are a good in themselves, but not the power for good in this war that a great and firmly established free country like the United States can be. The President's address and the way it has been followed up in your country is a splendid instance of great action finely inspired. I glow with admiration.

Yours sincerely,
GREY OF FALLODON

One Englishman who was especially touched by the action of the United States was His Majesty the King. Few men had watched the course of America during the war with more intelligent interest than the head of the British royal house. Page had had many interviews with King George at Buckingham Palace and at Windsor, and his notes contain many appreciative remarks on the King's high character and conscientious devotion to his duties. That Page in general did not believe in kings and emperors as institutions his letters reveal; yet even so profound a Republican as he recognized sterling character, whether in a crowned head or in a humble citizen, and he had seen enough of King George to respect him. Moreover, the peculiar limitations of the British monarchy certainly gave it an unusual position and even saved it from much of the criticism that was fairly lavished upon such nations as Germany and Austria. Page especially admired King George's frankness in recognizing these limitations and his readiness to accommodate himself to the British Constitution. On most occasions, when these two men met, their intercourse was certainly friendly or at least not formidable. After all formalities had been exchanged, the King would frequently draw the Ambassador aside; the two would retire to the smoking room, and there, over their cigars, discuss a variety of matters—submarines, international politics, the Irish question and the like. His Majesty was not averse even to bringing up the advantages of the democratic and the monarchical system. The King and Ambassador would chat, as Page himself would say, like "two human beings"; King George is an emphatic and vivacious talker, fond of emphasizing his remarks by pounding the table; he has the liveliest sense of humour, and enjoys nothing quite so much as a good story. Page found that, on the subject of the Germans, the King entertained especially robust views. "They are my kinsmen," he would say, "but I am ashamed of them."

Probably most Englishmen, in the early days of the war, preferred that the United States should not engage in hostilities; even after the *Lusitania,* the majority in all likelihood held this view. There are indications, however, that King George favoured American participation. A few days after the *Lusitania* sinking, Page had an audience for the purpose of presenting a medal sent by certain societies in New Orleans. Neither man was thinking much about medals that morning. The thoughts uppermost in their minds, as in the minds of most Americans and

Englishmen, were the *Lusitania* and the action that the United States was likely to take concerning it.   After the formalities of presentation, the King asked Page to sit down and talked with him for more than half an hour. "He said that Germany was evidently trying to force the United States into the war; that he had no doubt we would soon be in it and that, for his part, he would welcome us heartily.   The King also said he had reliable information from Germany, that the Emperor had wished to return a conciliatory answer to our *Lusitania* note, but that Admiral von Tirpitz had prevented it, even going so far as to 'threaten' the Kaiser.   It appears that the Admiral insisted that the submarine was the only weapon the Germans could use with effect against England and that they could not afford to give it up.   He was violent and the Kaiser finally yielded."[1]

The statement from the King at that crisis, that he would "heartily welcome the United States into the war," was interpreted by the Ambassador as amounting practically to an invitation—and certainly as expressing a wish that such an intervention should take place.

That the American participation would rejoice King George could therefore be taken for granted.   Soon after this event, the Ambassador and Mrs. Page were invited to spend the night at Windsor.

"I arrived during the middle of the afternoon," writes Page, "and he sent for me to talk with him in his office.

"'I've a good story on you,' said he.   'You Americans have a queer use of the word "some," to express mere bigness or emphasis.   We are taking that use of the word from you over here.   Well, an American and an Englishman were riding in the same railway compartment.   The

---

[1]The quotation is from a memorandum of the conversation made by one of the secretaries of the American Embassy.

American read his paper diligently—all the details of a big battle. When he got done, he put the paper down and said: "Some fight!" "And some don't!" said the Englishman.'

"And the King roared. 'A good one on you!'

"'The trouble with that joke, sir,' I ventured to reply, 'is that it's out of date.'

"He was in a very gay mood, surely because of our entry into the war. After the dinner—there were no guests except Mrs. Page and me, the members of his household, of course, being present—he became even familiar in the smoking room. He talked about himself and his position as king. 'Knowing the difficulties of a limited monarch, I thank heaven I am spared being an absolute one.'

"He went on to enumerate the large number of things he was obliged to do, for example, to sign the death warrant of every condemned man—and the little real power that he had—not at all in a tone of complaint, but as a merely impersonal explanation.

"Just how much power—perhaps 'influence' is a better word—the King has, depends on his personality. The influence of the throne—and of him on the throne, being a wholly thoughtful, industrious, and conscientious man— is very great—greatest of all in keeping the vested interests of the aristocratic social structure secure.

"Earlier than this visit to Windsor he sent for me to go to Buckingham Palace very soon after we declared war. He went over the whole course of events—and asked me many questions. After I had risen and said 'good-bye' and was about to bow myself out the door, he ran toward me and waving his hand cried out, 'Ah—Ah!—we knew where *you* stood all the time.'

"When General Pershing came along on his way to France, the King summoned us to luncheon. The luncheon was eaten (here, as everywhere, strict war rations are observed) to a flow of general talk, with the Queen, Princess Mary, and one of the young Princes. When they had gone from the luncheon room, the King, General Pershing, and I stood smoking by the window; and the King at once launched into talk about guns, rifles, ammunition, and the American place in the battle line. Would our place be with the British or with the French or between the two?

"General Pershing made a diplomatic reply. So far as he knew the President hadn't yet made a final decision, but there was a feeling that, since we were helping the British at sea, perhaps we ought to help the French on land.

"Then the King expressed the earnest hope that our guns and ammunition would match either the British or the French. Else if we happened to run out of ammunition we could not borrow from anybody. He thought it most unfortunate that the British and French guns and rifles were of different calibres."

To Arthur W. Page

Brighton, England,
April 28, 1917.

DEAR ARTHUR:

. . . Well, the British have given us a very good welcome into the war. They are not very skillful at such a task: they do not know how to say "Welcome" very vociferously. But they have said it to the very best of their ability. My speeches (which I send you, with some comment) were very well received indeed. Simple and obvious as they were, they meant a good deal of work.

I cannot conceal nor can I express my gratification that we are in the war. I shall always wonder but never find out what influence I had in driving the President over. All I know is that my letters and telegrams for nearly two years—especially for the last twelve months—have put before him every reason that anybody has expressed why we should come in—in season and out of season. And there is no new reason—only more reason of the same old sort—why we should have come in now than there was why we should have come in a year ago. I suspect that the pressure of the press and of public opinion really became too strong for him. And, of course, the Peace-Dream blew up—was torpedoed, mined, shot, captured, and killed. I trust, too, much enlightenment will be furnished by the two Commissions now in Washington.[1] Yet it's comical to think of the attitude of the poor old Department last September and its attitude now. But thank God for it! Every day now brings a confession of the blank idiocy of its former course and its long argument! Never mind that, so long as we are now right.

I have such a sense of relief that I almost feel that my job is now done. Yet, I dare say, my most important work is still to come.

The more I try to reach some sort of rational judgment about the war, the more I find myself at sea. It does look as if the very crisis is near. And there can be no doubt now—not even, I hope, in the United States—about the necessity of a clear and decisive victory, nor about punishment. All the devastation of Northern France, which outbarbarizes barbarism, all the ships sunk, including hospital ships, must be paid for; that's all. There'll be famine in Europe whenever it end. Not only must these destructions be paid for, but the Hohenzollerns and all they stand for must go. Trust your Frenchman for that, if nobody else!

---

[1] The British and French Commissions, headed by Mr. Balfour and M. Viviani.

If Europe had the food wasted in the United States, it would make the difference between sustenance and famine. By the way, the submarine has made every nation a danger zone except those few that have self-feeding continents, such as ours. It can bring famine to any other kind of a country.

You are now out in the country again—good. Give Mollie my love and help her with the garden. I envy you the fresh green things to eat. Little Mollie, kiss her for granddaddy. The Ambassador, I suppose, waxes even sturdier, and I'm glad to hear that A. W. P., Jr., is picking up. Get him fed right at all costs. If Frank stays at home and Ralph and his family come up, you'll all have a fine summer. We've the very first hint of summer we've had, and it's cheerful to see the sky and to feel the sunshine.

Affectionately,

W. H. P.

To Frank N. Doubleday

American Embassy,
London, May 3, 1917.

DEAR EFFENDI:

I aim this at you. It may hit a German submarine. But we've got to take our chances in these days of risk. Your letter from the tropics—a letter from you from any place is as scarce as peace!—gave me a pleasant thrill and reminder of a previous state of existence, a long way back in the past. I wonder if, on your side the ocean you are living at the rate of a century a year, as we are here? Here in bountiful England we are living on rations. I spent a night with the King a fortnight ago, and he gave us only so much bread, one egg apiece, and—lemonade. We are to begin bread tickets next week. All this is perfectly healthful and wholesome and as much as I ever eat. But the hard part of it is that it's necessary. We haven't more than six weeks' food supply and the submarines sunk eighty-eight ships—237,000 tons—last week. These English do not publish these harrowing facts, and nobody knows them but a few official people. And they are destroying the submarines at a most beggarly slow rate. They work far out at sea—100 to 200 miles—and it's as hard to find them as it would be to find whales. The simple truth is we are in a dangerous plight. If they could stop this submarine warfare, the war would pretty quickly be won, for the Germans are in a far worse plight for food and materials and they are getting much the worst of it on land. The war would be won this summer or autumn if the submarine could be put out of business. If it isn't, the Germans may use this success to keep their spirits up and go on till next year.

We (the United States) have about 40 destroyers. We are sending over 6! I'm doing my best to persuade the Government at Washington to send every one we have. But, since the British conceal the facts from their own press and the people and from all the world, the full pressure of the situation is hard to exert on Washington. Our Admiral (Sims) and I are trying our best, and we are spending enough on cables to build a destroyer. All this, you must, of course, regard as a dark secret; but it's a devilish black secret.

I don't mean that there's any danger of losing the war. Even if the British armies have to have their food cut down and people here go hungry, they'll win; but the winning may be a long time off. Nothing but their continued success can keep the Germans going. Their people are war-weary and hungry. Austria is knocked out and is starving. Turkey is done up but can go on living on nothing, but not fighting much more. When peace comes, there'll be a general famine, on the continent at least, and no ships to haul food. This side of the world will have to start life all over again—with insufficient men to carry things on and innumerable maimed men who'll have (more or less) to be cared for. The horror of the whole thing nobody realizes. We've all got used to it here; and nobody clearly remembers just what the world was like in peace times; those times were so far away. All this I write not to fill you with horrors but to prove that I speak the literal truth when I say that it seems a hundred years since I had before heard from you.

Just how all this affects a man, no man can accurately tell. Of how much use I'll be when I can get home, I don't know. Sometimes I think that I shall be of vastly greater use than ever. Plans and publishing ambitions pop up in my mind at times which look good and promising. I see books and series of books. I see most useful magazine stuff. Then, before I can think anything out to a clear plan or conclusion, the ever-increasing official duties and responsibilities here knock everything else out of my head, perhaps for a whole month. It's a literal fact that many a month I do not have an hour to do with as I please nor to think about what I please, from the time I wake up till I go to bed. In spite of twenty-four secretaries (the best fellows that ever were and the best staff that any Embassy ever had in the world) more and more work comes to me. I thank Heaven we no longer have the interests of Germany, Austria, and Turkey to look after; but with our coming into the war, work in general has increased enormously. I have to spend very much more time with the different departments of the British Government on war plans and such like things. They have welcomed us in very handsomely; and one form of their welcome is consulting with me about—navy plans, war plans, loans of billions, ships, censorship, secret service—everything you ever heard of. At first it seemed a little comical for the admirals and generals and the Governor of the Bank of England to come and ask for advice. But when I gave it and it worked out well, I went on and, after all, the thing's easier than it looks. With a little practice you can give these fellows several points in the game and play a pretty good hand. They don't know half as much as you might suppose they'd know. All these years of lecturing the State Department and the President got my hand in! The whole game is far easier than any small business. You always play with blue chips better than you play with white ones.

This country and these people are not the country and the people they were three years ago. They are very different. They are much more democratic, far less cocksure, far less haughty, far humbler. The man at the head of the army rose from the ranks. The Prime Minister is a poor Welsh schoolteacher's son, without early education. The man who controls all British shipping began life as a shipping "clark," at ten shillings a week. Yet the Lords and Ladies, too, have shown that they were made of the real stuff. This experience is making England over again. There never was a more interesting thing to watch and to be part of.

There are about twenty American organizations here— big, little, rag-tag, and bobtail. When we declared war, every one of 'em proceeded to prepare for some sort of celebration. There would have been an epidemic of Fourth-of-July oratory all over the town—before we'd done anything—Americans spouting over the edges and killing Kruger with their mouths. I got representatives of 'em all together and proposed that we hold our tongues

till we'd won the war—then we can take London. And
to give one occasion when we might all assemble and dedicate ourselves to this present grim business, I arranged for
an American Dedicatory Service at St. Paul's Cathedral.
The royal family came, the Government came, the Allied
diplomats came, my Lords and Ladies came, one hundred
wounded American (Canadian) soldiers came—the pick
of the Kingdom; my Navy and Army staff went in full
uniform, the Stars and Stripes hung before the altar, a
double brass band played the Star Spangled Banner and
the Battle Hymn of the Republic, and an American bishop
(Brent) preached a red-hot American sermon, the Archbishop of Canterbury delivered the benediction; and (for
the first time in English history) a foreign flag (the Stars
and Stripes) flew over the Houses of Parliament. It was
the biggest occasion, so they say, that St. Paul's ever had.
And there's been no spilling of American oratory since!
If you had published a shilling edition of the words and
music of the Star Spangled Banner and the Battle Hymn
you could have sent a cargo of 'em here and sold them.
There isn't paper enough in this Kingdom to get out an
edition here.

Give my love to all the Doubledays and to all the fellows
in the shop, and (I wonder if you will) try your hand at
another letter. You write very legibly these days!

Sincerely yours,
WALTER H. PAGE.

"Curiously enough," Page wrote about this time, "these
most exciting days of the war are among the most barren
of exciting topics for private correspondence. The 'atmosphere' here is unchanging—to us—and the British are
turning their best side to us continuously. They are
increasingly appreciative, and they see more and more

clearly that our coming into the war is all that saved them
from a virtual defeat—I mean the public sees this more
and more clearly, for, of course, the Government has
known it from the beginning. I even find a sort of mor-
bid fear lest they do not sufficiently show their appreciation. The Archbishop last night asked me in an appre-
hensive tone whether the American Government and
public felt that the British did not sufficiently show their
gratitude. I told him that we did not come into the war
to win compliments but to whip the enemy, and that we
wanted all the help the British can give: that's the main
thing; and that thereafter of course we liked appreciation,
but that expressions of appreciation had not been lacking.
Mr. Balfour and Sir Edward Carson also spoke to me
yesterday much in the same tone as the Archbishop of
Canterbury.

"Try to think out any line of action that one will, or
any future sequence or events or any plan touching the
war, one runs into the question whether the British are
doing the best that could be done or are merely plugging
away. They are, as a people, slow and unimaginative,
given to over-much self-criticism; but they eternally hold
on to a task or to a policy. Yet the question forever
arises whether they show imagination, to say nothing of
genius, and whether the waste of a slow, plodding policy
is the necessary price of victory.

"Of course such a question is easy to ask and it is easy
to give dogmatic answers. But it isn't easy to give an
answer based on facts. Our General Lassiter,[1] for instance—a man of sound judgment—has in general been
less hopeful of the military situation in France than most
of the British officers. But he is just now returned from
the front, much cheered and encouraged. 'Lassiter,' I

---

[1] American military attaché in London.

asked, 'have the British in France or has any man among them what we call genius, or even wide vision; or are they merely plodding along at a mechanical task?' His answer was, 'We don't see genius till it has done its job. It is a mechanical task—yes, that's the nature of the struggle—and they surely do it with intelligence and spirit. There is waste. There is waste in all wars. But I come back much more encouraged.'

"The same sort of questions and answers are asked and given continuously about naval action. Every discussion of the possibility of attacking the German naval bases ends without a plan. So also with preventing the submarines from coming out. These subjects have been continuously under discussion by a long series of men who have studied them; and the total effect so far has been to leave them among the impossible tasks. So far as I can ascertain all naval men among the Allies agree that these things can't be done.

"Here again—Is this a merely routine professional opinion—a merely traditional opinion—or is it a lack of imagination? The question will not down. Yet it is impossible to get facts to combat it. What are the limits of the practicable?

"Mr. Balfour told me yesterday his personal conviction about the German colonies, which, he said, he had not discussed with his associates in the Cabinet. His firm opinion is that they ought not to be returned to the Germans, first for the sake of humanity. 'The natives—the Africans especially—have been so barbarously treated and so immorally that it would be inhuman to permit the Germans to rule and degrade them further. But Heaven forbid that we should still further enlarge the British Empire. As a practical matter I do not care to do that. Besides, we should incur the criticism of fighting in order to get more territory, and that was not and is not our aim. If the United States will help us, my wish is that these German Colonies that we have taken, especially in Africa, should be "internationalized." There are great difficulties in such a plan, but they are not insuperable if the great Powers of the Allies will agree upon it.' And much more to the same effect. The parts of Asiatic Turkey that the British have taken, he thought, might be treated in the same way."

CHAPTER XXII

THE BALFOUR MISSION TO THE UNITED STATES

I

PAGE now took up a subject which had been near his heart for a long time. He believed that one of the most serious causes of Anglo-American misunderstanding was the fact that the leading statesmen of the two countries had never had any personal contact with one another. At one time, as this correspondence shows, the Ambassador had even hoped that President Wilson himself might cross the ocean and make the British people an official visit. The proposal, however, was made before the European war broke out, the occasion which Page had in mind being the dedication of Sulgrave Manor, the old English home of the Washington family, as a perpetual memorial to the racial bonds and common ideals uniting the two countries. The President found it impossible to act upon this suggestion and the outbreak of war made the likelihood of such a visit still more remote. Page had made one unsuccessful attempt to bring the American State Department and the British Foreign Office into personal contact. At the moment when American irritation had been most keen over the blockade and the blacklist, Page had persuaded the Foreign Office to invite to England Mr. Frank L. Polk, at that time Counsellor of the Department; the Ambassador believed that a few conversations between such an intelligent gentleman as Mr. Polk and the British statesmen would smooth out all the points which were then making things so difficult.   Unfortunately the pressure of work at Washington prevented Mr. Polk from accepting Sir Edward Grey's invitation.

But now a greater necessity for close personal association had arisen.   The United States had entered the war, and this declaration had practically made this country an ally of Great Britain and France.   The British Government wished to send a distinguished commission to the United States, for two reasons: first, to show its appreciation of the stand which America had taken, and second, to discuss plans for coöperation in the common task.   Great Britain frankly admitted that it had made many mistakes in the preceding three years—mistakes naval, military, political, and economic; it would welcome an opportunity to display these errors to Washington, which might naturally hope to profit from them.   As soon as his country was in the war, Page took up this suggestion with the Foreign Office.   There was of course one man who was preëminently fitted, by experience, position, and personal qualities, to head such a commission; on this point there was no discussion.   Mr. Balfour was now in his seventieth year; his activities in British politics dated back to the times of Disraeli; his position in Great Britain had become as near that of an "elder statesman" as is tolerable under the Anglo-Saxon system.   By this time Page had established the friendliest possible relations with this distinguished man.   Mr. Balfour had become Foreign Secretary in December, 1916, in succession to Lord Grey.   Greatly as Page regretted the resignation of Grey, he was much gratified that Mr. Balfour had been selected to succeed him.   Mr. Balfour's record for twenty-five years had been one of consistent friendliness toward the United States. When President Cleveland's Venezuelan message, in 1896, had precipitated a crisis in the relations of the two countries, it was Mr. Balfour's influence which was especially potent in causing Great Britain to modify its attitude and to accept the American demand for arbitration. That action not only amicably settled the Venezuelan question; it marked the beginning of a better feeling between the English-speaking countries and laid the basis for that policy of benevolent neutrality which Great Britain had maintained toward the United States in the Spanish War. The excellent spirit which Mr. Balfour had shown at this crisis he had manifested on many occasions since. In the criticisms of the United States during the *Lusitania* troubles Mr. Balfour had never taken part. The era of "neutrality" had not ruffled the confidence which he had always felt in the United States. During all this time the most conspicuous dinner tables of London had rung with criticisms of American policy; the fact was well known, however, that Mr. Balfour had never sympathized with these reproaches; even when he was not in office, no unfriendly word concerning the United States had ever escaped his lips. His feeling toward this country was well shown in a letter which he wrote Page, in reply to one congratulating him on his seventieth birthday. "I have now lived a long life," said Mr. Balfour, "and most of my energies have been expended in political work, but if I have been fortunate enough to contribute, even in the smallest degree, to drawing closer the bonds that unite our two countries, I shall have done something compared with which all else that I may have attempted counts in my eyes as nothing."

Page's letters and notes contain many references to Mr. Balfour's kindly spirit. On the day following the dismissal of Bernstorff the American Ambassador lunched with the Foreign Secretary at No. 4 Carlton Gardens.

"Mr. Balfour," Page reported to Washington, "gave expression to the hearty admiration which he entertained for the President's handling of a difficult task.   He said that never for a moment had he doubted the President's wisdom in the course he was pursuing.   He had the profoundest admiration for the manner in which he had promptly broken with Germany after receiving Germany's latest note.   Nor had he ever entertained the slightest question of the American people's ready loyalty to their Government or to their high ideals.   One of his intellectual pleasures, he added, had long been contemplation of the United States as it is and, even more, as its influence in the world will broaden.   'The world,' said Mr. Balfour, 'will more and more turn on the Great Republic as on a pivot.'"

Occasionally Mr. Balfour's discussion of the United States would take a more pensive turn.   A memorandum which Page wrote a few weeks after the above touches another point:

March 27, 1917.

I had a most interesting conversation with Mr. Balfour this afternoon.   "It's sad to me," said he, "that we are so unpopular, so much more unpopular than the French, in your country.   Why is it?   The old school books?"

I doubted the school-book influence.

"Certainly their influence is not the main cause.   It is the organized Irish.   Then it's the effect of the very fact that the Irish question is not settled.   You've had that problem at your very door for 300 years.   What's the matter that you don't solve it?"

"Yes, yes,"—he saw it.   But the plaintive tone of such a man asking such a question was significant and interesting and—sad.

Then I told him the curious fact that a British Government made up of twenty individuals, every one of whom is most friendly to the United States, will, when they act together as a Government, do the most offensive things. I mentioned the blacklist; I mentioned certain complaints that I then held in my hand—of Americans here who are told by the British Government that they must turn over to the British Government's agent in New York their American securities which they hold in America!

There's a sort of imperious, arrogant, Tory action that comes natural to the English Government, even when not natural to the individual Englishman.

On April 5th, the day before the United States formally declared war, Page notified Washington that the British Government wished Mr. Balfour to go to the United States as the head of a Commission to confer with our Government. "Mr. Balfour is chosen for this mission," Page reported, "not only because he is Secretary of State for Foreign Affairs, but because he is personally the most distinguished member of the Government." Page tells the story in more detail in a letter to Mr. Polk, at that time Counsellor of the State Department.

To Frank L. Polk

London, May 3, 1917.

DEAR MR. POLK:

. . . Mr. Balfour accurately represents British character, British opinion, and the British attitude. Nobody who knows him and knows British character and the British attitude ever doubted that. I know his whole tribe, his home-life, his family connections, his friends; and, of course, since he became Foreign Secretary, I've come to know him intimately. When the question first came up here of his going, of course I welcomed it enthusiastically. About that time during a two-hour conversation he asked me why the British were so unpopular in the United States. Among other reasons I told him that our official people on both sides steadfastly refused to visit one another and to become acquainted. Neither he nor Lord Grey, nor Mr. Asquith, nor Mr. Lloyd George, had ever been to the United States, nor any other important British statesman in recent times, and not a single member of the Administration was personally known to a single member of the British Government. "I'll go," said he, "if you are perfectly sure my going will be agreeable to the President." He himself recalled the fact, during one of our several conversations just before he left, that you had not come when he and Lord Grey had invited you. If you had come, by the way, this era of a better understanding would have begun then, and half our old troubles would then have been removed. Keeping away from one another is the best of all methods of keeping all old misunderstandings alive and of making new ones.

I have no doubt that Mr. Balfour's visit will cause visits of many first-class British statesmen during the war or soon afterward. That's all we need to bring about a perfect understanding.

You may remember how I tried to get an official report about the behaviour of the *Benham*,[1] and how, in the absence of that, Lord Beresford made a disagreeable speech about our Navy in the House of Lords, and how, when

---

[1]The reference is to the attack made in October, 1916, by the German Submarine *U*-53, off Nantucket on several British ships. An erroneous newspaper account said that the *Benham*, an American destroyer, had moved in a way that facilitated the operations of the German submarine. This caused great bitterness in England, until Page showed the Admiralty a report from the Navy Department proving that the story was false.

months later you sent me Roosevelt's[1] letter, Lord Beresford expressed regret to me and said that he would explain in another speech. I hadn't seen the old fellow for a long time till a fortnight ago. He greeted me cheerily, and I said, "I don't think I ought to shake hands with you till you retract what you said about our navy." He insisted on my dining with him. He invited Admiral Sims also, and those two sailors had a jolly evening of it. Sims's coming has straightened out all that naval misunderstanding and more. He is of immense help to them and to us. But I'm going to make old Beresford's life a burden till he gets up in the Lords and takes that speech back —publicly. He's really all right; but it's just as well to keep the records right. The proceedings of the House of Lords are handsomely bound and go into every gentleman's library. I have seen two centuries of them in many a house.

We can now begin a distinctly New Era in the world's history and in its management if we rise to the occasion: there's not a shadow of doubt about that. And the United States can play a part bigger than we have yet dreamed of if we prove big enough to lead the British and the French instead of listening to Irish and Germans. Neither England nor France is a democracy—far from it. We can make them both democracies and develop their whole people instead of about 10 per cent. of their people. We have simply to conduct our affairs by a large national policy and not by the complaints of our really non-American people. See how a declaration of war has cleared the atmosphere!

We're happy yet, on rations. There are no potatoes. We have meatless days. Good wheat meantime is sunk

[1]This, of course, is Franklin D. Roosevelt, Assistant Secretary of the Navy in 1917.

every day. The submarine must be knocked out. Else the earth will be ruled by the German bayonet and natural living will be *verboten*. We'll all have to goose-step as the Crown Prince orders or—be shot. I see they now propose that the United States shall pay the big war indemnity in raw materials to the value of hundreds of billions of dollars! Not just yet, I guess!

As we get reports of what you are doing, it's most cheerful. I assure you, God has yet made nothing or nobody equal to the American people; and I don't think He ever will or can.

Sincerely yours,

WALTER H. PAGE.

One of the curious developments of this Balfour Mission was a request from President Wilson that Great Britain should take some decisive step for the permanent settlement of the Irish question. "The President," this message ran, "wishes that, when you next meet the Prime Minister, you would explain to him that only one circumstance now appears to stand in the way of perfect coöperation with Great Britain. All Americans who are not immediately connected with Germany by blood ties find their one difficulty in the failure of Great Britain so far to establish a satisfactory form of self-government in Ireland. In the recent debates in Congress on the War Resolution, this sentiment was especially manifest. It came out in the speeches of those enemies of the Declaration who were not Irish themselves nor representatives of sections in which Irish voters possessed great influence— notably members from the Southern States.

"If the American people were once convinced that there was a likelihood that the Irish question would soon be settled, great enthusiasm and satisfaction would result and it would also strengthen the coöperation which we are now about to organize between the United States and Great Britain.   Say this in unofficial terms to Mr. Lloyd George, but impress upon him its very great significance. If the British Government should act successfully on this matter, our American citizens of Irish descent and to a great extent the German sympathizers who have made common cause with the Irish, would join hands in the great common cause."

To the President

London, May 4, 1917.

DEAR MR. PRESIDENT:

. . .   It is a remarkable commentary on the insularity of the British and on our studied isolation that till Mr. Balfour went over not a member of this Government had ever met a member of our Administration!   Quite half our misunderstandings were due to this.   If I had the making of the laws of the two governments, I'd have a statutory requirement that at least one visit a year by high official persons should be made either way.   We should never have had a blacklist, etc., if that had been done.   When I tried the quite humble task of getting Polk to come and the excuse was made that he couldn't be spared from his desk—Mr. President, I fear we haven't half enough responsible official persons in our Government.   I should say that no man even of Polk's rank ought to have a desk: just as well give him a mill-stone. Even I try not to have a desk: else I'd never get anything of importance done; for I find that talks and conferences in my office and in the government offices and wherever else I can find out things take all my waking hours.   The Foreign Office here has about five high position men to every one in the State Department.   God sparing me,

I'm going one of these days to prepare a paper for our Foreign Affairs Committee on the Waste of Having too Few High Grade Men in the Department of State; a Plea for Five Assistant Secretaries for Every One Now Existing and for Provision for International Visits by Them.

Here's an ancient and mouldy precedent that needs shattering—for the coming of our country into its proper station and influence in the world.

I am sure that Mr. Balfour's visit has turned out as well as I hoped, and my hopes were high. He is one of the most interesting men that I've ever had the honour to know intimately—he and Lord Grey. Mr. Balfour is a Tory, of course; and in general I don't like Tories, yet liberal he surely is—a sort of high-toned Scotch demo-crat. I have studied him with increasing charm and interest. Not infrequently when I am in his office just before luncheon he says, "Come, walk over and we'll have lunch with the family." He's a bachelor. One sister lives with him. Another (Lady Rayleigh, the wife of the great chemist and Chancellor of Cambridge University) frequently visits him. Either of those ladies could rule this Empire. Then there are nieces and cousins always about—people of rare cultivation, every one of 'em. One of those girls confirmed the story that "Uncle Arthur" one day concluded that the niblick was something more than a humble necessity of a bad golfer—that it had positive virtues of its own and had suffered centuries of neglect. He, therefore, proceeded to play with the niblick only, till he proved his case and showed that it is a club entitled to the highest respect.

A fierce old Liberal fighter in Parliamentary warfare, who entered politics about the time Mr. Balfour did, told me this story the other day. "I've watched Balfour for about forty years as a cat watches a rat. I hate his party. I hated him till I learned better, for I hated that whole Salisbury crowd. They wanted to Cecil everything. But I'll tell you, Sir, apropos of his visit to your country, that in all those years he has never spoken of the United States except with high respect and often with deep affection. I should have caught him, if he had."

I went with him to a college in London one afternoon where he delivered a lecture on Dryden, to prove that poetry can carry a certain cargo of argument but that argument can't raise the smallest flight of poetry. Dry as it sounds, it was as good a literary performance as I recall I ever heard.

At his "family" luncheon, I've found Lord Milner or Lord Lansdowne, or some literary man who had come in to find out from Lady Rayleigh how to conduct the Empire or to write a great book; and the modest old chemical Lord sits silent most of the time and now and then breaks loose to confound them all with a pat joke. This is a vigorous family, these Balfours. There's one of them (a cousin of some sort, I think, of the Foreign Secretary) who is a Lord of much of Scotland, about as tall as Ben Nevis is high—a giant of a man. One of his sons was killed early in the war and one was missing—whether dead or not he did not know. Mrs. Page expressed her hope one day to the old man that he had had news from his missing son. "No, no," said he simply, "and me lady is awearying."

We've been lucky, Mr. President, in these days of immortal horrors and of difficulties between two governments that did not know one another—uncommonly lucky, in the large chances that politics gives for grave errors, to have had two such men in the Foreign Office here as Lord Grey and Mr. Balfour. There are men who were

mentioned for this post that would have driven us mad—
or to war with them.   I'm afraid I've almost outgrown
my living hero worship.   There isn't worshipful material
enough lying around in the world to keep a vigorous reverence in practice.   But these two gentlemen by birth
and culture have at least sometimes seemed of heroic size
to me.   It has meant much to know them well.   I shall
always be grateful to them, for in their quiet, forceful
way they helped me much to establish right relations
with these people—which, pray God, I hope to retain
through whatever new trials we may yet encounter.   For
it will fall to us yet to loose and to free the British, and a
Briton set free is an American.   That's all you can do for
a man or for a nation of men.

These Foreign Secretaries are not only men of much
greater cultivation than their Prime Ministers but of
greater moral force.   But I've come to like Lloyd George
very much.   He'd never deliver a lecture on Dryden, and
he doesn't even play a good game of golf; but he has what
both Lord Grey and Mr. Balfour lack—a touch of genius
—whatever that is—not the kind that takes infinite pains,
but the kind that acts as an electric light flashed in the
dark.   He said to me the other day that experts have
nearly been the death of him.   "The Government has
experts, experts, experts, everywhere.   In any department where things are not going well, I have found boards
and committees and boards of experts.   But in one department at least I've found a substitute for them.   I let
twenty experts go and I put in one Man, and things
began to move at once.   Do you know any real Men?
When you hear of any, won't you let me know?"

A little while ago he dined with me, and, after dinner, I
took him to a corner of the drawing room and delivered
your message to him about Ireland.   "God knows, I'm try-

ing," he replied. "Tell the President that. And tell him to talk to Balfour." Presently he broke out—"Madmen, madmen—I never saw any such task," and he pointed across the room to Sir Edward Carson, his First Lord of the Admiralty—"Madmen." "But the President's right. We've got to settle it and we've got to settle it now." Carson and Jellicoe came across the room and sat down with us. "I've been telling the Ambassador, Carson, that we've got to settle the Irish question now—in spite of you."

"I'll tell you something else we've got to settle now," said Carson. "Else it'll settle us. That's the submarines. The press and public are working up a calculated and concerted attack on Jellicoe and me, and, if they get us, they'll get you. It's an attack on the Government made on the Admiralty. Prime Minister," said this Ulster pirate whose civil war didn't come off only because the big war was begun—"Prime Minister, it may be a fierce attack. Get ready for it." Well, it has been developing ever since. But I can't for the life of me guess at the possible results of an English Parliamentary attack on a government. It's like a baseball man watching a game of cricket. He can't see when the player is out or why, or what caused it. Of course, the submarine *may* torpedo Lloyd George and his Government. It looks very like it may overturn the Admiralty, as Gallipoli did. If this public finds out the whole truth, it will demand somebody's head. But I'm only a baseball man; cricket is beyond me.

But Lloyd George will outlive the war as an active force, whatever happen to him in the meantime. He's too heavily charged with electricity to stop activity. The war has ended a good many careers that seemed to have long promise. It is ending more every day. But there is only one Lloyd George, and, whatever else he lack, he doesn't lack life.

I heard all the speeches in both Houses on the resolution of appreciation of our coming into the war—Bonar Law's, Asquith's (one of the best), Dillon's, a Labour man's, and, in the Lords, Curzon's, Crewe's, the Archbishop's (who delivered in the course of his remarks a benediction on me) and Bryce's (almost the best of all). It wasn't "oratory," but it was well said and well meant. They know how badly they need help and they do mean to be as good to us as their benignant insularity will permit. They are changing. I can't describe the great difference that the war has made in them. They'll almost become docile in a little more time.

And we came in in the nick of time for them—in very truth. If we hadn't, their exchange would have gone down soon and they know it. I shall never forget the afternoon I spent with Mr. Balfour and Mr. Bonar Law on that subject. They saw blue ruin without our financial help. And now, if we can save them from submarines, those that know will know how vital our help was. Again, the submarine is the great and grave and perhaps the only danger now. If that can be scotched, I believe the whole Teutonic military structure would soon tumble. If not, the Germans may go on as long as they can feed their army, allowing their people to starve.

Of course, you know, we're on rations now—yet we suffer no inconvenience on that score. But these queer people (they *are* the most amusing and confusing and contradictory of all God's creatures, these English, whose possibilities are infinite and whose actualities, in many ways, are pitiful)—these queer people are fiercely pursuing food-economy by discussing in the newspapers whether a hen consumes more food than she produces, and whether what dogs eat contains enough human food to justify the shooting of every one in the Kingdom. That's the way we are coming down to humble fare. But nothing can quite starve a people who all live near the sea which yields fish enough near shore to feed them wastefully.

All along this South shore, where I am to-day,[1] I see the Stars and Stripes; and everywhere there is a demand for the words and music of the Battle Hymn of the Republic and the Star Spangled Banner.

This our-new-Ally business is bringing me a lot of amusing troubles. Theatres offer me boxes, universities offer me degrees, hospitals solicit visits from me, clubs offer me dinners—I'll have to get a new private secretary or two well-trained to say "No" politely, else I shall not have my work done. But all that will presently wear away as everything wears away (quickly, too) in the grim face of this bloody monster of war which is consuming men as a prairie fire consumes blades of grass. There's a family that lives around the corner from this hotel. One son is in the trenches, another is in a madhouse from shell-shock, a third coming home wounded the other day was barely rescued when a torpedo sunk a hospital ship and may lose his reason. I suppose I saw one hundred men this afternoon on a single mile of beach who had lost both legs. Through the wall from my house in London is a hospital. A young Texan has been there, whose legs are gone at the thighs and one arm at the elbow. God pity us for not having organized the world better than this! We'll do it, yet, Mr. President—*you'll* do it; and thank God for you. If we do not organize Europe

---

[1] This letter is dated London and was probably begun there. It is evident, however, that the latter part was written at Brighton, where the Ambassador was taking a brief holiday.

and make another such catastrophe impossible, life will not be worth being born into except to the few whose days happen to fall between recurring devastations of the world.

Yours sincerely,

WALTER H. PAGE.

"I hope that the English people," Colonel House wrote to Page about this time, "realize how successful Mr. Balfour's visit to America really was. There is no man they could have sent who could have done it better. He and the President got along marvellously well. The three of us dined and spent the evening together and it was delightful to see how sympathetic their minds were."

A letter from Mr. Polk also discloses the impression which Mr. Balfour made upon Washington:

From Frank L. Polk

Washington, May 25, 1917.

MY DEAR MR. PAGE:

I just want to get off a line to catch the pouch.

You probably know what a wonderful success the British Mission has been, but I do not think you can realize what a deep impression they have made on all of us. Mr. Balfour really won the affection of us all, and I do not know when I was more sorry to have a man leave than I was to have him go last night. He expressed himself as having been very much impressed with his reception and the way he was treated. He was most fair in all discussions, and I think has a better understanding of our point of view. I had the good fortune of being present at the financial and the diplomatic conferences, and I think we all felt that we were dealing with a sympathetic friend.

He and the President got on tremendously. The best evidence of that was the fact that the President went up to Congress and sat in the gallery while Mr. Balfour addressed the House. This is without precedent.

The difficult problem of course was the blacklist and bunkering agreement, but I think we are by that. The important thing now is for the British to make all the concessions possible in connection with the release of goods in Rotterdam and the release of goods in Prize Court, though the cases have not been begun. Of course I mean cases of merely suspicion rather than where there is evidence of wrongdoing.

The sending of the destroyers and troops abroad is going to do a great deal toward impressing our people with the fact that we really are in the war. I do not think it is thoroughly borne home on the majority yet what a serious road we have chosen.

With warm regards,

Yours faithfully,

FRANK L. POLK.

Mr. Polk's reference to the blacklist recalls an episode which in itself illustrates the changed character of the relations that had now been established between the American and the British governments. Mr. Balfour discussed shipping problems for the most part with Mr. Polk, under whose jurisdiction these matters fell. As one of these conferences was approaching its end Mr. Balfour slightly coughed, uttered an "er," and gave other indications that he was about to touch upon a ticklish question.

"Before I go," he said, "there—er—is one subject I would—er—like to say something about."

Mr. Polk at once grasped what was coming.

"I know what you have in mind," said Mr. Polk in his

characteristically quick way. "You want us to apply your blacklist to neutrals."

In other words, the British hoped that the United States, now that it was in the war, would adopt against South America and other offenders those same discriminations which this country had so fiercely objected to, when it was itself a neutral.

The British statesman gave Mr. Polk one of his most winning smiles and nodded.

"Mr. Balfour," said Mr. Polk, "it took Great Britain three years to reach a point where it was prepared to violate all the laws of blockade. You will find that it will take us only two months to become as great criminals as you are!"

Mr. Balfour is usually not explosive in his manifestations of mirth, but his laughter, in reply to this statement, was almost uproarious. And the State Department was as good as its word. It immediately forgot all the elaborate "notes" and "protests" which it had been addressing to Great Britain. It became more inexorable than Great Britain had ever been in keeping foodstuffs out of neutral countries that were contiguous to Germany. Up to the time the United States entered the war, Germany, in spite of the watchful British fleet, had been obtaining large supplies from the United States through Holland, Denmark, and the Scandinavian peninsula. But the United States now immediately closed these leaks. In the main this country adopted a policy of "rationing"; that is, it would furnish the little nations adjoining Germany precisely the amount of food which they needed for their own consumption. This policy was one of the chief influences in undermining the German people and forcing their surrender. The American Government extended likewise the blacklist to South America and other coun-

tries, and, in doing so, it bettered the instruction of Great
Britain herself.

Though the whole story of the blockade thus seems finally to have ended in a joke, the whole proceeding has its
serious side.   The United States had been posing for three
years as the champion of neutral rights; the point of view
of Washington had been that there was a great principle
at stake.   If such a principle were involved, it was certainly present in just the same degree after the United
States became belligerent as in the days when we were
neutrals.   The lofty ideals by which the Administration
had professed to be guided should have still controlled its
actions; the mere fact that we, as a belligerent, could obtain certain advantages would hardly have justified a
great and high-minded nation in abandoning its principles.
Yet abandon them we did from the day that we declared
war.   We became just as remorseless in disregarding the
rights of small states as Great Britain—according to our
numerous blockade notes—had been.   Possibly, therefore, Mr. Balfour's mirth was not merely sympathetic or
humorous; it perhaps echoed his discovery that our position for three years had really been nothing but a sham;
that the State Department had been forcing points in
which it did not really believe, or in which it did not believe when American interests were involved.   At any rate,
this ending of our long argument with Great Britain was
a splendid justification for Page; his contention had always been that the preservation of civilization was more
important than the technicalities of the international
lawyers.   And now the Wilson Administration, by throwing into the waste basket all the finespun theories with
which it had been embarrassing the Allied cause since
August 4, 1914, accepted—and accepted joyously—his
point of view.

II

One of the first things which Mr. Balfour did, on his arrival in Washington, was personally to explain to President Wilson about the so-called "secret treaties." The "secret treaty" that especially preyed upon Mr. Wilson's mind, and which led to a famous episode at the Versailles Conference, was that which had been made with Italy in 1915, as consideration for Italy's participation in the war. Mr. Balfour, in telling the President of these territorial arrangements with Italy, naturally did not criticise his ally, but it was evident that he regarded the matter as something about which the United States should be informed.

"This is the sort of thing you have to do when you are engaged in a war," he explained, and then he gave Mr. Wilson the details.

Probably the most important information which Mr. Balfour and the French and Italian Commissions brought to Washington was the desperate situation of the Allied cause. On that point not one of the visiting statesmen or military and naval advisers made the slightest attempt at concealment. Mr. Balfour emphasized the seriousness of the crisis in one of his earliest talks with Mr. McAdoo, Secretary of the Treasury. The British statesman was especially interested in the financial situation and he therefore took up this matter at an early date with the Treasury Department.

"Mr. Balfour," said Mr. McAdoo, "before we make any plans of financial assistance it is absolutely necessary that we know precisely where we stand. The all-important thing is the question as to how long the war is likely to last. If it is only to last a few months, it is evident that we need to make very different arrangements than if it is

to last several years.   Just what must we make provision
for?   Let us assume that the United States goes in with
all its men and resources—that we dedicate all our money,
our manufacturing plants, our army, our navy, everything
we have got, to bringing the war to an end.   How long
will it take?"

Mr. Balfour replied that it would be necessary to consult his naval and military advisers before he answered
that question.   He said that he would return in a day or
two and make an explicit statement.   He did so and his
answer was this: Under these circumstances—that the
United States should make war to the full limit of its
power, in men and resources—the war could not be ended
until the summer or the autumn of 1919.   Mr. McAdoo
put the same question in the same form to the French
and Italian Missions and obtained precisely the same
answer.

Page's papers show that Mr. Balfour, in the early stages
of American participation, regarded the financial situation as the thing which chiefly threatened the success of
the Allied cause.   So much greater emphasis has been
laid upon the submarine warfare that this may at first
seem rather a misreading of Great Britain's peril.   Yet
the fact is that the high rate of exchange and the dep-
redatory U-boat represented almost identically the same
danger.   The prospect that so darkened the horizon in
the spring of 1917 was the possible isolation of Great
Britain.   England's weakness, as always, consisted in the
fact that she was an island, that she could not feed herself
with her own resources and that she had only about six
weeks' supply of food ahead of her at any one time.   If
Germany could cut the lines of communication and so
prevent essential supplies from reaching British ports,
the population of Great Britain could be starved into

surrender in a very brief time, France would be over-whelmed, and the triumph of the Prussian cause would be complete.   That the success of the German submarine campaign would accomplish this result was a fact that the popular mind readily grasped.   What it did not so clearly see, however, was that the financial collapse of Great Britain would cut these lines of communication quite as effectually as the submarine itself.   The British were practically dependent for their existence upon the food brought from the United States, just as the Allied armies were largely dependent upon the steel which came from the great industrial plants of this country.   If Great Britain could not find the money with which to purchase these supplies, it is quite apparent that they could not be shipped.   The collapse of British credit therefore would have produced the isolation of the British Isles and led to a British surrender, just as effectively as would the success of the German submarine campaign.

As soon as Bernstorff was sent home, therefore, and the participation of this country in the war became extremely probable, Mr. Balfour took up the financial question with Page.

To the President

March 5, 1917.

The inquiries which I have made here about financial conditions disclose an international situation which is most alarming to the financial and industrial outlook of the United States.   England has not only to pay her own war bills, but is obliged to finance her Allies as well.   Up to the present time she has done these tasks out of her own capital.   But she cannot continue her present exten-sive purchases in the United States without shipping gold as payment for them, and there are two reasons why she cannot make large shipments of gold. In the first place, both England and France must keep the larger part of the gold they have to maintain issues of their paper at par; and, in the second place, the German U-boat has made the shipping of gold a dangerous procedure even if they had it to ship. There is therefore a pressing danger that the Franco-American and Anglo-American exchange will be greatly disturbed; the inevitable consequence will be that orders by all the Allied Governments will be reduced to the lowest possible amount and that trans-Atlantic trade will practically come to an end. The result of such a stoppage will be a panic in the United States. The world will therefore be divided into two hemispheres, one of them, our own, will have the gold and the commodities: the other, Great Britain and Europe, will need these commodities, but it will have no money with which to pay for them. Moreover, it will have practically no commodities of its own to exchange for them. The financial and commercial result will be almost as bad for the United States as for Europe. We shall soon reach this condition unless we take quick action to prevent it. Great Britain and France must have a credit in the United States which will be large enough to prevent the collapse of world trade and the whole financial structure of Europe.

If the United States declare war against Germany, the greatest help we could give Great Britain and its Allies would be such a credit. If we should adopt this policy, an excellent plan would be for our Government to make a large investment in a Franco-British loan. Another plan would be to guarantee such a loan. A great advantage would be that all the money would be kept in the United States. We could keep on with our trade and increase it, till the war ends, and after the war Europe would purchase food and an enormous supply of materials with

which to reëquip her peace industries. We should thus
reap the profit of an uninterrupted and perhaps an en-
larging trade over a number of years and we should hold
their securities in payment.

On the other hand, if we keep nearly all the gold and
Europe cannot pay for reëstablishing its economic life,
there may be a world-wide panic for an indefinite period.

Of course we cannot extend such a credit unless we go
to war with Germany. But is there no way in which our
Government might immediately and indirectly help the
establishment in the United States of a large Franco-
British credit without violating armed neutrality? I do
not know enough about our own reserve bank law to form
an opinion. But these banks would avert such a danger
if they were able to establish such a credit. Danger for
us is more real and imminent, I think, than the public on
either side the Atlantic understands. If it be not averted
before its manifestations become apparent, it will then be
too late to save the day.

The pressure of this approaching crisis, I am certain,
has gone beyond the ability of the Morgan financial agency
for the British and French governments. The financial
necessities of the Allies are too great and urgent for any
private agency to handle, for every such agency has to
encounter business rivalries and sectional antagonisms.

It is not improbable that the only way of maintaining
our present preëminent trade position and averting a
panic is by declaring war on Germany. The submarine
has added the last item to the danger of a financial world
crash. There is now an uncertainty about our being
drawn into the war; no more considerable credits can be
privately placed in the United States. In the meantime
a collapse may come.

PAGE.

Urgent as this message was, it really understated the desperate condition of British and Allied finances. That the warring powers were extremely pressed for money has long been known; but Page's papers reveal for the first time the fact that they were facing the prospect of bankruptcy itself. "The whole Allied combination on this side the ocean are very much nearer the end of their financial resources," he wrote in July, "than anybody has guessed or imagined. We only can save them. . . . The submarines are steadily winning the war. Pershing and his army have bucked up the French for the moment. But for his coming there was more or less danger of a revolution in Paris and of serious defection in the army. Everybody here fears that the French will fail before another winter of the trenches. Yet—the Germans must be still worse off."

The matter that was chiefly pressing at the time of the Balfour visit was the fact that the British balances in the New York banks were in a serious condition. It should always be remembered, however, that Great Britain was financing not only herself, but her Allies, and that the difficult condition in which she now found herself was caused by the not too considerate demands of the nations with which she was allied in the war. Thus by April 6, 1917, Great Britain had overdrawn her account with J. P. Morgan to the extent of $400,000,000 and had no cash available with which to meet this overdraft. This obligation had been incurred in the purchase of supplies, both for Great Britain and the allied governments; and securities, largely British owned stocks and bonds, had been deposited to protect the bankers. The money was now coming due; if the obligations were not met, the credit of Great Britain in this country would reach the vanishing point. Though at first there was a slight misunderstanding about this matter, the American Government finally paid this over-draft out of the proceeds of the first Liberty Loan. This act saved the credit of the allied countries; it was, of course, only the beginning of the financial support that America brought to the allied cause; the advances that were afterward furnished from the American Treasury made possible the purchases of food and supplies in enormous quantities. The first danger that threatened, the isolation and starvation of Great Britain, was therefore overcome. It was the joint product of Page's work in London and that of the Balfour Commission in the United States.

III

Until these financial arrangements had been made there was no certainty that the supplies which were so essential to victory would ever leave the United States; this obstruction at the source had now been removed. But the greater difficulty still remained. The German submarines were lying off the waters south and west of Ireland ready to sink the supply ships as soon as they entered the prohibited zone.   Mr. Balfour and his associates were working also on this problem in Washington; and, at the same time, Page and Admiral Sims and the British Admiralty were bending all their energies in London to obtain immediate coöperation.

A remark which Mr. Balfour afterward made to Admiral Sims shows the frightful nature of the problem which was confronting Great Britain at that time.

"That was a terrible week we spent at sea in that voyage to the United States," Mr. Balfour said. "We knew that the German submarine campaign was succeeding. Their submarines were destroying our shipping and we had no means of preventing it.   I could not help thinking that we were facing the defeat of Great Britain."

Page's papers show that as early as February 25th he understood in a general way the disheartening proportions of the German success.   "It is a momentous crisis," he wrote at that time.   "The submarines are destroying shipping at an appalling rate."   Yet it was not until Admiral Sims arrived in London, on April 9th, that the Ambassador learned all the details.   In sending the Admiral to England the Navy Department had acted on an earnest recommendation from Page.   The fact that the American Navy was inadequately represented in the British capital had long been a matter of embarrassment to him.   The ability and personal qualifications of our attachés had been unquestioned; but none of them during the war had been men of high rank, and this in itself proved to be a constant impediment to their success. While America was represented by Commanders, Japan, Italy, and France had all sent Admirals to London. Page's repeated requests for an American Admiral had so far met with no response, but the probability that this country would become involved in the war now gave new point to his representations.   In the latter part of March, Page renewed his request in still more urgent form, and this time the President and the Navy Department responded favourably.   The result was that, on April 9th, three days after the American declaration of war, Admiral Sims and his flag-lieutenant, Commander Babcock, presented themselves at the American Embassy.   There was little in the appearance of these men to suggest a violent naval demonstration against Germany.   Both wore civilian dress, their instructions having commanded them not to bring uniforms; both were travelling under assumed names, and both had no more definite orders than to investigate the naval situation and cable the results to Washington.   In spite of these attempts at secrecy, the British had learned that Admiral Sims was on the way; they rejoiced not only in this fact, but in the fact that Sims had been chosen, for there was no American naval officer whose professional reputation stood so high in the British Navy or who was so personally acceptable to British officialdom and the British public.   The Admiralty therefore met Admiral Sims at Liverpool, brought him to London in a special train, and, a few hours after his arrival, gave him the innermost secrets on the submarine situation—secrets which were so dangerous that not all the members of the British Cabinet had been let into them.

Page welcomed Admiral Sims with a cordiality which that experienced sea veteran still gratefully remembers. He at once turned over to him two rooms in the Embassy. "You can have everything we've got," the Ambassador said.   "If necessary to give you room, we'll turn the whole Embassy force out into the street."   The two men had not previously met, but in an instant they became close friends.   A common sympathy and a common enthusiasm were greatly needed at that crisis.   As soon as Admiral Sims had finished his interview with Admiral Jellicoe, he immediately sought out the Ambassador and laid all the facts before him.   Germany was winning the war.   Great Britain had only six weeks' food supply on hand, and the submarines were sinking the ships at a rate which, unless the depredations should be checked, meant an early and unconditional surrender of the British Empire.   Only the help of the United States could prevent this calamity.

Page, of course, was aghast: the facts and figures Admiral Sims gave him disclosed a situation which was even more desperate than he had imagined.   He advised the Admiral to cable the whole story immediately to Washington.   Admiral Sims at first had some difficulty in obtaining the Admiralty's consent to doing this, and the reason was the one with which Page had long been familiar—the fear, altogether too justified, that the news would "leak" out of Washington.   Of course there was no suspicion in British naval circles of the good faith of the Washington officials, but important facts had been sent so many times under the seal of the strictest secrecy and had then found their way into the newspapers that there was a deep distrust of American discretion.   Certainly no greater damage could have been done the allied cause at that time than to have the Germans learn how successfully their submarine campaign was progressing.   The question was referred to the Imperial War Council and its consent obtained.   The report, however, was sent to the Navy Department in the British naval code, and decoded in the British Embassy in Washington.

Admiral Sims's message gave all the facts about the submarine situation, and concluded with the recommendation that the United States should assemble all floating craft that could be used in the anti-submarine warfare, destroyers, tugs, yachts, light cruisers, and similar vessels, and send them immediately to Queenstown, where they would do valuable service in convoying merchant vessels and destroying the U-boats.   At that time the American Navy had between fifty and sixty destroyers that were patrolling the American coast; these could have been despatched, almost immediately, to the scene of operations; but, in response to this request, the Department sent six to Queenstown.

The next few months were very unhappy ones for Admiral Sims.   He was the representative in London of one of the world's greatest naval powers, participating in the greatest war that had ever enlisted its energies, yet his

constant appeals for warships elicited the most inade-
quate response, his well-reasoned recommendations for
meeting the crisis were frequently unanswered and at other
times were met with counter-proposals so childish that
they seemed almost to have originated in the brains of
newspaper amateurs, and his urgent pictures of a civilization rapidly going to wreck were apparently looked upon
with suspicion as the utterances of a man who had been
completely led astray by British guile.   To give a fair
idea of Washington's neglect during this period it is only
necessary to point out that, for four months, Admiral
Sims occupied the two rooms in the Embassy directly
above Page's, with Commander Babcock as his only aid.
Sims's repeated requests to Secretary Daniels for an
additional staff went unheeded.   Had it not been for the
Admiral's constant daily association with Page and the
comfort and encouragement which the Ambassador gave
him, this experience would have been almost unbearable.
In the latter part of April, the Admiral's appeals to Washington having apparently fallen on deaf ears, he asked
Page to second his efforts.   The Admiral and Commander
Babcock wrote another message, and drove in a motor
car to Brighton, where Page was taking a little rest.   The
Admiral did not know just how strong a statement the
Ambassador would care to sponsor, and so he did not make
this representation as emphatic as the judgment of both
men would have preferred.

The Admiral handed Page the paper, saying that he
had prepared it with the hope that the Ambassador would
sign it and send it directly to President Wilson.

"It is quite apparent," Admiral Sims said, "that the
Department doesn't believe what I have been saying.
Or they don't believe what the British are saying.   They
think that England is exaggerating the peril for reasons

of its own. They think I am hopelessly pro-British and that I am being used. But if you'll take it up directly with the President, then they may be convinced."

Page put on his spectacles, took the paper, and read it through. Then, looking over the rim of his glasses in his characteristic way, he leaned toward Admiral Sims and said:

"Admiral, it isn't half strong enough! I think I can write a better despatch than that, myself! At least let me try."

He immediately took a pen and paper and in a few minutes he had written his own version which he gave the Admiral to read. The latter was delighted with it and in a brief time it was on its way to Washington.

From: Ambassador Page.
To: Secretary of State.
Sent: 27 April, 1917.

Very confidential for Secretary and President

There is reason for the greatest alarm about the issue of the war caused by the increasing success of the German submarines. I have it from official sources that during the week ending 22nd April, 88 ships of 237,000 tons, allied and neutral, were lost. The number of vessels unsuccessfully attacked indicated a great increase in the number of submarines in action.

This means practically a million tons lost every month till the shorter days of autumn come. By that time the sea will be about clear of shipping. Most of the ships are sunk to the westward and southward of Ireland. The British have in that area every available anti-submarine craft, but their force is so insufficient that they hardly discourage the submarines.

The British transport of troops and supplies is already strained to the utmost, and the maintenance of the armies in the field is threatened.   There is food enough here to last the civil population only not more than six weeks or two months.

Whatever help the United States may render at any time in the future, or in any theatre of the war, our help is now more seriously needed in this submarine area for the sake of all the Allies than it can ever be needed again, or anywhere else.

After talking over this critical situation with the Prime Minister and other members of the Government, I cannot refrain from most strongly recommending the immediate sending over of every destroyer and all other craft that can be of anti-submarine use.   This seems to me the sharpest crisis of the war, and the most dangerous situation for the Allies that has arisen or could arise.

If enough submarines can be destroyed in the next two or three months, the war will be won, and if we can contribute effective help immediately, it will be won directly by our aid.   I cannot exaggerate the pressing and increasing danger of this situation.   Thirty or more destroyers and other similar craft sent by us immediately would very likely be decisive.

There is no time to be lost.

(Signed) PAGE.

This cablegram had a certain effect.   The reply came from Washington that "eventually" thirty-six destroyers would be sent.

Page's letters of this period are full of the same subject.

To the President

London, May 4, 1917.

DEAR MR. PRESIDENT:

The submarines have become a very grave danger. The loss of British and allied tonnage increases with the longer and brighter days—as I telegraphed you, 237,000 tons last week; and the worst of it is, the British are not destroying them. The Admiralty publishes a weekly report which, though true, is not the whole truth. It is known in official circles here that the Germans are turning out at least two a week—some say three; and the British are not destroying them as fast as new ones are turned out. If merely the present situation continue, the war will pretty soon become a contest of endurance under hunger, with an increasing proportion of starvation. Germany is yet much the worse off, but it will be easily possible for Great Britain to suffer to the danger point next winter or earlier unless some decided change be wrought in this situation.

The greatest help, I hope, can come from us—our destroyers and similar armed craft—provided we can send enough of them quickly. The area to be watched is so big that many submarine hunters are needed. Early in the war the submarines worked near shore. There are very many more of them now and their range is one hundred miles, or even two hundred, at sea.

The public is becoming very restive with its half-information, and it is more and more loudly demanding all the facts. There are already angry threats to change the personnel of the Admiralty; there is even talk of turning out the Government. "We must have results, we must have results." I hear confidentially that Jellicoe has threatened to resign unless the Salonica expedition is brought back: to feed and equip that force requires too many ships.

And there are other troubles impending.   Norway has lost so many of her ships that she dare not send what are left to sea.   Unarmed they'll all perish.   If she arm them, Germany will declare war against her.   There is a plan on foot for the British to charter these Norwegian ships and to arm them, taking the risk of German war against Norway.   If war come (as it is expected) England must then defend Norway the best she can.   And *then England may ask for our big ships to help in these waters.*   All this is yet in the future, but possibly not far in the future.

For the present the only anti-submarine help is the help we may be able to give to patrol the wide area off Ireland. If we had one hundred destroyers to send, the job there could, I am told, be quickly done.   A third of that number will help mightily.   At the present rate of destruction more than four million tons will be sunk before the summer is gone.

Such is this dire submarine danger.   The English thought that they controlled the sea; the Germans, that they were invincible on land.   Each side is losing where it thought itself strongest.

Admiral Sims is of the greatest help imaginable.   Of course, I gave him an office in one of our Embassy buildings, and the Admiralty has given him an office also with them.   He spends much of his time there, and they have opened all doors and all desks and drawers to him.   He strikes me (and the English so regard him) as a man of admirable judgment—unexcitable and indefatigable.   I hope we'll soon send a general over, to whom the War Department will act similarly.   Hoover, too, must have a good man here as, I dare say, he has already made known. These will cover the Navy, the Army, Food, and Shipping.

Perhaps a Censor and an Intelligence (Secret Service) group ought to come. I mean these for permanent—at least indefinite—service. Exchange visits by a Congressional Committee (such as the French and British make) and by high official persons such as members of your Cabinet (such also as the French and British make)—you will have got ideas about these from Mr. Balfour.

W. H. P.

In the latter part of June Admiral Sims went to Queenstown. Admiral Bayly, who directed the operation of the anti-submarine forces there, had gone away for a brief rest, and Admiral Sims had taken over the command of both the British and American forces at that point. This experience gave Admiral Sims a first-hand picture of a really deplorable situation. The crisis was so desperate that he made another appeal to Page.

From Admiral William S. Sims

Admiralty House, Queenstown,
June 25, 1917.

MY DEAR MR. PAGE:

I enclose herewith a letter on the submarine situation.[1]

I think I have made it plain therein that the Allies are losing the war; that it will be already lost when the loss of shipping reaches the point where fully adequate supplies cannot be maintained on the various battle fronts.

I cannot understand why our Government should hesitate to send the necessary anti-submarine craft to this side.

There are at least seventeen more destroyers employed on our Atlantic coast, *where there is no war*, not to mention numerous other very useful anti-submarine craft, including sea-going tugs, etc.

---

[1]This was a long document describing conditions in great detail.

Can you not do something to bring our Government to an understanding of how very serious the situation is?

Would it not be well to send another telegram to Mr. Lansing and the President, and also send them the enclosed correspondence?

I am sending this by mail because I may be somewhat delayed in returning to London.

Very sincerely yours,
WM. S. SIMS.

Page immediately acted on this suggestion.

Most confidential for the Secretary of State and President only

Sims sends me by special messenger from Queenstown the most alarming reports of the submarine situation which are confirmed by the Admiralty here. He says that the war will be won or lost in this submarine zone within a few months. Time is of the essence of the problem, and anti-submarine craft which cannot be assembled in the submarine zone almost immediately may come too late. There is, therefore, a possibility that this war may become a war between Germany and the United States alone. Help is far more urgently and quickly needed in this submarine zone than anywhere else in the whole war area.

PAGE.

The United States had now been in the war for three months and only twenty-eight of the sixty destroyers which were available had been sent into the field. Yet this latest message of Page produced no effect, and, when Admiral Sims returned from Queenstown, the two men, almost in despair, consulted as to the step which they should take next. What was the matter? Was it that

Washington did not care to get into the naval war with its full strength, or was it that it simply refused to believe the representations of its Admiral and its Ambassador? Admiral Sims and Page went over the whole situation and came to the conclusion that Washington regarded them both as so pro-British that their reports were subject to suspicion. Just as Page had found that the State Department, and its "trade advisers," had believed that the British were using the blockade as a means of destroying American trade for the benefit of Britain, so now he believed that Mr. Daniels and Admiral Benson, the Chief of Naval Operations, evidently thought that Great Britain was attempting to lure American warships into European waters, to undergo the risk of protecting British commerce, while British warships were kept safely in harbour. Page suggested that there was now only one thing left to do, and that was to request the British Government itself to make a statement to President Wilson that would substantiate his own messages.

"Whatever else they think of the British in Washington," he said, "they know one thing—and that is that a British statesman like Mr. Balfour will not lie."

Mr. Balfour by this time had returned from America. The fact that he had established these splendid personal relations with Mr. Wilson, and that he had impressed the American public so deeply with his sincerity and fine purpose, made him especially valuable for this particular appeal. Page and Admiral Sims therefore went to the Foreign Office and laid all the facts before him. Their own statements, Page informed the Foreign Secretary, were evidently regarded as hysterical and biased by an unreasoning friendliness to Great Britain. If Mr. Balfour would say the same things over his own signature, then they would not be disbelieved.

Mr. Balfour gladly consented. He called in Admiral Jellicoe and asked him to draft a despatch, so that all the technical facts would be completely accurate. He also consulted with Sir Edward Carson, the First Lord of the Admiralty. Then Mr. Balfour put the document in its final shape and signed it. It was as follows:

Mr. Balfour to the President

June 30, 1917.

The forces at present at the disposal of the British Admiralty are not adequate to protect shipping from submarine attack in the danger zone round the British Islands. Consequently shipping is being sunk at a greater rate than it can be replaced by new tonnage of British origin.

The time will come when, if the present rate of loss continues, the available shipping, apart from American contribution, will be insufficient to bring to this country sufficient foodstuffs and other essentials, including oil fuel. The situation in regard to our Allies, France, and Italy, is much the same.

Consequently, it is absolutely necessary to add to our forces as a first step, pending the adoption or completion of measures which will, it is hoped, eventually lead to the destruction of enemy submarines at a rate sufficient to ensure safety of our sea communications.

The United States is the only allied country in a position to help. The pressing need is for armed small craft of every kind available in the area where commerce concentrates near the British and French coasts. Destroyers, submarines, gunboats, yachts, trawlers, and tugs would all give invaluable help, and if sent in sufficient numbers would undoubtedly save a situation which is manifestly critical. But they are required now and in as great numbers as possible. There is no time for delay.

The present method of submarine attack is almost entirely by torpedo with the submarine submerged. The gun defense of merchant ships keeps the submarine below the surface but does no more; offensively against a submerged submarine it is useless, and the large majority of the ships torpedoed never see the attacking submarine until the torpedo has hit the ship.[1]

The present remedy is, therefore, to prevent the submarine from using its periscope for fear of attack by bomb or ram from small craft, and this method of defense for the shipping and offense against the submarine requires small craft in very large numbers.

The introduction of the convoy system, provided there are sufficient destroyers to form an adequate screen to the convoy, will, it is hoped, minimize losses when it is working, and the provision of new offensive measures is progressing; but for the next few months there is only one safeguard, viz., the immediate addition to patrols of every small vessel that can possibly be sent to European waters.

Page, moreover, kept up his own appeal:

To the President

July 5th.

Strictly confidential to the President and the Secretary

The British Cabinet is engaging in a threatening controversy about the attitude which they should take toward the submarine peril. There is a faction in the Admiralty which possesses the indisputable facts and which takes

---

[1]The Navy Department had taken the position that arming merchantmen was the best protection against the submarine. This statement was intended to refute this belief.

a very disheartening view of the situation.   This group insists that the Cabinet should make a confession at least to us of the full extent of the danger and that it should give more information to the public.   The public does not feel great alarm simply because it has been kept in too great ignorance.   But the political faction is so far the stronger.   It attempts to minimize the facts, and, probably for political reasons, it refuses to give these discouraging facts wide publicity.   The politicians urge that it is necessary to conceal the full facts from the Germans.   They also see great danger in throwing the public into a panic.

Mr. Lloyd George is always optimistic and he is too much inclined to yield his judgment to political motives. In his recent address in Glasgow he gave the public a comforting impression of the situation.   But the facts do not warrant the impression which he gave.

This dispute among the political factions is most unfortunate and it may cause an explosion of public feeling at any time.   Changes in the Cabinet may come in consequence.   If the British public knew all the facts or if the American people knew them, the present British Government would probably fall.   It is therefore not only the submarine situation which is full of danger.   The political situation is in a dangerous state also.

PAGE.

To Arthur W. Page

Wilsford Manor, Salisbury,
July 8, 1917.

DEAR ARTHUR:
Since admirals and generals began to come from home, they and the war have taken my time so completely, day and night, that I haven't lately written you many things that I should like to tell you.   I'll try here—a house of a

friend of ours where the only other guest besides your mother and me is Edward Grey. This is the first time I've seen him since he left office. Let me take certain big subjects in order and come to smaller things later:

1. The German submarines are succeeding to a degree that the public knows nothing about. These two things are true: (a) The Germans are building submarines faster than the English sink them. In this way, therefore, they are steadily gaining. (b) The submarines are sinking freight ships faster than freight ships are being built by the whole world. In this way, too, then, the Germans are succeeding. Now if this goes on long enough, the Allies' game is up. For instance, they have lately sunk so many fuel oil ships, that this country may very soon be in a perilous condition—even the Grand Fleet may not have enough fuel. Of course the chance is that oil ships will not continue to fall victims to the U-boats and we shall get enough through to replenish the stock. But this illustrates the danger, and it is a very grave danger.

The best remedy so far worked out is the destroyer. The submarines avoid destroyers and they sink very, very few ships that are convoyed. If we had destroyers enough to patrol the whole approach (for, say, 250 miles) to England, the safety of the sea would be very greatly increased; and if we had enough to patrol and to convoy every ship going and coming, the damage would be reduced to a minimum. The Admiral and I are trying our best to get our Government to send over 500 improvised destroyers—yachts, ocean-going tugs—any kind of swift craft that can be armed. Five hundred such little boats might end the war in a few months; for the Germans are keeping the spirit of their people and of their army up by their submarine success. If that success were stopped they'd have no other cry half so effective. If they could see this in Washington as we see it, they'd do it and do it not halfway but with a vengeance.   If they don't do it, the war may be indefinitely prolonged and a wholly satisfactory peace may never be made.   The submarine is the most formidable thing the war has produced—by far —and it gives the German the only earthly chance he has to win.   And he *may* substantially win by it yet.   That's what the British conceal.   In fact, half of them do not see it or believe it.   But nothing is truer, or plainer.   One hundred thousand submarine chasers next year may be worth far less than 500 would be worth now, for next year see how few ships may be left!   The mere arming of ships is not enough.   Nearly all that are sunk are armed.   The submarine now carries a little periscope and a big one, each painted the colour of the sea.   You can't see a little periscope except in an ocean as smooth as glass.   It isn't bigger than a coffee cup.   The submarine thus sinks its victims without ever emerging or ever being seen.   As things now stand, the Germans are winning the war, and they are winning it on the sea; that's the queer and the most discouraging fact.   My own opinion is that all the facts ought to be published to all the world.   Let the Germans get all the joy they can out of the confession. No matter, if the Government and the people of the United States knew all the facts, we'd have 1,000 improvised destroyers (yachts, tugs, etc., etc.) armed and over here very quickly.   Then the tide would turn.

Then there'd be nothing to fear in the long run.   For the military authorities all agree that the German Army is inferior to the British and French and will be whipped. That may take a long time yet; but of the result nobody who knows seems to have any doubt—unless the French get tired and stop.   They have periods of great war weariness and there is real danger that they may quit and make a separate peace.   General Pershing's presence has made the situation safe for the moment.   But in a little while something else spectacular and hopeful may be required to keep them in line.

Such is an accurate picture of the war as it is now, and it is a dangerous situation.

2.   The next grave danger is financial.   The European Allies have so bled the English for money that the English would by this time probably have been on a paper money basis (and of course all the Allies as well) if we had not come to their financial aid.   And we've got to keep our financial aid going to them to prevent this disastrous result.   That wouldn't at once end the war, if they had all abandoned specie payments; but it would be a frightfully severe blow and it might later bring defeat.   That is a real danger.   And the Government at Washington, I fear, does not know the full extent of the danger.   They think that the English are disposed to lie down on them.   They don't realize the cost of the war.   This Government has bared all this vast skeleton to me; but I fear that Washington imagines that part of it is a deliberate scare.   It's a very real danger.

Now, certain detached items:

Sims is the idol of the British Admiralty and he is doing his job just as well as any man could with the tools and the chance that he has.   He has made the very best of the chance and he has completely won the confidence and admiration of this side of the world.

Pershing made an admirable impression here, and in France he has simply set them wild with joy.   His coming and his little army have been worth what a real army will be worth later.   It is well he came to keep the French in line.

The army of doctors and nurses have had a similar effect.

Even the New England saw-mill units have caused a furor of enthusiasm. They came with absolute Yankee completeness of organization—with duplicate parts of all their machinery, tents, cooks, pots, and pans, and everything ship-shape. The only question they asked was: "Say, where the hell are them trees you want sawed up?" That's the way to do a job! Yankee stock is made high here by such things as that.

We're getting a crowd of Yankee lecturers on the United States to go up and down this Kingdom. There's the greatest imaginable curiosity to hear about the United States in all kinds of society from munition workers to universities. I got the British Government to write Buttrick[1] to come as its guest, and the Rockefeller Boards rose to the occasion. He'll probably be along presently. If he hasn't already sailed when you get this, see him and tell him to make arrangements to have pictures sent over to him to illustrate his lectures. Who else could come to do this sort of a job?

I am myself busier than I have ever been. The kind of work the Embassy now has to do is very different from the work of the days of neutrality. It continues to increase—especially the work that I have to do myself. But it's all pleasant now. We are trying to help and no longer to hinder. To save my life I don't see how the Washington crowd can look at themselves in a mirror and keep their faces straight. Yesterday they were bent on sending everything into European neutral states. The foundations of civilization would give way if neutral trade were interfered with. Now, nothing must go in except on a ration basis. Yesterday it must be a peace without victory. Now it must be a complete victory, every man

---

[1] Dr. Wallace Buttrick, President of the General Education Board, who was sent at this time to deliver lectures throughout Great Britain on the United States.

and every dollar thrown in, else no peace is worth having. I don't complain. I only rejoice. But I'm glad that kind of a rapid change is not a part of my record. The German was the same beast yesterday that he is to-day; and it makes a simple-minded, straight-minded man like me wonder which attitude was the (or is the) attitude of real conviction. But this doesn't bother me now as a real problem—only as a speculation. What we call History will, I presume, in time work this out. But History is often a kind of lie. But never mind that. The only duty of mankind now is to win. Other things can wait.

I walked over to Stonehenge and back (about six miles) with Lord Grey (Sir Edward, you know) and we, like everybody else, fell to talking about when the war may end. We know as well as anybody and no better than anybody else. I have very different moods about it—no convictions. It seems to me to depend, as things now are, more on the submarines than on anything else. If we could effectually discourage them so that the Germans would have to withdraw them and could no more keep up the spirit of their people by stories of the imminent starvation of England, I have a feeling that the hunger and the war weariness of the German people would lead them to force an end. But, the more they are called on to suffer the more patriotic do they think themselves and they *may* go on till they drop dead in their tracks.

What I am really afraid of is that the Germans may, before winter, offer all that the Western Allies most want —the restoration of Belgium and France, the return of Alsace-Lorraine, etc., in the West and the surrender of the Colonies—provided Austria is not dismembered. That would virtually leave them the chance to work out their Middle Europe scheme and ultimately there'd probably have to be another war over that question. That's the real eventuality to be feared—a German defeat in the West but a German victory in the Southeast.   Everybody in Europe is so war weary that such a plan *may* succeed.

On the other hand, what Hoover and Northcliffe fear may come true—that the Germans are going to keep up the struggle for years—till their armies are practically obliterated, as Lee's army was.   If the Allies were actually to kill (not merely wound, but actually kill) 5,000 Germans a day for 300 days a year, it would take about four years to obliterate the whole German Army.   There is the bare possibility, therefore, of a long struggle yet. But I can't believe it.   My dominant mood these days is an end within a very few months after the submarines are knocked out.   Send over, therefore, 1,000 improvised destroyers the next two months, and I'll promise peace by Christmas.   Otherwise I can make no promises. That's all that Lord Grey and I know, and surely we are two wise men.   What, therefore, is the use in writing any more about this?

The chief necessity that grows upon me is that all the facts must be brought out that show the kinship in blood and ideals of the two great English-speaking nations. We were actually coming to believe ourselves that we were part German and Slovene and Pole and What-not, instead of essentially being Scotch and English.   Hence the unspeakable impudence of your German who spoke of eliminating the Anglo-Saxon element from American life!   The truth should be forcibly and convincingly told and repeated to the end of the chapter, and our national life should proceed on its natural historic lines, with its proper historic outlook and background.   We can do something to bring this about.

Affectionately,

W. H. P.

The labour of getting the American Navy into the war was evidently at first a difficult one, but the determination of Page and Admiral Sims triumphed, and, by August and September, our energies were fully engaged. And the American Navy made a record that will stand everlastingly to its glory. Without its help the German submarines could never have been overcome.

CHAPTER XXIII

PAGE — THE MAN

THE entrance of America into the war, followed by the successful promotion of the Balfour visit, brought a period of quiet into Page's life. These events represented for him a personal triumph; there were many things still to be done, it is true, and Page, as always, was active in advancing the interests that were nearest his heart; yet the mighty relief that followed the American declaration was the kind that one experiences after accomplishing the greatest task of a lifetime. Page's letters have contained many references to the sense of moral isolation which his country's policy had forced upon him; he probably exaggerated his feeling that there was a tendency to avoid him; this was merely a reflection of his own inclination to keep away from all but the official people. He now had more leisure and certainly more interest in cultivating the friends that he had made in Great Britain. For the fact is that, during all these engrossing years, Page had been more than an Ambassador; by the time the United States entered the war he had attained an assured personal position in the life of the British capital. He had long since demonstrated his qualifications for a post, which, in the distinction of the men who have occupied it, has few parallels in diplomacy. The scholarly Lowell, the courtly Bayard, the companionable Hay, the ever-humorous Choate, had set a standard for American Ambassadors which had made the place a difficult one for their successors. Though Page had characteristics in common with all these men, his personality had its own distinctive tang; and it was something new to the political and social life of London. And the British capital, which is extremely exacting and even merciless in its demands upon its important personages, had found it vastly entertaining. "I didn't know there could be anything so American as Page except Mark Twain," a British literary man once remarked; and it was probably this strong American quality, this directness and even breeziness of speech and of method, this absence of affectation, this almost openly expressed contempt for finesse and even for tradition, combined with those other traits which we like to think of as American—an upright purpose, a desire to serve not only his own country but mankind—which made the British public look upon Page as one of the most attractive and useful figures in a war-torn Europe.

There was a certain ruggedness in Page's exterior which the British regarded as distinctly in keeping with this American flavour. The Ambassador was not a handsome man. To one who had heard much of the liveliness of his conversation and presence a first impression was likely to be disappointing. His figure at this time was tall, gaunt, and lean—and he steadily lost weight during his service in England; his head was finely shaped—it was large, with a high forehead, his thin gray hair rather increasing its intellectual aspect; and his big frank brown eyes reflected that keen zest for life, that unsleeping interest in everything about him, that ever-working intelligence and sympathy which were the man's predominant traits. But a very large nose at first rather lessened the pleasing effects of his other features, and a rather weather-beaten, corrugated face gave a preliminary suggestion of roughness. Yet Page had only to begin talking and the impression immediately changed. "He puts his mind to yours," Dr. Johnson said, describing the sympathetic qualities of a friend, and the same was true of Page. Half a dozen sentences, spoken in his quick, soft, and ingratiating accents, accompanied by the most genial smile, at once converted the listener into a friend. Few men have ever lived who more quickly responded to this human relationship. The Ambassador, at the simple approach of a human being, became as a man transformed. Tired though he might be, low in spirits as he not infrequently was, the press of a human hand at once changed him into an animated and radiating companion. This responsiveness deceived all his friends in the days of his last illness. His intimates who dropped in to see Page invariably went away much encouraged and spread optimistic reports about his progress. A few minutes' conversation with Page would deceive even his physicians. The explanation was a simple one: the human presence had an electric effect upon him, and it is a revealing sidelight on Page's character that almost any man or woman could produce this result. As an editor, the readiness with which he would listen to suggestions from the humblest source was a constant astonishment to his associates. The office boy had as accessible an approach to Page as had his partners. He never treated an idea, even a grotesque one, with contempt; he always had time to discuss it, to argue it out, and no one ever left his presence thinking that he had made an absurd proposal. Thus Page had a profound respect for a human being simply because he was a human being; the mere fact that a man, woman, or child lived and breathed, had his virtues and his failings, constituted in Page's imagination a tremendous fact. He could not wound such a living creature any more than he could wound a flower or a tree; conse-

quently he treated every person as an important member
of the universe. Not infrequently, indeed, he stormed
at public men, but his thunder, after all, was not very
terrifying; his remarks about such personages as Mr.
Bryan merely reflected his indignation at their policies and
their influence but did not indicate any feeling against the
victims themselves. Page said "Good morning" to his
doorman with the same deference that he showed to Sir
Edward Grey, and there was not a little stenographer in
the building whose joys and sorrows did not arouse in him
the most friendly interest. Some of the most affecting
letters written about Page, indeed, have come from these
daily associates of more humble station. "We so often
speak of Mr. Page," writes one of the Embassy staff—
"Findlater, Short, and Frederick"—these were all English
servants at the Embassy; "we all loved him equally,
and hardly a day passes that something does not remind
us of him, and I often fancy that I hear his laugh, so full
of kindness and love of life." And the impression left
on those in high position was the same. "I have seen
ladies representing all that is most worldly in Mayfair,"
writes Mr. Ellery Sedgwick, the editor of the *Atlantic
Monthly*, "start at the sudden thought of Page's illness,
their eyes glistening with tears."

Perhaps what gave most charm to this human side was
the fact that Page was fundamentally such a scholarly
man. This was the aspect which especially delighted
his English friends. He preached democracy and Americanism with an emphasis that almost suggested the back-
woodsman—the many ideas on these subjects that appear
in his letters Page never hesitated to set forth with all due
resonance at London dinner tables—yet he phrased his
creed in language that was little less than literary style,
and illuminated it with illustrations and a philosophy

that were the product of the most exhaustive reading. "Your Ambassador has taught us something that we did not know before," an English friend remarked to an American. "That is that a man can be a democrat and a man of culture at the same time." The Greek and Latin authors had been Page's companions from the days when, as the holder of the Greek Fellowship at Johns Hopkins, he had been a favourite pupil of Basil L. Gildersleeve. British statesmen who had been trained at Balliol, in the days when Greek was the indispensable ear-mark of a gentleman, could thus meet their American associate on the most sympathetic terms. Page likewise spoke a brand of idiomatic English which immediately put him in a class by himself. He regarded words as sacred things. He used them, in his writing or in his speech, with the utmost care and discrimination; yet this did not result in a halting or stilted style; he spoke with the utmost ease, going rapidly from thought to thought, choosing invariably the one needful word, lighting up the whole with whimsicalities all his own, occasionally emphasizing a good point by looking downward and glancing over his eyeglasses, perhaps, if he knew his companion intimately, now and then giving him a monitory tap on the knee. Page, in fact, was a great and incessant talker; hardly anything delighted him more than a companionable exchange of ideas and impressions; he was seldom so busy that he would not push aside his papers for a chat; and he would talk with almost any one, on almost any subject—his secretaries, his stenographers, his office boys, and any crank who succeeded in getting by the doorman—for, in spite of his lively warnings against the breed, Page did really love cranks and took a collector's joy in uncovering new types. Page's voice was normally quiet; though he had spent all his early life in the South, the characteristic

Southern accents were ordinarily not observable; yet his intonation had a certain gentleness that was probably an inheritance of his Southern breeding. Thus, when he first began talking, his words would ripple along quietly and rapidly; a characteristic pose was to sit calmly, with one knee thrown over the other, his hands folded; as his interest increased, however, he would get up, perhaps walk across the room, or stand before the fireplace, his hands behind his back; a large cigar, sometimes unlighted, at other times emitting huge clouds of smoke, would oscillate from one side of his mouth to the other; his talk would grow in earnestness, his voice grow louder, his words come faster and faster, until finally they would gush forth in a mighty torrent.

All Page's personal traits are explained by that one characteristic which tempered all others, his sense of humour. That Page was above all a serious-minded man his letters show; yet his spirits were constantly alert for the amusing, the grotesque, and the contradictory; like all men who are really serious and alive to the pathos of existence, he loved a hearty laugh, especially as he found it a relief from the gloom that filled his every waking moment in England. Page himself regarded this ability to smile as an indispensable attribute to a well-rounded life. "No man can be a gentleman," he once declared, "who does not have a sense of humour." Only he who possessed this gift, Page believed, had an imaginative insight into the failings and the virtues of his brothers; only he could have a tolerant attitude toward the stupidities of his fellows, to say nothing of his own. And humour with him assumed various shades; now it would flash in an epigram, or smile indulgently at a passing human weakness; now and then it would break out into genial mockery; occasionally it would manifest itself as sheer horse-play; and less frequently it would become sardonic or even savage. It was in this latter spirit that he once described a trio of Washington statesmen, whose influence he abhorred as, "three minds that occupy a single vacuum." He once convulsed a Scottish audience by describing the national motto of Scotland—and doing so with a broad burr in his voice that seemed almost to mark the speaker a native to the heath—as "Liber-r-ty, fra-a-ternity and f-r-r-u-gality." The policy of his country occasioned many awkward moments which, thanks to his talent for amiable raillery, he usually succeeded in rendering harmless. Not infrequently Page's fellow guests at the dinner table would think the American attitude toward Germany a not inappropriate topic for small talk. "Mr. Page," remarked an exaltedly titled lady in a conversational pause, "when is your country going to get into the war?" The more discreet members of the company gasped, but Page was not disturbed. "Please give us at least ninety days," he answered, and an exceedingly disagreeable situation was thus relieved by general laughter.

On another occasion his repudiation of this flippant spirit took a more solemn and even more effective form. The time was a few days before the United States had declared war. Bernstorff had been dismissed; events were rapidly rushing toward the great climax; yet the behaviour of the Washington Administration was still inspiring much caustic criticism. The Pages were present at one of the few dinners which they attended in the course of this crisis; certain smart and tactless guests did not seem to regard their presence as a bar to many gibes against the American policy. Page sat through it all impassive, never betraying the slightest resentment.

Presently the ladies withdrew. Page found himself sitting next to Mr. Harold Nicolson, an important official in the Foreign Office. It so happened that Mr. Nicolson and Page were the only two members of the company who were the possessors of a great secret which made ineffably silly all the chatter that had taken place during the dinner; this was that the United States had decided on war against Germany and would issue the declaration in a few days.

"Well, Mr. Nicolson," said Page, "I think that you and I will drink a glass of wine together."

The two men quietly lifted their glasses and drank the silent toast. Neither made the slightest reference to the forthcoming event. Perhaps the other men present were a little mystified, but in a few days they understood what it had meant, and also learned how effectively they had been rebuked.

"Is it any wonder," says Mr. Nicolson, telling this story, "that I think that Mr. Page is perhaps the greatest gentleman I have ever known? He has only one possible competitor for this distinction—and that is Arthur Balfour."

The English newspapers took delight in printing Page's aphorisms, and several anecdotes that came from America afforded them especial joy. One went back to the days when the Ambassador was editor of the *Atlantic Monthly*. A woman contributor had sent him a story; like most literary novices she believed that editors usually rejected the manuscripts of unknown writers without reading them. She therefore set a trap for Page by pasting together certain sheets. The manuscript came back promptly, and, as the prospective contributor had hoped, these sheets had not been disturbed. These particular sections had certainly not been read. The angry author triumphantly wrote to Page, explaining how she had caught him and denouncing the whole editorial tribe as humbugs. "Dear

Madam," Page immediately wrote in reply, "when I break an egg at breakfast, I do not have to eat the whole of it to find out that it is bad." Page's treatment of authors, however, was by no means so acrimonious as this little note might imply. Indeed, the urbanity and consideration shown in his correspondence with writers had long been a tradition in American letters. The remark of O. Henry in this regard promises to become immortal: "Page could reject a story with a letter that was so complimentary," he said, "and make everybody feel so happy that you could take it to a bank and borrow money on it."

Another anecdote reminiscent of his editorial days was his retort to S. S. McClure, the editor of *McClure's Magazine*.

"Page," said Mr. McClure, "there are only three great editors in the United States."

"Who's the third one, Sam?" asked Page.

Plenty of stories, illustrating Page's quickness and aptness in retort, have gathered about his name in England. Many of them indicate a mere spirit of boyish fun. Early in his Ambassadorship he was spending a few days at Stratford-on-Avon, his hostess being an American woman who had beautifully restored an Elizabethan house; the garden contained a mulberry tree which she liked to think had been planted by Shakespeare himself. The dignitaries of Stratford, learning that the American Ambassador had reached town, asked permission to wait upon him; the Lord Mayor, who headed the procession, made an excellent speech, to which Page appropriately replied, and several hundred people were solemnly presented. After the party had left Page turned to his hostess:

"Have they all gone?"

"Yes."

"All?"

"Yes."

"Are you sure?"

"Yes."

"Then let's take hands and dance around the mulberry tree!"

Page was as good as his word; he danced as gaily as the youngest member of the party, to the singing of the old English song.

The great service in St. Paul's Cathedral, in commemoration of America's entry into the war, has already been described. A number of wounded Americans, boys whose zeal for the Allies had led them to enlist in the Canadian Army, were conspicuous participants in this celebration. After the solemn religious ceremonies, the Ambassador and these young men betook themselves for lunch to a well-known London restaurant. In an interval of the conversation one of the Americans turned to Page.

"Mr. Ambassador, there was just one thing wrong with that service."

"What was that?"

"We wanted to yell, and we couldn't."

"Then why don't you yell now?"

The boy jumped on a chair and began waving his napkin. "The Ambassador says we may yell," he cried. "Let's yell!"

"And so," said Page, telling the story, "they yelled for five minutes and I yelled with them. We all felt better in consequence."

This geniality, this disposition not to take life too solemnly, sometimes lightened up the sombre atmosphere of the Foreign Office itself. "Mr. Balfour went on a sort of mild rampage yesterday," Page records. "The British and American navies had come to an arrangement whereby the Brazilian ships that are coming over to help us fight should join the American unit, not the British, as was at first proposed. Washington telegraphed me that the British Minister at Rio was blocking the game by standing out for the first British idea—that the Brazilian ships should join the British. It turned out in the conversation that the British Minister had not been informed of the British-American naval arrangement. Mr. Balfour sent for Lord Hardinge. He called in one of the private secretaries. Was such a thing ever heard of?

"'Did you ever know,' said the indignant Mr. Balfour, turning to me, 'of such a thing as a minister not even being informed of his Government's decisions?' 'Yes,' I said, 'if I ransack my memory diligently, I think I could find such cases.' The meeting went into laughter!"

Evidently the troubles which Page was having with his own State Department were not unfamiliar to British officialdom.

Page's letters sufficiently reveal his fondness for Sir Edward Grey and the splendid relations that existed between them. The sympathetic chords which the two men struck upon their first meeting only grew stronger with time. A single episode brings out the bonds that drew them together. It took place at a time when the tension over the blockade was especially threatening. One afternoon Page asked for a formal interview; he had received another exceedingly disagreeable protest from Washington, with instructions to push the matter to a decision; the Ambassador left his Embassy with a grave expression upon his face; his associates were especially worried over the outcome. So critical did the situation seem that the most important secretaries gathered in the Ambassador's room, awaiting his return, their nerves strung almost to the breaking point. An hour went by and nothing was heard from Page; another hour slowly passed and still the Ambassador did not return. The faces of the assembled staff lengthened as the minutes went by; what was the Ambassador doing at the Foreign Office? So protracted an interview could portend only evil; already, in the minds of these nervous young men, ultimatums were flying between the United States and Great Britain, and even war might be hanging in the balance. Another hour drew out its weary length; the room became dark, dinner time was approaching, and still Page failed to make his appearance. At last, when his distracted subordinates were almost prepared to go in search of their chief, the Ambassador walked jauntily in, smiling and apparently carefree. What had happened? What was to be done about the detained ships?

"What ships?" asked Page, and then suddenly he remembered. "Oh, yes—those." That was all right; Sir Edward had at once promised to release them; it had all been settled in a few minutes.

"Then why were you so long?"

The truth came out: Sir Edward and Page had quickly turned from intercepted cargoes to the more congenial subject of Wordsworth, Tennyson, and other favourite poets, and the rest of the afternoon had been consumed in discussing this really important business.

Perhaps Page was not so great a story-teller as many Americans, but he excelled in a type of yarn that especially delights Englishmen, for it is the kind that is native to the American soil. He possessed an inexhaustible stock of Negro anecdotes, and he had the gift of bringing them out at precisely the right point. There was one which the Archbishop of York never tired of repeating. Soon after America entered the war, the Archbishop asked Page how long his country was "in for." "I can best answer that by telling you a story," said Page. "There were two Negroes who had just been sentenced to prison terms. As they were being taken away in the carriage placed at their disposal by the United States Government, one said to the other, 'Sam, how long is you in fo'?' 'I guess dat it's a yeah or two yeahs,' said Sam. 'How long is you in fo'?' 'I guess it's from now on,' said the other darky." "From now on," remarked the Archbishop, telling this story. "What could more eloquently have described America's attitude toward the war?"

The mention of the Archbishop suggests another of Page's talents—the aptness of his letters of introduction. In the spring of 1918 the Archbishop, at the earnest recommendation of Page and Mr. Balfour, came to the United States. Page prepared the way by letters to several distinguished Americans, of which this one, to Theodore Roosevelt, is a fair sample:

To Theodore Roosevelt

London, January 16, 1918.

DEAR MR. ROOSEVELT:

The Archbishop of York goes to the United States to make some observations of us and of our ways and to deliver addresses—on the invitation of some one of our church organizations; a fortunate event for us and, I have ventured to tell him, for him also.

During his brief stay in our country, I wish him to make your acquaintance, and I have given him a card of introduction to you, and thus I humbly serve you both.

The Archbishop is a man and a brother, a humble, learned, earnest, companionable fellow, with most charming manners and an attractive personality, a good friend of mine, which argues much for him and (I think) implies also something in my behalf.   You will enjoy him.

I am, dear Mr. Roosevelt,

Sincerely yours,

WALTER H. PAGE.

Greatly as Page loved England he never ceased to preach his Americanism.   That he preferred his own country to any other and that he believed that it was its greatest destiny to teach its institutions to the rest of the world, Page's letters show; yet this was with him no cheap spread-eagleism; it was a definite philosophy which the Ambassador had completely thought out.   He never hesitated to express his democratic opinions in any company, and only once or twice were there any signs that these ideas jarred a little in certain strongholds of conservatism. Even in the darkest period of American neutrality Page's faith in the American people remained complete.   After this country had entered the war and the apparent slowness of the Washington Administration had raised certain questionings, Page never doubted that the people themselves, however irresolute and lukewarm their representatives might be, would force the issue to its only logical end.   Even so friendly a man as Mr. Balfour once voiced a popular apprehension that the United States might not get into the war with all its strength or might withdraw prematurely.   This was in the early period of our participation.   "Who is going to stop the American people and how?" Page quickly replied.   "I think that was a good answer," he said, as he looked back at the episode in the summer of 1918, when hundreds of thousands of Americans were landing in France every month. A scrap of his writing records a discussion at a dinner party on this question: "If you could have a month in any time and any country, what time and what country would you choose?" The majority voted for England in the time of Elizabeth, but Page's preference was for Athens in the days of Pericles. Then came a far more interesting debate: "If you could spend a second lifetime when and where would you choose to spend it?" On this Page had not a moment's hesitation: "In the future and in the U. S. A.!" and he upheld his point with such persuasiveness that he carried the whole gathering with him. His love of anything suggesting America came out on all occasions. One of his English hostesses once captivated him by serving corn bread at a luncheon. "The American Ambassador and corn bread!" he exclaimed with all the delight of a schoolboy. Again he was invited, with another distinguished American, to serve as godfather at the christening of the daughter of an American woman who had married an Englishman. When the ceremony was finished he leaned over the font toward his fellow godfather. "Born on July 4th," he exclaimed, "of an American mother! And we two Yankee godfathers! We'll see that this child is taught the Constitution of the United States!"

One day an American duchess came into Page's office.

"I am going home for a little visit and I want a passport," she said.

"But you don't get a passport here," Page replied. "You must go to the Foreign Office."

His visitor was indignant.

"Not at all," she answered. "I am an American: you know that I am; you knew my father. I want an American passport."

Page patiently explained the citizenship and naturalization laws and finally convinced his caller that she was now a British subject and must have a British passport. As this American duchess left the room he shook at her a menacing forefinger.

"Don't tell me," was the Ambassador's parting shot, "that you thought that you could have your Duke and Uncle Sam, too!"

The judgments which Page passed on men and things were quick and they were not infrequently wise. One of these judgments had historic consequences the end of which cannot even yet be foreseen. On the outbreak of hostilities, as already related, an American Relief Committee was organized in London to look out for the interests of stranded Americans. Page kept a close eye on its operations, and soon his attention was attracted by the noiseless efficiency of an American engineer of whom he had already caught a few fleeting glimpses in the period of peace. After he had finished his work with the American Committee, Mr. Herbert C. Hoover began to make his arrangements to leave for the United States. His private affairs had been disorganized; he had already sent his family home, and his one ambition was to get on the first ship sailing for the United States. The idea of Belgian relief, or of feeding starving people anywhere, had never occurred to him. At this moment an American, Mr. Millard K. Shaler, came from Brussels and gave the most harrowing account of conditions in Belgium. Mr. Hoover took Mr. Shaler to Page, who immediately became sympathetic. The Ambassador arranged an interview between Mr. Hoover and Sir Edward Grey, who likewise showed great interest and promised government support. Soon afterward three Belgians arrived and described the situation as immediately alarming: Brussels had only food enough to feed the people for thirty-six hours; after that, unless help were forthcoming, the greatest distress would set in. Five men—Page, the three Belgians, and Mr. Hoover—at once got together at the American Embassy. Upon the result of that meeting hung the fate of millions of people. Who before had ever undertaken a scheme for feeding an entire nation for an indefinite period? That there were great obstacles in the way all five men knew; the British Admiralty in particular were strongly opposed; there was a fear that the food, if it could be acquired and sent to Belgium, would find its way to the German Army. Unless the British Government could be persuaded that this could be prevented, the enterprise would fail at the start. How could it be done?

"There is only one way," said Page. "Some government must give its guarantee that this food will get to the Belgian people." "And, of course," he added, "there is only one government that can do that. It must be the American Government."

Mr. Hoover pointed out that any such guarantee involved the management of transportation; only by controlling the railroads could the American Government make sure that this food would reach its destination.

And that, added Page, involved a director—some one man who could take charge of the whole enterprise. Who should it be?

Then Page turned quickly to the young American.

"Hoover, you're It!"

Mr. Hoover made no reply; he neither accepted nor rejected the proposal. He merely glanced at the clock, then got up and silently left the room. In a few minutes he returned and entered again into the discussion.

"Hoover, why did you get up and leave us so abruptly?" asked Page, a little puzzled over this behaviour.

"I saw by the clock," came the answer—and it was a story that Page was fond of telling, as illustrating the rapidity with which Mr. Hoover worked—"that there was an hour left before the Exchange closed in New York. So I went out and cabled, buying several millions of bushels of wheat—for the Belgians, of course."

For what is usually known as "society" Page had little inclination. Yet for social intercourse on a more genuine plane he had real gifts. Had he enjoyed better health, week ends in the country would have afforded him welcome entertainment. He also liked dinner parties but indulged in them very moderately. He was a member of many London clubs but he seldom visited any of them. There were a number of organizations, however, which he regularly attended. The Society of Dilettanti, a company of distinguished men interested in promoting the arts and improving the public taste, which has been continuously in existence since 1736, enrolling in each generation the greatest painters and writers of the time, elected Page to membership. He greatly enjoyed its dinners in the Banquet Hall of the Grafton Gallery. "Last night," he writes, describing his initial appearance, "I attended my first Dilettanti dinner and was inducted, much as a new Peer is inducted into the House of Lords. Lord Mersey in the chair—in a red robe. These gay old dogs have had a fine time of it for nearly 200 years—good wine, high food, fine satisfaction. The oldest dining society in the Kingdom. The blue blood old Briton has the art of enjoying himself reduced to a very fine point indeed." Another gathering whose meetings he seldom missed was that of the Kinsmen, an informal club of literary men who met occasionally for food and converse in the Trocadero Restaurant. Here Page would meet such congenial souls as Sir James Barrie and Sir Arthur Pinero, all of whom retain lively memories of Page at these gatherings. "He was one of the most lovable characters I have ever had the good fortune to encounter," says Sir Arthur Pinero, recalling these occasions. "In what special quality or qualities lay the secret of his charm and influence? Surely in his simplicity and transparent honesty, and in the possession of a disposition which, without the smallest loss of dignity, was responsive and affectionate. Distinguished American Ambassadors will come and go, and will in their turn win esteem and admiration. But none, I venture to say, will efface the recollection of Walter Page from the minds of those who were privileged to gain his friendship."

One aspect of Page that remains fixed in the memory of his associates is his unwearied industry with the pen. His official communications and his ordinary correspondence Page dictated; but his personal letters he wrote with his own hand. He himself deplored the stenographer as a deterrent to good writing; the habit of dictating, he argued, led to wordiness and general looseness of thought. Practically all the letters published in these volumes were therefore the painstaking work of Page's own pen. His handwriting was so beautiful and clear that, in his editorial days, the printers much preferred it as "copy" to typewritten matter. This habit is especially surprising in view of the Ambassador's enormous epistolary output. It must be remembered that the letters included in the present book are only a selection from the vast number that he wrote during his five years in England; many of these letters fill twenty and thirty pages of script; the labour involved in turning them out, day after day, seems fairly astounding. Yet with Page this was a labour of love. All through his Ambassadorship he seemed hardly contented unless he had a pen in his hand. As his secretaries would glance into his room, there they would see the Ambassador bending over his desk—writing, writing, eternally writing; sometimes he would call them in, and read what he had written, never hesitating to tear up the paper if their unfavourable criticisms seemed to him well taken. The Ambassador kept a desk also in his bedroom, and here his most important correspondence was attended to. Page's all-night self-communings before his wood fire have already been described, and he had another nocturnal occupation that was similarly absorbing. Many a night, after returning late from his office or from dinner, he would put on his dressing gown, sit at his bedroom desk, and start pouring forth his inmost thoughts in letters to the President, Colonel House, or some other correspondent. His pen flew over the paper with the utmost rapidity and the Ambassador would sometimes keep at his writing until two or three o'clock in the morning. There is a frequently expressed fear that letter writing is an art of the past; that the intervention of the stenographer has destroyed its spontaneity; yet it is evident that in Page the present generation has a letter writer of the old-fashioned kind, for he did all his writing with his own hand and under circumstances that would assure the utmost freshness and vividness to the result.

An occasional game of golf, which he played badly, a trip now and then to rural England—these were Page's only relaxations from his duties. Though he was not especially fond of leaving his own house, he was always delighted when visitors came to him. And the American Embassy, during the five years from 1913 to 1918, extended a hospitality which was fittingly democratic in its quality but which gradually drew within its doors all that was finest in the intellect and character of England. Page himself attributed the popularity of his house to his wife. Mrs. Page certainly embodied the traits most desirable in the Ambassadress of a great Republic. A woman of cultivation, a tireless reader, a close observer of people and events and a shrewd commentator upon them, she also had an unobtrusive dignity, a penetrating sympathy, and a capacity for human association, which, while more restrained and more placid than that of her husband, made her a helpful companion for a sorely burdened man. The American Embassy under Mr. and Mrs. Page was not one of London's smart houses as that word is commonly understood in this great capital. But No. 6 Grosvenor Square, in the spaciousness of its rooms, the simple beauty of its furnishings, and especially in its complete absence of ostentation, made it the worthy abiding place of an American Ambassador. And the people who congregated there were precisely the kind that appeal to the educated American. "I didn't know I was getting into an assembly of immortals," exclaimed Mr. Hugh Wallace, when he dropped in one Thursday afternoon for tea, and found himself foregathered with Sir Edward Grey, Henry James, John Sargent, and other men of the same type. It was this kind of person who most naturally gravitated to the Page establishment, not the ultra-fashionable, the merely rich, or the many titled. The formal functions which the position demanded the Pages scrupulously gave; but the affairs which Page most enjoyed and which have left the most lasting remembrances upon his guests were the informal meetings with his chosen favourites, for the most part literary men. Here Page's sheer brilliancy of conversation showed at its best. Lord Bryce, Sir John Simon, John Morley, the inevitable companions, Henry James and John Sargent—"What things have I seen done at the Mermaid"; and certainly these gatherings of wits and savants furnished as near an approach to its Elizabethan prototype as London could then present.

Besides his official activities Page performed great services to the two countries by his speeches. The demands of this kind on an American Ambassador are always numerous, but Page's position was an exceptional one; it was his fortune to represent America at a time when his own country and Great Britain were allies in a great war. He could therefore have spent practically all his time in speaking had he been so disposed. Of the hundreds of invitations received he was able to accept only a few, but most of these occasions became memorable ones. In any spectacular sense Page was not an orator; he rather despised the grand manner, with its flourishes and its tricks; the name of public speaker probably best describes his talents on the platform. Here his style was earnest and conversational: his speech flowed with the utmost readiness; it was invariably quiet and restrained; he was never aiming at big effects, but his words always went home. Of the series of speeches that stand to his credit in England probably the one that will be longest remembered is that delivered at Plymouth on August 4, 1917, the third anniversary of the war. This not only reviewed the common history of the two nations for three hundred years, and suggested a programme for making the bonds tighter yet, but it brought the British public practical assurances as to America's intentions in the conflict. Up to that time there had been much vagueness and doubt; no official voice had spoken the clear word for the United States; the British public did not know what to expect from their kinsmen overseas. But after Page's Plymouth speech the people of Great Britain looked forward with complete confidence to the coöperation of the two countries and to the inevitable triumph of this coöperation.

To Arthur W. Page

Knebworth House, Knebworth,
August 11, 1917.

DEAR ARTHUR:

First of all, these three years have made me tired. I suppose there's no doubt about that, if there were any scientific way of measuring it. While of course the strain now is nothing like what it was during the days of neutral·ity, there's yet some strain.

I went down to Plymouth to make a speech on the anniversary of the beginning of the war—went to tell them in the ‚west of England something about relations with the United States and something about what the United States is doing in the war. It turned out to be a great success. The Mayor met me at the train; there was a military company, the Star Spangled Banner and real American applause. All the way through the town the streets were lined with all the inhabitants and more— apparently millions of 'em. They made the most of it for five solid days.

On the morning of August 4th the Mayor gave me an official luncheon. Thence we went to the esplanade facing the sea, where soldiers and sailors were lined up for half a mile. The American Flag was flung loose, the Star Spangled Banner broke forth from the band, and all the people in that part of the world were there gathered to see the show. After all this salute the Mayor took me to the stand and he and I made speeches, and the background was a group of dozens of admirals and generals and many smaller fry. Then I reviewed the troops; then they marched by me and in an hour or two the show was over.

Then the bowling club—the same club and the same green as when Drake left the game to sail out to meet the Armada.

Then a solemn service in the big church, where the prayers were written and the hymns selected with reference to our part in the war.

Then, of course, a dinner party. At eight o'clock at night, the Guildhall, an enormous town hall, was packed with people and I made my speech at 'em. A copy (somewhat less good than the version I gave them) goes to you, along with a leader from the *Times*. They were vociferously grateful for any assuring word about the United States. It's strange how very little the provincial Englander knows about what we have done and mean to do. They took the speech finely, and I have had good letters about it from all sorts of people in every part of the Kingdom.

Then followed five days of luncheons and dinners and garden parties—and (what I set out to say) I got back to London last night dead tired. To-day your mother and I came here—about twenty-five miles from London—for a fortnight.

This is Bulwer-Lytton's house—a fine old English place hired this year by Lady Strafford, whom your mother is visiting for a fortnight or more, and they let me come along, too. They have given me the big library, as good a room as I want—with as bad pens as they can find in the Kingdom.

Your mother is tired, too. Since the American Red Cross was organized here, she has added to her committee and hospitals. But she keeps well and very vigorous. A fortnight here will set her up. She enjoyed Plymouth very much in spite of the continual rush, and it was a rush.

What the United States is doing looks good and large at

this distance. The gratitude here is unbounded; but I detect a feeling here and there of wonder whether we are going to keep up this activity to the end.

I sometimes feel that the German collapse *may* come next winter. Their internal troubles and the lack of sufficient food and raw materials do increase. The breaking point may be reached before another summer. I wish I could prove it or even certainly predict it. But it is at least conceivable. Alas, no one can *prove* anything about the war. The conditions have no precedents. The sum of human misery and suffering is simply incalculable, as is the loss of life; and the gradual and general brutalization goes on and on and on far past any preceding horrors.

With all my love to you and Mollie and the trio,

W. H. P.

And so for five busy and devastating years Page did his work. The stupidities of Washington might drive him to desperation, ill-health might increase his periods of despondency, the misunderstandings that he occasionally had with the British Government might add to his discouragements, but a naturally optimistic and humorous temperament overcame all obstacles, and did its part in bringing about that united effort which ended in victory. And that it was a great part, the story of his Ambassadorship abundantly proves. Page was not the soldier working in the blood and slime of Flanders, nor the sea fighter spending day and night around the foggy coast of Ireland, nor the statesman bending parliaments to his will and manipulating nations and peoples in the mighty game whose stake was civilization itself. But history will indeed be ungrateful if it ever forget the gaunt and pensive figure, clad in a dressing gown, sitting long into the morning before the smouldering fire at 6 Grosvenor Square, seeking to find some way to persuade a reluctant and hesitating President to lead his country in the defense of liberty and determined that, so far as he could accomplish it, the nation should play a part in the great assize that was in keeping with its traditions and its instincts.

CHAPTER XXIV

A RESPITE AT ST. IVES

To Edward M. House

Knebworth House
Sunday, September, [sic] 1917.

DEAR HOUSE:

. . . By far the most important peace plan or utterance is the President's extraordinary answer to the Pope.[1] His flat and convincing refusal to take the word of the present rulers of Germany as of any value has had more effect here than any other utterance and it is, so far, the best contribution we have made to the war. The best evidence that I can get shows also that it has had more effect in Germany than anything else that has been said by anybody. That hit the bull's-eye with perfect accuracy; and it has been accepted here as *the* war aim and *the* war condition. So far as I can make out it is working in Germany toward peace with more effect than any other deliverance made by anybody. And it steadied the already unshakable resolution here amazingly.

I can get any information here of course without danger of the slightest publicity—an important point, because even the mention of peace now is dangerous. All the world, under this long strain, is more or less off the normal,

[1] On August 1, 1917, Pope Benedict XV sent a letter to the Powers urging them to bring the war to an end and outlining possible terms of settlement. On August 29th President Wilson sent his historic reply. This declared, in memorable language, that the Hohenzollern dynasty was unworthy of confidence and that the United States would have no negotiations with its representatives. It inferentially took the stand that the Kaiser must abdicate, or be deposed, and the German autocracy destroyed, as part of the conditions of peace.

and all my work—even routine work—is done with the profoundest secrecy: it has to be.

Our energetic war preparations call forth universal admiration and gratitude here on all sides and nerve up the British and hearten them more than I know how to explain. There is an eager and even pathetic curiosity to hear all the details, to hear, in fact, anything about the United States; and what the British do not know about the United States would fill the British Museum. They do know, however, that they would soon have been obliged to make an unsatisfactory peace if we hadn't come in when we did and they freely say so. The little feeling of jealousy that we should come in and win the war at the end has, I think, been forgotten, swallowed up in their genuine gratitude.

Sincerely yours,

WALTER H. PAGE.

To Arthur W. Page

American Embassy,
London, Sept. 3, 1917.

DEAR ARTHUR:

. . . The President has sent Admiral Mayo over to study the naval situation. So far as I can learn the feeling at Washington is that the British Navy has done nothing. Why, it hasn't attacked the German naval bases and destroyed the German navy and ended the war! Why not? I have a feeling that Mayo will supplement and support Sims in his report. Then gradually the naval men at Washington may begin to understand and they may get the important facts into the President's head. Meantime the submarine work of the Germans continues to win the war, although the government and the people here and in the United States appear not to believe it.

They are still destroying seventy-five British ships a month besides an additional (smaller) number of allied and neutral ships. And all the world together is not turning out seventy-five ships a month; nor are we all destroying submarines as fast as the Germans are turning *them* out. Yet all the politicians are putting on a cheerful countenance about it because the Germans are not starving England out and are not just now sinking passenger ships. They may begin this again at any time. They have come within a few feet of torpedoing two of our American liners. The submarine *is* the war yet, but nobody seems disposed to believe it. They'll probably wake up with a great shock some day—or the war may possibly end before the destruction of ships becomes positively fatal.

The President's letter to the Pope gives him the moral and actual leadership now. The Hohenzollerns must go. Somehow the subjects and governments of these Old World kingdoms have not hitherto laid emphasis on this. There's still a divinity that doth hedge a king in most European minds. To me this is the very queerest thing in the whole world. What again if Germany, Austria, Spain should follow Russia? Whether they do or not crowns will not henceforth be so popular. There is an unbounded enthusiasm here for the President's letter and for the President in general.

In spite of certain details which it seems impossible to make understood on the Potomac, the whole American preparation and enthusiasm seem from this distance to be very fine. The *people* seem in earnest. When I read about tax bills, about the food regulation and a thousand other such things, I am greatly gratified. And it proves that we were right when we said that during the days of neutrality the people were held back. It all looks exceedingly good from this distance, and it makes me homesick.

To Frank N. Doubleday

American Embassy.

[Undated, but written about October 1, 1917]

DEAR EFFENDI:

. . . The enormous war work and war help that everybody seems to be doing in the United States is heartily appreciated here—most heartily. The English eat out of our hands. You can see American uniforms every day in London. Every ship brings them. Everybody's thrilled to see them. The Americans here have great houses opened as officers' clubs, and scrumptious huts for men where countesses and other high ladies hand out sandwiches and serve ice cream and ginger beer. Our two admirals are most popular with all classes, from royalty down. English soldiers salute our officers in the street and old gentlemen take off their hats when they meet nurses with the American Red Cross uniform. My Embassy now occupies four buildings for offices, more than half of them military and naval. And my own staff, proper, is the biggest in the world and keeps growing. When I go, in a little while, to receive the Freedom of the City of Edinburgh, I shall carry an Admiral or a General as my aide!

That's the way we keep a stiff upper lip.

And Good Lord! it's tiresome. Peace? We'd all give our lives for the right sort of peace, and never move an eyelid. But only the wrong sort has yet come within reach. The other sort is coming, however; for these present German contortions are the beginning of the end. But the weariness of it, and the tragedy and the cost. No human creature was ever as tired as I am. Yet I keep well and keep going and keep working all my waking hours. When it ends, I shall collapse and go home and have to rest a while. So at least I feel now. And, if I outlive the work and the danger and the weariness, I'll praise God for that. And it doesn't let up a single day. And I'm no worse off than everybody else.

So this over-weary world goes, dear Effendi; but the longest day shades at last down to twilight and rest; and so this will be. And poor old Europe will then not be worth while for the rest of our lives—a vast grave and ruin where unmated women will mourn and starvation will remain for years to come.

God bless us.

Sincerely yours, with my love to all the boys,

W. H. P.

To Frank N. Doubleday

London, November 9, 1917.

DEAR EFFENDI:

. . . This infernal thing drags its slow length along so that we cannot see even a day ahead, not to say a week, or a year. If any man here allowed the horrors of it to dwell on his mind he would go mad, so we have to skip over these things somewhat lightly and try to keep the long, definite aim in our thoughts and to work away distracted as little as possible by the butchery and by the starvation that is making this side of the world a shambles and a wilderness. There is hardly a country on the Continent where people are not literally starving to death, and in many of them by hundreds of thousands; and this state of things is going to continue for a good many years after the war. God knows we (I mean the American people) are doing everything we can to alleviate it but there is so much more to be done than any group of forces can possibly do, that I have a feeling that we have hardly touched the borders of the great problem itself. Of course here in London we are away from all that. In spite of the rations we get quite enough to eat and it's as good as it is usually in England, but we have no right to complain. Of course we are subject to air raids, and the wise air people here think that early next spring we are going to be bombarded with thousands of aeroplanes, and with new kinds of bombs and gases in a well-organized effort to try actually to destroy London. Possibly that will come; we must simply take our chance, every man sticking to his job. Already the slate shingles on my roof have been broken, and bricks have been knocked down my chimney; the skylight was hit and glass fell down all through the halls, and the nose of a shrapnel shell, weighing eight pounds, fell just in front of my doorway and rolled in my area. This is the sort of thing we incidentally get, not of course from the enemy directly, but from the British guns in London which shoot these things at German aeroplanes. What goes up must come down. Between our own defences and the enemy, God knows which will kill us first!

In spite of all this I put my innocent head on my pillow every night and get a good night's sleep after the bombing is done, and I thank Heaven that nothing interrupts my sleep. This, and a little walking, which is all I get time to do in these foggy days, constitute my life outdoors and precious little of it is outdoors.

Then on every block that I know of in London there is a hospital or supply place and the ambulances are bringing the poor fellows in all the time. We don't get any gasolene to ride so we have to walk. We don't get any white bread so we have to eat stuff made of flour and corn meal ground so fine that it isn't good. While everybody gets a little thinner, the universal opinion is that they also get a little better, and nobody is going to die here of hunger.

We feel a little more cheerful about the submarines than we did some time ago. For some reason they are not getting so many ships. One reason, I am glad to believe, is that they are getting caught themselves. If I could remember all the stories that I hear of good fighting with the submarines I could keep you up two nights when I get home, but in these days one big thing after another crowds so in men's minds that the Lord knows if, when I get home, I shall remember anything.

Always heartily yours,

W. H. P.

To the President

London, December 3, 1917.

DEAR MR. PRESIDENT:

. . .. Some of the British military men in London are not hopeful of an early end of the war nor even cheerful about the result. They are afraid of the war-weariness that overcame Russia and gave Italy a setback. They say the military task, though long and slow and hard, can be done if everybody will pull together and keep at the job without weariness—*be done by our help*. But they have fits of fear of France. They are discouraged by the greater part of Lord Lansdowne's letter.[1] I myself do not set great value on this military feeling in London, for the British generals in France do not share it. Lord French once said to me and General Robertson, too, that when they feel despondent in London, they go to the front and get cheered up. But it does seem to be a long job. Evidently the Germans mean to fight to the last man

---

[1] On November 29, 1917, the London *Daily Telegraph* published a letter from the Marquis of Lansdowne, which declared that the war had lasted too long and suggested that the British restate their war aims. This letter was severely condemned by the British press and by practically all representative British statesmen. It produced a most lamentable impression in the United States also.

unless they can succeed in inducing the Allies to meet them to talk it over without naming their terms in advance. That is what Lord Lansdowne favours, and no public outgiving by any prominent man in England has called forth such a storm of protest since the war began. I think I see the genesis of his thought, and it is this: there is nothing in his letter and there was nothing in the half dozen or more rather long conversations that I have had with him on other subjects to show that he has the slightest conception of democracy as a social creed or as a political system. He is, I think, the most complete aristocrat that I have ever met. He doesn't see the war at all as a struggle between democracy and its opposite. He sees it merely as a struggle between Germany and the Allies; and inferentially he is perfectly willing the Kaiser should remain in power. He is of course a patriotic man and a man of great cultivation. But he doesn't see the deeper meaning of the conflict. Add to this defect of understanding, a long period of bad health and a lasting depression because of the loss of his son, and his call to the war-weary ceases to be a surprise.

I am, dear Mr. President,

Sincerely yours,

WALTER H. PAGE.

To Arthur W. Page

American Embassy,
London, December 23, 1917.

DEAR ARTHUR:

I sent you a Christmas cable yesterday for everybody. That's about all I can send in these days of slow mail and restricted shipping and enormously high prices; and you gave all the girls each $100 for me, for the babies and themselves? That'll show 'em that at least we haven't forgotten them. Forgotten? Your mother and I are always talking of the glad day when we can go home and live among them. We get as homesick as small boys their first month at a boarding school. Do you remember the day I left you at Lawrenceville, a forlorn and lonely kid?— It's like that.

A wave of depression hangs over the land like a London fog. And everybody on this tired-out side of the world shows a disposition to lean too heavily on us—to depend on us so completely that the fear arises that they may unconsciously relax their own utmost efforts when we begin to fight. Yet they can't in the least afford to relax, and, when the time comes, I dare say they will not. Yet the plain truth is, the French may give out next year for lack of men. I do not mean that they will quit, but that their fighting strength will have passed its maximum and that they will be able to play only a sort of second part. Except the British and the French, there's no nation in Europe worth a tinker's damn when you come to the real scratch. The whole continent is rotten or tyrannical or yellow-dog. I wouldn't give Long Island or Moore County for the whole of continental Europe, with its kings and itching palms.

. . . Waves of depression and of hope—if not of elation—come and go. I am told, and I think truly, that waves of weariness come in London far oftener and more depressingly than anywhere else in the Kingdom. There is no sign nor fear that the British will give up; they'll hold on till the end. Winston Churchill said to me last night: "We can hold on till next year. But after 1918, it'll be your fight. We'll have to depend on you." I told him that such a remark might well be accepted in some quarters as a British surrender. Then he came up to the scratch: "Surrender? Never." But I fear we need—in some practical and non-ostentatious way—now and then to remind all these European folk that we get no particular encouragement by being unduly leaned on.

It is, however, the weariest Christmas in all British annals, certainly since the Napoleonic wars. The untoward event after the British advance toward Cambrai caused the retirement of six British generals and deepened the depression here. Still I can see it now passing. Even a little victory will bring back a wave of cheerfulness.

Depression or elation show equally the undue strain that British nerves are under. I dare say nobody is entirely normal. News of many sorts can now be circulated only by word of mouth. The queerest stories are whispered about and find at least temporary credence. For instance: The report has been going around that the revolution that took place in Portugal the other day was caused by the Germans (likely enough); that it was a monarchical movement and that the Germans were going to put the King back on the throne as soon as the war ended. Sensation-mongers appear at every old-woman's knitting circle. And all this has an effect on conduct. Two young wives of noble officers now in France have just run away with two other young noblemen—to the scandal of a large part of good society in London. It is universally said that the morals of more hitherto good people are wrecked by the strain put upon women by the absence of their husbands than was ever before heard of. Everybody is overworked. Fewer people are literally truthful than ever before. Men and women break down and fall out of working ranks continuously. The number of men in the government who have disappeared from public view is amazing, the number that would like to disappear is still greater—from sheer overstrain. The Prime Minister is tired. Bonar Law in a long conference that Crosby and I had with him yesterday wearily ran all round a circle rather than hit a plain proposition with a clear decision. Mr. Balfour has kept his house from overwork a few days every recent week. I lunched with Mr. Asquith yesterday; even he seemed jaded; and Mrs. Asquith assured me that "everything is going to the devil damned fast." Some conspicuous men who have always been sober have taken to drink. The very few public dinners that are held are served with ostentatious meagreness to escape criticism. I attended one last week at which there was no bread, no butter, no sugar served. All of which doesn't mean that the world here is going to the bad—only that it moves backward and forward by emotions; and this is normally a most unemotional race. Overwork and the loss of sons and friends—the list of the lost grows—always make an abnormal strain. The churches are fuller than ever before. So, too, are the "parlours" of the fortune-tellers. So also the theatres—in the effort to forget one's self. There are afternoon dances for young officers at home on leave: the curtains are drawn and the music is muffled. More marriages take place—blind and maimed, as well as the young fellows just going to France—than were ever celebrated in any year within men's memory. Verse-writing is rampant. I have received enough odes and sonnets celebrating the Great Republic and the Great President to fill a folio volume. Several American Y. M. C. A. workers lately turned rampant Pacifists and had to be sent home. Colonial soldiers and now and then an American sailor turn up at our Y. M. C. A. huts as full as a goat and swear after the event that they never did such a thing before. Emotions and strain everywhere!

Affectionately,

W. H. P.

In March Page, a very weary man—as these letters indicate—took a brief holiday at St. Ives, on the coast of Cornwall. As he gazed out on the Atlantic, the yearning for home, for the sandhills and the pine trees of North Carolina, again took possession of his soul. Yet it is evident, from a miscellaneous group of letters written at this time, that his mind revelled in a variety of subjects, ranging all the way from British food and vegetables to the settlement of the war and from secret diplomacy to literary style.

To Mrs. Charles G. Loring

St. Ives, Cornwall, March 3, 1918.

DEAR KITTY:

Your mother of course needed a rest away from London after the influenza got done with her; and I discovered that I had gone stale. So she and I and the golf clubs came here yesterday—as near to the sunlit land of Uncle Sam as you can well get on this island. We look across the ocean—at least out into it—in your direction, but I must confess that Labrador is not in sight. The place is all right, the hotel uncommonly good, but it's Greenlandish in its temperature—a very cold wind blowing. The golf clubs lean up against the wall and curse the weather. But we are away from the hordes of people and will have a little quiet here. It's as quiet as any far-off place by the sea, and it's clean. London is the dirtiest town in the world.

By the way that picture of Chud came (by Col. Honey) along with Alice Page's adorable little photograph. As for the wee chick, I see how you are already beginning to get a lot of fun with her. And you'll have more and more as she gets bigger. Give her my love and see what she'll say. You won't get so lonesome, dear Kitty, with little Alice; and I can't keep from thinking as well as hoping that the war will not go on as long as it sometimes seems that it must. The utter collapse of Russia has given Germany a vast victory on that side and it may turn out that this will make an earlier peace possible than would otherwise have come. And the Germans may be—in fact, *must* be, very short of some of the essentials of war in their metals or in cotton. They are in a worse internal plight than has been made known, I am sure. I can't keep from hoping that peace may come this year. Of course, my guess may be wrong; but everything I hear points in the direction of my timid prediction.

Bless you and little Alice,
Affectionately,
W. H. P.

Page's oldest son was building a house and laying out a garden at Pinehurst, North Carolina, a fact which explains the horticultural and gastronomical suggestions contained in the following letter:

To Ralph W. Page

Tregenna Castle Hotel,
St. Ives, Cornwall, England,
March 4, 1918.

DEAR RALPH:
  Asparagus
  Celery
  Tomatoes
  Butter Beans
  Peas
  Sweet Corn
  Sweet Potatoes

Squash—the sort you cook in the rind
Cantaloupe
Peanuts
Egg Plant
Figs
Peaches
Pecans
Scuppernongs
Peanut-bacon, in glass jars
Razor-back hams, divinely cured
Raspberries
Strawberries
etc. etc. etc. etc.

You see, having starved here for five years, my mind, as soon as it gets free, runs on these things and my mouth waters. All the foregoing things that grow can be put up in pretty glass jars, too.

Add cream, fresh butter, buttermilk, fresh eggs. Only one of all the things on page one grows with any flavour here at all—strawberries; and only one or two more grow at all. Darned if I don't have to confront Cabbage every day. I haven't yet surrendered, and I never shall unless the Germans get us. Cabbage and Germans belong together: God made 'em both the same stinking day.

Now get a bang-up gardener no matter what he costs. Get him started. Put it up to him to start toward the foregoing programme, to be reached in (say) three years —two if possible. He must learn to grow these things absolutely better than they are now grown anywhere on earth. He must get the best seed. He must get muck out of the swamp, manure from somewhere, etc. etc. He must have the supreme flavour in each thing. Let him take room enough for each—plenty of room. He doesn't want much room for any one thing, but good spaces between.

This will be the making of the world. Talk about fairs! If he fails to get every prize he must pay a fine for every one that goes to anybody else.

How we'll live! I can live on these things and nothing else. But (just to match this home outfit) I'll order tea from Japan, ripe olives from California, grape fruit and oranges from Florida. Then poor folks will hang around, hoping to be invited to dinner!

Plant a few fig trees now; and pecans? Any good?

The world is going to come pretty close to starvation not only during the war but for five or perhaps ten years afterward. An acre or two *done right*—divinely right—will save us. An acre or two on my land in Moore County —no king can live half so well if the ground be got ready this spring and such a start made as one natural-born gardener can make. The old Russian I had in Garden City was no slouch. Do you remember his little patch back of the house? That far, far, far excelled anything in all Europe. And you'll recall that we jarred 'em and had good things all winter.

This St. Ives is the finest spot in England that I've ever seen. To-day has been as good as any March day you ever had in North Carolina—a fine air, clear sunshine, a beautiful sea—looking out toward the United States; and this country grows—the best golf links that I've ever seen in the world, and nothing else worth speaking of but —tin. Tin mines are all about here. Tin and golf are good crops in their way, but they don't feed the belly of man. As matters stand the only people that have fit things to eat now in all Europe are the American troops in France, and their food comes out of tins chiefly. Ach! Heaven! In these islands man is amphibious and carnivorous. It rains every day and meat, meat, meat is the only human idea of food. God bless us, one acre of the Sandhills is worth a vast estate of tin mines and golf links to feed the innards of

Yours affectionately,

W. H. P.

P. S. And cornfield peas, of just the right rankness, cooked with just the right dryness.

When I become a citizen of the Sandhills I propose to induce some benevolent lover of good food to give substantial prizes to the best grower of each of these things and to the best cook of each and to the person who serves each of them most daintily.

We can can and glass jar these things and let none be put on the market without the approval of an expert employed by the community. Then we can get a reputation for Sandhill Food and charge double price.

W. H. P.

To Arthur W. Page

St. Ives, Cornwall,
England, March 8, 1918.

DEAR ARTHUR:

Your letter, written from the University Club, is just come. It makes a very distinct impression on my mind which my own conclusions and fears have long confirmed. Let me put it at its worst and in very bald terms: The Great White Chief is at bottom pacifist, has always been so and is so now. Of course I do not mean a pacifist at any price, certainly not a cowardly pacifist. But (looked at theoretically) war is, of course, an absurd way of settling any quarrel, an irrational way. Men and nations are wasteful, cruel, pigheaded fools to indulge in it. Quite true. But war is also the only means of adding to a nation's territory the territory of other nations which they do not wish to sell or to give up—the robbers' only way to get more space or to get booty. This last explains this war. Every Hohenzollern (except the present Emperor's father, who reigned only a few months) since Frederick the Great has added to Prussian and German area of rule. Every one, therefore, as he comes to the throne, feels an obligation to make his addition to the Empire. For this the wars of Prussia with Austria, with Denmark, with France were brought on. They succeeded and won the additions that old William I made to the Empire. Now William II must make *his* addition. He prepared for more than forty years; the nation prepared before he came to the throne and his whole reign has been given to making sure that he was ready. It's a robber's raid. Of course, the German case has been put so as to direct attention from this bald fact.

Now the philosophical pacifists—I don't mean the cowardly, yellow-dog ones—have never quite seen the war in this aspect. They regard it as a dispute about something—about trade, about more seaboard, about this or that, whereas it is only a robber's adventure. They want other people's property. They want money, treasure, land, indemnities, minerals, raw materials; and they set out to take them.

Now confusing this character of the war with some sort of rational dispute about something, the pacifists try in every way to stop it, so that the "issue" may be reasoned out, debated, discussed, negotiated. Surely the President tried to reach peace—tried as hard and as long as the people would allow him. The Germans argued away time with him while they got their submarine fleet built. Then they carried out the programme they had always had in mind and had never thought of abandoning. Now they wish to gain more time, to slacken the efforts of the Allies, if possible to separate them by asking for "discussions"—peace by "negotiation." When you are about to kill the robber, he cries out, "For God's sake, let's discuss the question between us. We can come to terms."—Now here's where the danger comes from the philosophical pacifist—from any man who does not clearly understand the nature of the war and of the enemy. To discuss the difference between us is so very reasonable in sound—so very reasonable in fact if there were a discussable difference. It is a programme that would always be in order except with a burglar or a robber.

The yet imperfect understanding of the war and of the nature of the German in the United States, especially at Washington—more especially in the White House—herein lies the danger.

. . . This little rest down here is a success. The weather is a disappointment—windy and cold. But to be away from London and away from folks that's much. Shoecraft is very good.[1] He sends us next to nothing. Almost all we've got is an invitation to lunch with Their Majesties and they've been good enough to put that off. It's a far-off country, very fine, I'm sure in summer, and with most beautiful golf links. The hill is now so windy that no sane man can play there.

We're enjoying the mere quiet. And your mother is quite well again.

Affectionately,

W. H. P.

---

[1]Eugene C. Shoecraft, the Ambassador's secretary.

To Mrs. Charles G. Loring

St. Ives, Cornwall,
March 10, 1918.

DEAR KITTY:

A week here. No news. Shoecraft says we've missed nothing in London. What we came for we've got: your mother's quite well. She climbs these high hills quite spryly. We've had a remarkable week in this respect— we haven't carried on a conversation with any human being but ourselves. I don't think any such thing has ever happened before. I can stand a week, perhaps a fortnight of this now. But I don't care for it for any long period. At the bottom of this high and steep hill is the quaintest little town I ever saw. There are some streets so narrow that when a donkey cart comes along the urchins all have to run to the next corner or into doors. There is no sidewalk, of course; and the donkey cart takes the whole room between the houses. Artists take to the town, and they have funny little studios down by the water front in tiny houses built of stone in pieces big enough to construct a tidewater front. Imagine stone walls made of stone, each weighing tons, built into little houses about as big as your little back garden! There's one fellow here (an artist) whom I used to know in New York, so small has the world become!

On another hill behind us is a triangular stone monument to John Knill. He was once mayor of the town. When he died in 1782, he left money to the town. If the town is to keep the money (as it has) the Mayor must once in every five years form a procession and march up to this monument. There ten girls, natives of the town, and two widows must dance around the monument to the playing of a fiddle and a drum, the girls dressed in white. This ceremony has gone on, once in five years, all this time and the town has old Knill's money!

Your mother and I—though we are neither girls nor widows—danced around it this morning, wondering what sort of curmudgeon old John Knill was.

Don't you see how easily we fall into an idle mood?

Well, here's a photograph of little Alice looking up at me from the table where I write—a good, sweet face she has.

And you'll never get another letter from me in a time and from a place whereof there is so little to tell.

Affectionately, dear Kitty,

W. H. P.

To Ralph W. Page

Tregenna Castle Hotel,
St. Ives, Cornwall,
March 12, 1918.

My dear Ralph:

Arthur has sent me Gardiner's 37-page sketch of American-British Concords and Discords—a remarkable sketch; and he has reminded me that your summer plan is to elaborate (into a popular style) your sketch of the same subject. You and Gardiner went over the same ground, each in a very good fashion. That's a fascinating task, and it opens up a wholly new vista of our History and of Anglo-Saxon, democratic history. Much lies ahead of that. And all this puts it in my mind to write you a little discourse on *style*. Gardiner has no style. He put his facts down much as he would have noted on a blue print the facts about an engineering project that he sketched. The style of your article, which has much to be said for it as a magazine article, is not the best style for a book.

Now, this whole question of style—well, it's the gist of good writing. There's no really effective writing without it. Especially is this true of historical writing. Look at X Y Z's writings. He knows his American history and has written much on it. He's written it as an Ohio blacksmith shoes a horse—not a touch of literary value in it all; all dry as dust—as dry as old Bancroft.

Style is good breeding—and art—in writing. It consists of the arrangement of your matter, first; then, more, of the gait; the manner and the manners of your expressing it. Work every group of facts, naturally and logically grouped to begin with, into a climax. Work every group up as a sculptor works out his idea or a painter, each group complete in itself. Throw out any superfluous facts or any merely minor facts that prevent the orderly working up of the group—that prevent or mar the effect you wish to present.

Then, when you've got a group thus presented, go over what you've made of it, to make sure you've used your material and its arrangement to the best effect, taking away merely extraneous or superfluous or distracting facts, here and there adding concrete illustrations—putting in a convincing detail here, and there a touch of colour.

Then go over it for your vocabulary. See that you use no word in a different meaning than it was used 100 years ago and will be used 100 years hence. You wish to use only the permanent words—words, too, that will be understood to carry the same meaning to English readers in every part of the world. Your vocabulary must be chosen from the permanent, solid, stable parts of the language.

Then see that no sentence contains a hint of obscurity.

Then go over the words you use to see if they be the

best. Don't fall into merely current phrases. If you have a long word, see if a native short one can be put in its place which will be more natural and stronger. Avoid a Latin vocabulary and use a plain English one—short words instead of long ones.

Most of all, use *idioms*—English idioms of force. Say an agreement was "come to." Don't say it was "consummated." For the difference between idioms and a Latin style, compare Lincoln with George Washington. One's always interesting and convincing. The other is dull in spite of all his good sense. How most folk do misuse and waste words!

Freeman went too far in his use of one-syllable words. It became an affectation. But he is the only man I can think of that ever did go too far in that direction. X— would have written a great history if he had had the natural use of idioms. As it is, he has good sense and no style; and his book isn't half so interesting as it would have been if he had some style—some proper value of short, clear-cut words that mean only one thing and that leave no vagueness.

You'll get a good style if you practice it. It is in your blood and temperament and way of saying things. But it's a high art and must be laboriously cultivated.

Yours affectionately,
W. H. P.

This glimpse of a changing and chastened England appears in a letter of this period:

The disposition shown by an endless number of such incidents is something more than a disposition of gratitude of a people helped when they are hard pressed. All these things show the changed and changing Englishman. It has already come to him that he may be weaker than he had thought himself and that he may need friends more than he had once imagined; and, if he must have helpers and friends, he'd rather have his own kinsmen. He's a queer "cuss," this Englishman. But he isn't a liar nor a coward nor any sort of "a yellow dog." He's true, and he never runs—a possible hero any day, and, when heroic, modest and quiet and graceful. The trouble with him has been that he got great world power too easily. In the times when he exploited the world for his own enrichment, there were no other successful exploiters. It became an easy game to him. He organized sea traffic and sea power. Of course he became rich—far, far richer than anybody else, and, therefore, content with himself. He has, therefore, kept much of his mediæval impedimenta, his dukes and marquesses and all that they imply—his outworn ceremonies and his mediæval disregard of his social inferiors. Nothing is well done in this Kingdom for the big public, but only for the classes. The railway stations have no warm waiting rooms. The people pace the platform till the train comes, and milord sits snugly wrapt up in his carriage till his footman announces the approach of the train. And occasional discontent is relieved by emigration to the Colonies. If any man becomes weary of his restrictions he may go to Australia and become a gentleman. The remarkable loyalty of the Colonies has in it something of a servant's devotion to his old master.

Now this trying time of war and the threat and danger of extinction are bringing—have in fact already brought —the conviction that many changes must come. The first sensible talk about popular education ever heard here is just now beginning. Many a gentleman has made up his mind to try to do with less than seventeen servants for the rest of his life since he now *has* to do with less. Privilege, on which so large a part of life here rests, is already pretty well shot to pieces. A lot of old baggage will never be recovered after this war: that's certain. During a little after-dinner speech in a club not long ago I indulged in a pleasantry about excessive impedimenta. Lord Derby, Minister of War and a bluff and honest aristocrat, sat near me and he whispered to me—"That's me." "Yes," I said, "that's you," and the group about us made merry at the jest. The meaning of this is, they now joke about what was the most solemn thing in life three years ago.

None of this conveys the idea I am trying to explain— the change in the English point of view and outlook—a half century's change in less than three years, radical and fundamental change, too. The mother of the Duke of X came to see me this afternoon, hobbling on her sticks and feeble, to tell me of a radiant letter she had received from her granddaughter who has been in Washington visiting the Spring Rices. "It's all very wonderful," said the venerable lady, "and my granddaughter actually heard the President make a speech!" Now, knowing this lady and knowing her son, the Duke, and knowing how this girl, his daughter, has been brought up, I dare swear that three years ago not one of them would have crossed the street to hear any President that ever lived. They've simply become different people. They were very genuine before. They are very genuine now.

It is this steadfastness in them that gives me sound hope for the future. They don't forget sympathy or help or friendship. Our going into the war has eliminated the Japanese question. It has shifted the virtual control of the world to English-speaking peoples. It will bring into the best European minds the American ideal of service.

Lord Robert Cecil, Minister of Blockade, 1916–18, Assistant Secretary of State for Foreign Affairs, 1918

General John J. Pershing, Commander-in-Chief of the American
Expeditionary Force in the Great War

It will, in fact, give us the lead and make the English in the long run our willing followers and allies. I don't mean that we shall always have plain sailing. But I do mean that the direction of events for the next fifty or one hundred years has now been determined.

Yet Page found one stolid opposition to his attempts to establish the friendliest relations between the two peoples. That offish attitude of the Washington Administration, to which reference has already been made, did not soften with the progress of events. Another experience now again brought out President Wilson's coldness toward his allies. About this time many rather queer Americans —some of the "international" breed—were coming to England on more or less official missions. Page was somewhat humiliated by these excursions; he knew that his country possessed an almost unlimited supply of vivid speakers, filled with zeal for the allied cause, whose influence, if they could be induced to cross the Atlantic, would put new spirit into the British. The idea of having a number of distinguished Americans come to England and tell the British public about the United States and especially about the American preparations for war, was one that now occupied his thoughts. In June, 1917, he wrote his old friend Dr. Wallace Buttrick, extending an invitation to visit Great Britain as a guest of the British Government. Dr. Buttrick made a great success; his speeches drew large crowds and proved a source of inspiration to the British masses. So successful were they, indeed, that the British Government desired that other Americans of similar type should come and spread the message. In November, therefore, Dr. Buttrick returned to the United States for the purpose of organizing such a committee. Among the eminent Americans whom he per-

suaded to give several months of their time to this work
of heartening our British allies were Mr. George E. Vincent,
President of the Rockefeller Foundation, Mr. Harry Pratt
Judson, President of Chicago University, Mr. Charles
R. Van Hise, President of the University of Wisconsin,
Mr. Edwin A. Alderman, President of the University of
Virginia, Mr. Harry Emerson Fosdick, and Bishop Law-
rence of Massachusetts. It was certainly a distinguished
group, but it was the gentleman selected to be its head
that gave it almost transcendent importance in the eyes
of the British Government. This was ex-President William H. Taft. The British lay greater emphasis upon
official rank than do Americans, and the fact that an ex-
President of the United States was to head this delegation
made it almost an historic event. Mr. Taft was exceedingly busy, but he expressed his willingness to give up all
his engagements for several months and to devote his
energies to enlightening the British public about America
and its purposes in the war. An official invitation was
sent him from London and accepted.

Inasmuch as Mr. Taft was an ex-President and a
representative of the political party opposed to the one
in power, he thought it only courteous that he call upon
Mr. Wilson, explain the purpose of his mission, and obtain
his approval. He therefore had an interview with the
President at the White House; the date was December 12,
1917. As soon as Mr. Wilson heard of the proposed visit
to Great Britain he showed signs of irritation. He at
once declared that it met with his strongest disapproval.
When Mr. Taft remarked that the result of such an enterprise would be to draw Great Britain and the United States
more closely together, Mr. Wilson replied that he seriously
questioned the desirability of drawing the two countries
any more closely together than they already were. He

was opposed to putting the United States in a position of seeming in any way to be involved with British policy. There were divergencies of purpose, he said, and there were features of the British policy in this war of which he heartily disapproved. The motives of the United States in this war, the President continued, "were unselfish, but the motives of Great Britain seemed to him to be of a less unselfish character." Mr. Wilson cited the treaty between Great Britain and Italy as a sample of British statesmanship which he regarded as proving this contention. The President's reference to this Italian treaty has considerable historic value; there has been much discussion as to when the President first learned of its existence, but it is apparent from this conversation with ex-President Taft that he must have known about it on December 12, 1917, for President Wilson based his criticism of British policy largely upon this Italian convention.[1]

The President showed more and more feeling about the matter as the discussion continued. "There are too many Englishmen," he said, "in this country and in Washington now and I have asked the British Ambassador to have some of them sent home."

Mr. Wilson referred to the jealousy of France at the close relations which were apparently developing between Great Britain and the United States. This was another reason, he thought, why it was unwise to make the bonds between them any tighter. He also called Mr. Taft's attention to the fact that there were certain elements in the United States which were opposed to Great Britain— this evidently being a reference to the Germans and the

[1]As related in Chapter XXII, page 267, President Wilson was informed of the so-called "secret treaties" by Mr. Balfour, in the course of his memorable visit to the White House.

Irish—and he therefore believed that any conspicuous attempts to increase the friendliness of the two countries for each other would arouse antagonism and resentment.

As Mr. Taft was leaving he informed Mr. Wilson that the plan for his visit and that of the other speakers had originated with the American Ambassador to Great Britain. This, however, did not improve the President's temper.

"Page," said the President, "is really an Englishman and I have to discount whatever he says about the situation in Great Britain."

And then he added, "I think you ought not to go, and the same applies to the other members of the party. I would like you to make my attitude on this question known to those having the matter in charge."

Despite this rebuff Dr. Buttrick and Mr. Taft were reluctant to give up the plan. An appeal was therefore made to Colonel House. Colonel House at once said that the proposed visit was an excellent thing and that he would make a personal appeal to Mr. Wilson in the hope of changing his mind. A few days afterward Colonel House called up Dr. Buttrick and informed him that he had not succeeded. "I am sorry," wrote Colonel House to Page, "that the Buttrick speaking programme has turned out as it has. The President was decidedly opposed to it and referred to it with some feeling."

CHAPTER XXV

GETTING THE AMERICAN TROOPS TO FRANCE

A GROUP of letters, written at this time, touch upon a variety of topics which were then engaging the interest of all countries:

To Arthur W. Page

London, January 19, 1918.

DEAR ARTHUR:

While your letter is still fresh in my mind I dictate the following in answer to your question about Palestine.

It has not been settled—and cannot be, I fancy, until the Peace Conference—precisely what the British will do with Palestine, but I have what I think is a correct idea of their general attitude on the subject. First, of course, they do not propose to allow it to go back into Turkish hands; and the same can be said also of Armenia and possibly of Mesopotamia. Their idea of the future of Palestine is that whoever shall manage the country, or however it shall be managed, the Jews shall have the same chance as anybody else. Of course that's quite an advance for the Jews there, but their idea is not that the Jews should have command of other populations there or control over them—not in the least. My guess at the English wish, which I have every reason to believe is the right guess, is that they would wish to have Palestine internationalized, whatever that means. That is to say, that it should have control of its own local affairs and be a free country but that some great Power, or number of Powers, should see to it that none of the races that live there should be allowed to impose upon the other races.   I don't know just how such a guarantee can be given by the great Powers or such a responsibility assumed except by an agreement among two or three of them, or barely possibly by the English keeping control themselves; but the control by the English after the war of the former German colonies will put such a large task on them that they will not be particularly eager to extend the area of their responsibility elsewhere.   Of course a difficult problem will come up also about Constantinople and the Dardanelles. The Dardanelles must be internationalized.

I have never been able to consider the Zionist movement seriously.   It is a mere religious sentiment which will express itself in action by very few people.   I have asked a number of Jews at various times who are in favour of the Zionist movement if they themselves are going there.   They always say no.   The movement, therefore, has fixed itself in my mind as a Jewish movement in which no Jew that you can lay your hands on will ever take part but who wants other Jews to take part in it.   Of course there might be a flocking to Palestine of Jews from Russia and the adjoining countries where they are not happy, but I think the thing is chiefly a sentiment and nothing else.   Morgenthau[1] is dead right.   I agree with him *in toto*.   I do not think anybody in the United States need be the least concerned about the Zionist movement because there isn't a single Jew in our country such a fool as to go to Palestine when he can stay in the United States. The whole thing is a sentimental, religious, more or less

---

[1]Mr. Henry Morgenthau, American Ambassador to Turkey, 1913–16, an American of Jewish origin who opposed the Zionist movement as un-American and deceptive.

unnatural and fantastic idea and I don't think will ever trouble so practical a people as we and our Jews are.

The following memorandum is dated February 10, 1918:

General Bliss[1] has made a profound and the best possible impression here by his wisdom and his tact.   The British have a deep respect for him and for his opinions, and in inspiring and keeping high confidence in us he is worth an army in himself.   I have seen much of him and found out a good deal about his methods.   He is simplicity and directness itself.   Although he is as active and energetic as a boy, he spends some time by himself to think things out and even to say them to himself to see how his conclusions strike the ear as well as the mind. He has been staying here at the house of one of our resident officers.   At times he goes to his room and sits long by the fire and argues his point—out loud—oblivious to everything else.   More than once when he was so engaged one of his officers has knocked at the door and gone in and laid telegrams on the table beside him and gone out without his having known of the officer's entrance.   Then he comes out and tries his conclusion on someone who enjoys his confidence.   And then he stands by it and when the time comes delivers it slowly and with precision; and there he is; and those who hear him see that he has thought the matter out on all sides and finally.

Our various establishments in London have now become big—the Embassy proper, the Naval and Army Headquarters, the Red Cross, the War Trade Board's representatives, and now (forthwith) the Shipping Board, besides Mr. Crosby of the Treasury.   The volume of work is

---

[1]American member of the Supreme War Council.   Afterward member of the American Commission to Negotiate Peace.

enormous and it goes smoothly, except for the somewhat halting Army Headquarters, the high personnel of which is now undergoing a change; and that will now be all right. I regularly make the rounds of all the Government Departments with which we deal to learn if they find our men and methods effective, and the rounds of all our centres of activity to find whether there be any friction with the British. The whole machine moves very well. For neither side hesitates to come to me whenever they strike even small snags. All our people are at work on serious tasks and (so far as I know) there are now none of those despicable creatures here who used during our neutrality days to come from the United States on peace errands and what-not to spy on the Embassy and me (their inquiries and their correspondence were catalogued by the police). I have been amazed at the activity of some of them whose doings I have since been informed of.

We now pay this tribute to the submarines—that we have entered the period of compulsory rations. There is enough to eat in spite of the food that has gone to feed the fishes. But no machinery of distribution to a whole population can be uniformly effective. The British worker with his hands is a greedy feeder and a sturdy growler and there will be trouble. But I know no reason to apprehend serious trouble.

The utter break-up of Russia and the German present occupation of so much of the Empire as she wants have had a contrary effect on two sections of opinion here, as I interpret the British mind. On the undoubtedly enormously dominant section of opinion these events have only stiffened resolution. They say that Germany now *must* be whipped to a finish. Else she will have doubled her empire and will hold the peoples of her new territory as vassals without regard to their wishes and the war lord caste will be more firmly seated than ever before.   If her armies be literally whipped she'll have to submit to the Allies' terms, which will dislodge her from overlordship over these new unwilling subjects—and she can be dislodged in no other way.   This probably means a long war, now that after a time she can get raw materials for war later and food from Rumania and the Ukraine, etc.   This will mean a fight in France and Belgium till a decisive victory is won and the present exultant German will is broken.

The minority section of public opinion—as I judge a small minority—has the feeling that such an out-and-out military victory cannot be won or is not worth the price; and that the enemies of Germany, allowing her to keep her Eastern accretions, must make the best terms they can in the East; that there's no use in running the risk of Italy's defeat and defection before some sort of bargain could be made about Belgium, Alsace-Lorraine, and Serbia. Of course this plan would leave the German warlordship intact and would bring no sort of assurance of a prolonged peace.   It would, too, leave European Russia at least to German mercy, and would leave the Baltic and the Black Seas practically wholly under German influence.   As for the people of Russia, there seems small chance for them in this second contingency.   The only way to save them is to win a decisive victory.

As matters stand to-day Lord Lansdowne and his friends (how numerous they are nobody knows) are the loudest spokesmen for such a peace as can be made.   But it is talked much of in Asquith circles that the time may come when this policy will be led by Mr. Asquith, in a form somewhat modified from the Lansdowne formula. Mr. Asquith has up to this time patriotically supported the government and he himself has said nothing in public which could warrant linking his name with an early peace-seeking policy. But his friends openly and incessantly predict that he will, at a favourable moment, take this cue. I myself can hardly believe it. Political victory in Great Britain doesn't now lie in that direction.

The dominant section of opinion is much grieved at Russia's surrender, but they refuse to be discouraged by it. They recall how Napoleon overran most of Europe, and the French held practically none of his conquests after his fall.

Such real political danger as exists here—if any exists, of which I am not quite sure—comes not only now mainly of this split in public opinion but also and to a greater degree from the personal enemies of the present government. Lloyd George is kept in power because he is the most energetic man in sight—by far. Many who support him do not like him nor trust him—except that nobody doubts his supreme earnestness to win the war. On all other subjects he has enemies of old and he makes new ones. His intense and superb energy has saved him in two notable crises. His dismissal of Sir William Robertson[1] has been accepted in the interest of greater unity of military control, but it was a dangerous rapids that he shot, for he didn't do it tactfully. Yet there's a certain danger to the present powers in the feeling that some of them are wearing out. Parliament itself—an old one now—is thought to have gone stale. Bonar Law is overworked and tired; Balfour is often said to be too philosophical and languid; but, when this feeling seems in danger of taking definite shape, he makes a clearer statement than anybody else and catches on his feet. The man of new energy, not yet fagged, is Geddes,[2] whose frankness carries conviction.

---

[1] Sir Henry Wilson had recently succeeded Sir William Robertson as Chief of the Imperial General Staff.

[2] First Lord of the Admiralty.

To the President

London, March 17, 1918.

DEAR MR. PRESIDENT:

The rather impatient and unappreciative remarks made by the Prime Minister before a large meeting of preachers of the "free" churches about a League of Nations reminds me to write you about the state of British opinion on that subject. What Lloyd George said to these preachers is regrettable because it showed a certain impatience of mind from which he sometimes suffers; but it is only fair to him to say that his remarks that day did not express a settled opinion. For on more than one previous occasion he has spoken of the subject in a wholly different tone— much more appreciatively. On that particular day he had in mind only the overwhelming necessity to win the war— other things, *all* other things must wait. In a way this is his constant mood—the mood to make everybody feel that the only present duty is to win the war. He has been accused of almost every defect in the calendar except of slackness about the war. Nobody has ever doubted his earnestness nor his energy about *that*. And the universal confidence in his energy and earnestness is what keeps him in office. Nobody sees any other man who can push and inspire as well as he does. It would be a mistake, therefore, to pay too much heed to any particular utterance of this electrical creature of moods, on any subject.

Nevertheless, he hasn't thought out the project of a league to enforce peace further than to see the difficulties. He sees that such a league might mean, in theory at least, the giving over in some possible crisis the command of the British Fleet to an officer of some other nationality. That's unthinkable to any red-blooded son of these islands. Seeing a theoretical possibility even of raising such a question, the British mind stops and refuses to go further—refuses in most cases even to inquire seriously whether any such contingency is ever likely to come.

The British Grand Fleet, in fact, is a subject that stands alone in power and value and in difficulties. It classifies itself with nothing else. Since over and over again it has saved these islands from invasion when nothing else could have saved them and since during this war in particular it has saved the world from German conquest—as every Englishman believes—it lies in their reverence and their gratitude and their abiding convictions as a necessary and perpetual shield so long as Great Britain shall endure. If the Germans are thrashed to a frazzle (and we haven't altogether done that yet) and we set about putting the world in order, when we come to discuss Disarmament, the British Fleet will be the most difficult item in the world to dispose of. It is not only a Fact, with a great and saving history, it is also a sacred Tradition and an Article of Faith.

The first reason, therefore, why the British general mind has not firmly got hold on a league is the instinctive fear that the formation of any league may in some conceivable way affect the Grand Fleet. Another reason is the general inability of a somewhat slow public opinion to take hold on more than one subject at a time or more than one urgent part of one subject. The One Subject, of course, is winning the war. Since everything else depends on that, everything else must wait on that.

The League, therefore, has not taken hold on the public imagination here as it has in the United States. The large mass of the people have not thought seriously about it: it has not been strongly and persistently presented to the mass of the people. There is no popular or general organization to promote it. There is even, here and there, condemnation of the idea.   The (London) *Morning Post*, for example, goes out of its way once in a while to show the wickedness of the idea because, so it argues, it will involve the sacrifice, more or less, of nationality.   But the *Morning Post* is impervious to new ideas and is above all things critical in its activities and very seldom constructive.   The typical Tory mind in general sees no good in the idea.   The typical Tory mind is the insular mind.

On the other hand, the League idea is understood as a necessity and heartily approved by two powerful sections of public opinion—(1) the group of public men who have given attention to it, such as Bryce, Lord Robert Cecil, and the like, and (2) some of the best and strongest leaders of Labour.   There is good reason to hope that whenever a fight and an agitation is made for a League these two sections of public opinion will win; but an agitation and a fight must come.   Lord Bryce, in the intervals of his work as chairman of a committee to make a plan for the reorganization of the House of Lords, which, he remarked to me the other day, "involves as much labour as a Government Department," has fits of impatience about pushing a campaign for a league, and so have a few other men. They ask me if it be not possible to have good American public speakers come here—privately, of course, and in no way connected with our Government nor speaking for it—to explain the American movement for a League in order to arouse a public sentiment on the subject.

Thus the case stands at present.

Truth and error alike and odd admixtures of them come in waves over this censored land where one can seldom determine what is true, before the event, from the newspapers.   "News" travels by word of mouth, and information that one can depend on is got by personal inquiry from sources that can be trusted.

There is a curious wave of fear just now about what Labour may do, and the common gossip has it that there is grave danger in the situation. I can find no basis for such a fear. I have talked with labour leaders and I have talked with members of the government who know most about the subject. There is not a satisfactory situation—there has not been since the war began. There has been a continuous series of labour "crises," and there have been a good many embarrassing strikes, all of which have first been hushed up and settled—at least postponed. One cause of continuous trouble has been the notion held by the Unions, sometimes right and sometimes wrong, that the employers were making abnormal profits and that they were not getting their due share. There have been and are also other causes of trouble. It was a continuous quarrel even in peace times. But I can find no especial cause of fear now. Many of the Unions have had such advances of wages that the Government has been severely criticized for giving in. Just lately a large wing of the Labour Party put forth its war aims which—with relatively unimportant exceptions—coincide with the best declarations made by the Government's own spokesmen.

Of course, no prudent man would venture to make dogmatic predictions. There have been times when for brief intervals any one would have been tempted to fear that these quarrels might cause an unsatisfactory conclusion of the war. But the undoubted patriotism of the British workman has every time saved the situation. While a danger point does lie here, there is no reason to be more fearful now than at any preceding time when no especial trouble was brewing. This wave of gossip and fear has no right to sweep over the country now.

Labour hopes and expects and is preparing to win the next General Election—whether with good reason or not

I cannot guess. But most men expect it to win the Government at some time—most of them *after* the war. I recall that Lord Grey once said to me, before the war began, that a general political success of the Labour Party was soon to be expected.

Another wave which, I hear, has swept over Rome as well as London is a wave of early peace expectation.   The British newspapers have lately been encouraging this by mysterious phrases.   Some men here of good sense and sound judgment think that this is the result of the so-called German "peace offensive," which makes the present the most dangerous period of the war.

W. H. P.

To David F. Houston[1]

London, March 23, 1918.

MY DEAR HOUSTON:

It is very kind of you indeed to write so generously about the British visitors who are invading our sacred premises, such as the Archbishop of York, and it is good to hear from you anyhow about any subject and I needn't say that it is quite a rare experience also.   I wish you would take a little of your abundant leisure and devote it to good letters to me.

And in some one of your letters tell me this.—The British send over men of this class that you have written about to see us, but they invite over here—and we permit to come—cranks on prohibition, experts in the investigation of crime, short-haired women who wish to see how British babies are reared, peace cranks and freaks of other kinds.[2] Our Government apparently won't let plain,

---

[1] Secretary of Agriculture.
[2] See Chapter XXIV.

honest, normal civilians come over, but if a fellow comes along who wants to investigate some monstrosity then one half of the Senate, one half of the House of Representatives, and a number of the executive offices of the Government give him the most cordial letters.   Now there are many things, of course, that I don't know, but it has been my fate to have a pretty extensive acquaintance with cranks of every description in the United States.   I don't think there is any breed of them that didn't haunt my office while I was an editor.   Now I am surely punished for all my past sins by having those fellows descend on me here.   I know them, nearly all, from past experience and now just for the sake of keeping the world as quiet as possible I have to give them time here far out of proportion to their value.

Now, out of your great wisdom, I wish you would explain to me why the deuce we let all this crew come over here instead of sending a shipload of perfectly normal, dignified, and right-minded gentlemen.   These thug reformers!—Baker will be here in a day or two and if I can remember it I am going to suggest to him that he round them all up and put them in the trenches in France where those of them who have so far escaped the gallows ought to be put.

I am much obliged to have the illuminating statement about our crops.   I am going to show it to certain gentlemen here who will be much cheered by it.   By gracious, you ought to hear their appreciation of what we are doing! We are not doing it for the sake of their appreciation, but if we were out to win it we could not do it better.   Down at bottom the Englishman is a good fellow.   He has his faults but he doesn't get tired and he doesn't suffer spasms of emotion.

Give my love to Mrs. Houston, and do sit down and

From a painting by Irving R. Wiles

Admiral William Sowden Sims, Commander of American naval
forces operating in European waters during the Great War

A silver model of the *Mayflower*, the farewell gift of the Plymouth
Council to Mr. Page

write me a good long letter—a whole series of them, in fact.

Believe me, always most heartily yours,

WALTER HINES PAGE.

To Frank L. Polk

London, March 22, 1918.

DEAR MR. POLK:

You are good enough to mention the fact that the Embassy has some sort of grievance against the Department. Of course it has, and you are, possibly, the only man that can remove it. It is this: You don't come here to see the war and this government and these people who are again saving the world as we are now saving them. I thank Heaven and the Administration for Secretary Baker's visit. It is a dramatic moment in the history of the race, of democracy, and of the world. The State Department has the duty to deal with foreign affairs—the especial duty—and yet no man in the State Department has been here since the war began. This doesn't look pretty and it won't look pretty when the much over-worked "future historian" writes it down in a book. Remove that grievance.

The most interesting thing going on in the world to-day —a thing that in History will transcend the war and be reckoned its greatest gain—is the high leadership of the President in formulating the struggle, in putting its aims high, and in taking the democratic lead in the world, a lead that will make the world over—and in taking the democratic lead of the English-speaking folk. Next most impressive to that is to watch the British response to that lead. Already they have doubled the number of their voters, and even more important definite

steps in Democracy will be taken. My aim—and it's
the only way to save the world—is to lead the British
in this direction. They are the most easily teachable
people in our way of thinking and of doing. Of
course everybody who works toward such an aim
provokes the cry from a lot of fools among us who
accuse him of toadying to the English and of "accepting
the conventional English conclusion." They had as
well talk of missionaries to India accepting Confucius
or Buddha. Their fleet has saved us four or five times.
It's about time we were saving them from this bloody
Thing that we call Europe, for our sake and for
theirs.

The bloody Thing will get us all if we don't fight our
level best; and it's only by *our* help that we'll be saved.
That clearly gives us the leadership. Everybody sees
that. Everybody acknowledges it. The President authoritatively speaks it—speaks leadership on a higher level
than it was ever spoken before to the whole world. As
soon as we get this fighting job over, the world procession
toward freedom—our kind of freedom—will begin under
our lead. This being so, can't you delegate the writing of
telegrams about "facilitating the license to ship poppy
seed to McKesson and Robbins," and come over and see
big world-forces at work?

I cannot express my satisfaction at Secretary Baker's
visit. It was historic—the first member of the Cabinet,
I think, who ever came here while he held office. He
made a great impression and received a hearty welcome.

That's the only grievance I can at the moment unload
on you. We're passing out of our old era of isolation.
These benighted heathen on this island whom we'll yet
save (since they are well worth saving) will be with us as

we need them in future years and centuries.   Come, help us heighten this fine spirit.

Always heartily yours,

WALTER HINES PAGE.

P. S. You'd see how big our country looks from a distance.   It's gigantic, I assure you.

The above letter was written on what was perhaps the darkest day of the whole war.   The German attack on the Western Front, which had been long expected, had now been launched, and, at the moment that Page was penning this cheery note to Mr. Polk, the German armies had broken through the British defenses, had pushed their lines forty miles ahead, and, in the judgment of many military men, had Paris almost certainly within their grasp.   A great German gun, placed about seventy miles from the French capital, was dropping shells upon the apparently doomed city.   This attack had been regarded as inevitable since the collapse of Russia, which had enabled the Germans to concentrate practically all their armies on the Western Front.

The world does not yet fully comprehend the devastating effect of this apparently successful attack upon the allied morale.   British statesmen and British soldiers made no attempt to conceal from official Americans the desperate state of affairs.   It was the expectation that the Germans might reach Calais and thence invade England.   The War Office discussed these probabilities most freely with Colonel Slocum, the American military attaché. The simple fact was that both the French and the British armies were practically bled white.

"For God's sake, get your men over!" they urged General Slocum.   "You have got to finish it."

Page was writing urgently to President Wilson to the same purpose. Send the men and send them at once. "I pray God," were his solemn words to Mr. Wilson, "that you will not be too late!"

One propitious event had taken place at the same time as the opening of the great German offensive. Mr. Newton D. Baker, the American Secretary of War, had left quietly for France in late February, 1918, and had reached the Western Front in time to obtain a first-hand sight of the great March drive. No visit in history has ever been better timed, and no event could have better played into Page's hands. He had been urging Washington to send all available forces to France at the earliest possible date; he knew, as probably few other men knew, the extent to which the Allies were depending upon American troops to give the final blow to Germany; and the arrival of Secretary Baker at the scene of action gave him the opportunity to make a personal appeal. Page immediately communicated with the Secretary and persuaded him to come at once to London for a consultation with British military and political leaders. The Secretary spent only three days in London, but the visit, brief as it was, had historic consequences. IIe had many consultations with the British military men; he entered into their plans with enthusiasm; he himself received many ideas that afterward took shape in action, and the British Government obtained from him first-hand information as to the progress of the American Army and the American determination to coöperate to the last man and the last dollar. "Baker went straight back to France," Page wrote to his son Arthur, "and our whole coöperation began."

Page gave a dinner to Mr. Baker at the Embassy on March 23rd—two days after the great March drive had begun. This occasion gave the visitor a memorable glimpse of the British temperament.   Mr. Lloyd George, Mr. Balfour, Lord Derby, the War Secretary, General Biddle, of the United States Army, and Admiral Sims were the Ambassador's guests.   Though the mighty issues then overhanging the world were not ignored in the conversation the atmosphere hardly suggested that the existence of the British Empire, indeed that of civilization itself, was that very night hanging in the balance.   Possibly it was the general sombreness of events that caused these British statesmen to find a certain relief in jocular small talk and reminiscence.   For the larger part of the evening not a word was said about the progress of the German armies in France.   Mr. Lloyd George and Mr. Balfour, seated on opposite sides of the table, apparently found relaxation in reviewing their political careers and especially their old-time political battles.   They would laughingly recall occasions when, in American parlance, they had put each other "in a hole"; the exigencies of war had now made these two men colleagues in the same government, but the twenty years preceding 1914 they had spent in political antagonism.   Page's guests on this occasion learned much political history of the early twentieth century, and the mutual confessions of Mr. Lloyd George and Mr. Balfour gave these two men an insight into each others' motives and manœuvres which was almost as revealing.   "Yes, you caught me that time," Mr. Lloyd George would say, and then he would counter with an episode of a political battle in which he had got the better of Mr. Balfour.   The whole talk was lively and bantering, and accompanied with much laughter; and all this time shells from that long-distance gun were dropping at fifteen minute intervals upon the devoted women and children of Paris and the Germans were every hour driving the British back in disorder.   At times the conversation took a more philosophic turn. Would the men present like to go back twenty-five years and live their lives all over again? The practically unanimous decision of every man was that he would not wish to do so.

All this, of course, was merely on the surface; despite the laughter and the banter, there was only one thing which engrossed the Ambassador's guests, although there were not many references to it. That was the struggle which was then taking place in France. At intervals Mr. Lloyd George would send one of the guests, evidently a secretary, from the room. The latter, on his return, would whisper something in the Prime Minister's ear, but more frequently he would merely shake his head. Evidently he had been sent to obtain the latest news of the battle.

At one point the Prime Minister did refer to the great things taking place in France.

"This battle means one thing," he said. "That is a generalissimo."

"Why couldn't you have taken this step long ago?" Admiral Sims asked Mr. Lloyd George.

The answer came like a flash.

"If the cabinet two weeks ago had suggested placing the British Army under a foreign general, it would have fallen. Every cabinet in Europe would also have fallen, had it suggested such a thing."

Memorandum on Secretary Baker's visit

Secretary Baker's visit here, brief as it was, gave the heartiest satisfaction. So far as I know, he is the first member of an American Cabinet who ever came to England while he held office, as Mr. Balfour was the first member of a British Cabinet who ever went to the United States while he held office. The great governments of the English-speaking folk have surely dealt with one another with mighty elongated tongs. Governments of democracies are not exactly instruments of precision. But they are at least human. But personal and human neglect of one another by these two governments over so long a period is an astonishing fact in our history. The wonder is that we haven't had more than two wars. And it is no wonder that the ignorance of Englishmen about America and the American ignorance of England are monumental, stupendous, amazing, passing understanding. I have on my mantelpiece a statuette of Benjamin Franklin, an excellent and unmistakable likeness which was made here during his lifetime; and the inscription burnt on its base is *Geo. Washington.* It serves me many a good turn with my English friends. I use it as a measure of their ignorance of us. Of course this is a mere little error of a statuette-maker, an error, moreover, of a hundred years ago. But it tells the story of to-day also. If I had to name the largest and most indelible impression that has been made on me during my five years' work here, I should say the ignorance and aloofness of the two peoples—not an ignorance of big essential facts but of personalities and temperaments—such as never occur except between men who had never seen one another.

But I was writing about Mr. Baker's visit and I've got a long way from that. I doubt if he knows himself what gratification it gave; for these men here have spoken to me about it as they could not speak to him.

Here is an odd fact: For sixty years, so far as I know, members of the Administration have had personal acquaintance with some of the men in power in Salvador, Costa Rica, Venezuela, Peru, etc., etc., and members of the British Government have had personal acquaintance with some men in authority in Portugal, Serbia, Montenegro and Monte Carlo; but during this time (with the single exception of John Hay) I think no member of any Administration had a real personal acquaintance while he held office with any member of the British Government while he held office, and vice versa—till Mr. Balfour's visit. Suspicion grows out of ignorance. The longer I live here the more astonished I become at the fundamental ignorance of the British about us and of our fundamental ignorance about them. So colossal is this ignorance that every American sent here is supposed to be taken in, to become Anglophile; and often when one undertakes to enlighten Englishmen about the United States one becomes aware of a feeling inside the English of unbelief, as if he said, "Oh, well! you are one of those queer people who believe in republican government." All this is simply amazing. Poor Admiral Sims sometimes has a sort of mania, a delusion that nobody at Washington trusts his judgment because he said seven or eight years ago that he liked the English. Yet every naval officer who comes here, I understand, shares his views about practically every important naval problem or question. I don't deserve the compliment (it's a very high one) that some of my secretaries sometimes pay me when they say that I am the only man they know who tries to tell the whole truth to our Government in favour of the Englishman as well as against him. It is certain that American public opinion is universally supposed to suspect any American who tries to do anything with the British lion except to twist his tail—a supposition that I never believed to be true.—But it is true that the mutual ignorance is as high as the Andes and as deep as the ocean. Personal acquaintance removes it and nothing else will.

To Arthur W. Page

American Embassy,
London, April 7, 1918.

DEAR ARTHUR:

I daresay you remember this epic:

Old Morgan's wife made butter and cheese;
  Old Morgan drank the whey.
There came a wind from West to East
  And blew Old Morgan away.

I'm Old Morgan and your mother got ashamed of my wheyness and made the doctor prescribe cream for me. There's never been such a luxury, and anybody who supposes that I am now going to get fat and have my cream stopped simply doesn't know me. So, you see why I'm intent on shredded wheat biscuits. That's about the best form of real wheat that will keep. And there's no getting real wheat-stuff, pure and simple, in any other form.

There's no use in talking about starving people—except perhaps in India and China. White men can live on anything. The English could fight a century on cabbage and Brussels sprouts. I've given up hope of starving the Germans. A gut of dogmeat or horse flesh and a potato will keep them in fighting trim forever. I've read daily for two years of impending starvation across the Rhine; but I never even now hear of any dead ones from hunger. Cold steel or lead is the only fatal dose for them.

Therefore I know that shredded wheat will carry me through.

You'll see, I hope, from the clippings that I enclose that I'm not done for yet anyhow. Two speeches a day is no small stunt; and I did it again yesterday—hand running; and I went out to dinner afterward. It was a notable occasion—this celebration of the anniversary of our coming into the war.[1]

Nobody here knows definitely just what to fear from the big battle; but everybody fears more or less. It's a critical time—very. I am told that that long-range gunning of Paris is the worst form of frightfulness yet tried. The shells do not kill a great many people. But their falling every fifteen minutes gets on people's nerves and they can't sleep. I hear they are leaving Paris in great numbers. Since the big battle began and the Germans have needed all their planes and more in France, they've let London alone. But nobody knows when they will begin again.

Nobody knows any future thing about the war, and everybody faces a fear.

Secretary Baker stayed with me the two days and three nights he was here. He made a good impression but he received a better one. He now knows something about the war. I had at dinner to meet him:

Lloyd George, Prime Minister.
Balfour, Foreign Secretary.
The Chief of Staff.
Lord Derby, War Secretary.
General Biddle, U. S. A., in command in London.
Admiral Sims, U. S. N.

The talk was to the point—good and earnest. Baker went straight back to France and our *whole* coöperation began. With the first group of four he had conferences besides for two days. His coming was an admirable move.

Yours affectionately,

W. H. P.

---

[1]This meeting, on April 6, 1918, was held at the Mansion House. Page and Mr. Balfour were the chief speakers.

To Ralph W. Page

London, April 13, 1918.

DEAR RALPH:

Your cheery letters about entertaining governors, planting trees and shrubbery and your mother's little orchard give us much pleasure. The Southern Pines paper brings news of very great damage to the peach crop. I hope it is much exaggerated. Is it?

We haven't any news here, and I send you my weekly note only to keep my record clear. The great battle—no one talks or thinks of anything else. We have suffered and still suffer a good deal of fear and anxiety, with real reason, too. But the military men are reassuring. Yet I don't know just how far to trust their judgment or to share their hopes. Certainly this is the most dangerous situation that modern civilization was ever put in. If we can keep them from winning any *great* objective, like Paris or a channel port, we ought to end the war this year. If not, either they win or at the least prolong the war indefinitely. It's a hazardous and trying time.

There were never such casualties on either side as now. Such a bloody business cannot keep up all summer. But before everybody is killed or a decisive conclusion is reached, the armies will, no doubt, dig themselves in and take a period of comparative rest. People here see and feel the great danger. But the extra effort now *may* come too late. Still we keep up good hope. The British are hard to whip. They never give up. And as for the French army, I always remember Verdun and keep my courage up.

The wounded are coming over by the thousand. We are incomparably busy and in great anxiety about the result (though still pretty firm in the belief that the Germans will lose), and luckily we keep very well.

Affectionately,

W. H. P.

To Ralph W. Page

London, April 7, 1918.

DEAR RALPH:

There used to be a country parson down in Wake County who, when other subjects were talked out, always took up the pleasing topic of saving your soul. That's the way your mother and I do—with the subject of going home. We talk over the battle, we talk over the boys, we talk over military and naval problems, we discuss the weather and all the babies, and then take up politics, and talk over the gossip of the wiseacres; but we seldom finish a conversation without discussing going home. And we reach just about as clear a conclusion on our topic as the country parson reached on his. I've had the doctors going over me (or rather your mother has) as an expert accountant goes over your books; and I tried to bribe them to say that I oughtn't to continue my arduous duties here longer. They wouldn't say any such thing. Thus that device failed—dead. It looks as if I were destined for a green old age and no martyr business at all.

All this is disappointing; and I don't see what to do but to go on. I can't keep from hoping that the big battle may throw some light on the subject; but there's no telling when the big battle will end. Nothing ends—that's the trouble. I sometimes feel that the war may never end, that it may last as the Napoleonic Wars did, for 20 years; and before that time we'll all have guns that shoot 100 miles. We can stay at home and indefinitely bombard the enemy across the Rhine—have an endless battle at long range.

So, we stick to it, and give the peach trees time to grow up.

We had a big day in London yesterday—the anniversary of our entry into the war. I send you some newspaper clippings about it.

The next best news is that we have a little actual sunshine—a very rare thing—and some of the weather is now almost decent. . . .

Affectionately,

W. H. P.

CHAPTER XXVI

LAST DAYS IN ENGLAND

IN SPITE of the encouraging tone of the foregoing letters, everything was not well with Page. All through the winter of 1917–1918 his associates at the Embassy had noticed a change for the worse in his health. He seemed to be growing thinner; his face was daily becoming more haggard; he tired easily, and, after walking the short distance from his house to his Embassy, he would drop listlessly into his chair. His general bearing was that of a man who was physically and nervously exhausted. It was hoped that the holiday at St. Ives would help him; that he greatly enjoyed that visit, especially the westward —homeward—outlook on the Atlantic which it gave him, his letters clearly show; there was a temporary improvement also in his health, but only a temporary one. The last great effort which he made in the interest of the common cause was Secretary Baker's visit; the activities which this entailed wearied him, but the pleasure he obtained from the resultant increase in the American participation made the experience one of the most profitable of his life. Indeed, Page's last few months in England, though full of sad memories for his friends, contained little but satisfaction for himself. He still spent many a lonely evening by his fire, but his thoughts were now far more pleasurable than in the old *Lusitania* days. The one absorbing subject of contemplation now was that America was "in." His country had justified his deep confidence. The American Navy had played a determining part in defeating the submarine, and American shipyards were turning out merchant ships faster than the Germans were destroying them. American troops were reaching France at a rate which necessarily meant the early collapse of the German Empire. Page's own family had responded to the call and this in itself was a cause of great contentment to a sick and weary man. The Ambassador's youngest son, Frank, had obtained a commission and was serving in France; his son-in-law, Charles G. Loring, was also on the Western Front; while from North Carolina Page's youngest brother Frank and two nephews had sailed for the open battle line. The bravery and success of the American troops did not surprise the Ambassador but they made his last days in England very happy.

Indeed, every day had some delightful experience for Page. The performance of the Americans at Cantigny especially cheered him. The day after this battle he and Mrs. Page entertained Mr. Lloyd George and other guests at lunch. The Prime Minister came bounding into the room with his characteristic enthusiasm, rushed up to Mrs. Page with both hands outstretched and shook hands joyously.

"Congratulations!" he exclaimed. "The Americans have done it! They have met the Prussian guard and defeated them!"

Mr. Lloyd George was as exuberant over the achievement as a child.

This was now the kind of experience that had become Page's daily routine. Lively as were his spirits, however, his physical frame was giving way. In fact Page, though he did not know it at the time, was suffering from a specific disease—nephritis; and its course, after Christmas of 1917, became rapid. His old friend, Dr. Wallace Buttrick, had noted the change for the worse and had attempted to persuade him to go home.

"Quit your job, Page," he urged. "You have other big tasks waiting you at home. Why don't you go back?"

"No—no—not now."

"But, Page," urged Dr. Buttrick, "you are going to lay down your life."

"I have only one life to lay down," was the reply. "I can't quit now."

To Mary E. Page[1]

London, May 12, 1918.

DEAR MARY:

You'll have to take this big paper and this paint brush pen—it's all the pen these blunt British have. This is to tell you how very welcome your letter to Alice is—how *very* welcome, for nobody writes us the family news and nothing is so much appreciated. I'll try to call the shorter roll of us in the same way:

After a miserable winter we, too, are having the rare experience of a little sunshine in this dark, damp world of London. The constant confinement in the city and *in the house* (that's the worst of it—no outdoor life or fresh air) has played hob with my digestion. It's not bad, but it's troublesome, and for some time I've had the feeling of being one half well. It occurred to me the other day that I hadn't had leave from my work for four years, except my short visit home nearly two years ago. I asked for two months off, and I've got it. We are going down by the shore where there is fresh air and where I can live outdoors and get some exercise. We have a house that we can get there and be comfortable. To get away from London

---

[1] Of Aberdeen, N. C., the Ambassador's sister.

when the weather promises to be good, and to get away from people seemed a joyous prospect. I can, at any time I must, come to London in two hours.

The job's too important to give up at this juncture. This, then, is the way we can keep it going. I've no such hard task now as I had during the years of our neutrality, which, praise God! I somehow survived, though I am now suffering more or less from the physical effects of that strain. Yet, since I have had the good fortune to win the confidence of this Government and these people, I feel that I ought to keep on now until some more or less natural time to change comes.

Alice keeps remarkably well—since her influenza late in the winter; but a rest away from London is really needed as much by her as by me. They work her to death. In a little while she is to go, by the invitation of the Government and the consent of the King, to christen a new British warship at Newcastle. It will be named the "Eagle." Meantime I'll be trying to get outdoor life at Sandwich.

Yesterday a regiment of our National Army marched through the streets of London and were reviewed by the King and me; and the town made a great day of it. While there is an undercurrent of complaint in certain sections of English opinion because we didn't come into the war sooner, there is a very general and very genuine appreciation of everything we have done and of all that we do. Nothing could be heartier than the welcome given our men here yesterday. Nor could any men have made a braver or better showing than they made. They made us all swell with pride.

They are coming over now, as you know, in great quantities. There were about 8,000 landed here last week and about 30,000 more are expected this week. I think that many more go direct to France than come through England. On their way through England they do not come to London. Only twice have we had them here, yesterday and one day last summer when we had a parade of a regiment of engineers. For the *army* London is on a sidetrack—is an out of the way place. For our navy, of course, it's the European headquarters, since Admiral Sims has his headquarters here. We thus see a good many of our sailors who are allowed to come to London on leave. A few days ago I had a talk with a little bunch of them who came from one of our superdreadnaughts in the North Sea. They had just returned from a patrol across to the coast of Norway. "Bad luck, bad luck," they said, "on none of our long patrol trips have we seen a single Hun ship!"

About the war, you know as much as I know. There is a general confidence that the Allies will hold the Germans in their forthcoming effort to get to Calais or to Paris. Yet there is an undercurrent of fear. Nobody knows just how to feel about it. Probably another prodigious onslaught will be made before you receive this letter. It seems to me that we can make no intelligent guess until this German effort is finished in France—no guess about the future. If the Germans get the French ports (Calais, for example) the war will go on indefinitely. If they are held back, it *may* end next autumn or winter —partly because of starvation in Germany and partly because the Germans will have to confess that they can't whip our armies in France. But, even then, since they have all Russia to draw on, they may keep going for a long time. One man's guess is as good as another's.

One sad thing is certain: we shall at once begin to have heavy American casualties. Our Red Cross and our army here are getting hospitals ready for such American wounded as are brought over to England—the parts of our army that are fighting with the British.

We have a lot of miserable politics here which interfere with the public feeling. The British politician is a worse yellow dog than the American—at times he is, at least; and we have just been going through such a time. Another such time will soon come about the Irish.

Well, we have an unending quantity of work and wear —no very acute bothers but a continuous strain, the strain of actual work, of uneasiness, of seeing people, of uncertainty, of great expense, of doubt and fear at times, of inability to make any plans—all which is only the common lot now all over the world, except that most persons have up to this time suffered incomparably worse than we. And there's nothing to do but to go on and on and on and to keep going with the stoutest hearts we can keep up till the end do at last come. But the Germans now (as the rest of us) are fighting for their lives. They are desperate and their leaders care nothing for human life.

The Embassy now is a good deal bigger than the whole State Department ever was in times of peace. I have three buildings for offices, and a part of our civil force occupies two other buildings. Even a general supervision of so large a force is in itself a pretty big job. The army and the Navy have each about the same space as the Embassy proper. Besides, our people have huts and inns and clubs and hospitals all over the town. Even though there be fewer vexing problems than there were while we were neutral, there is not less work—on the contrary, more. Nor will there be an end to it for a very long time—long after my time here. The settling of the war and the beginning of peace activities, whenever these come, will involve a great volume of work. But I've no ambition to have these things in hand. As soon as a natural time of relief shall come, I'll go and be happier in my going than you or anybody else can guess.

Now we go to get my digestion stiffened up for another long tug—unless the Germans proceed forthwith to knock us out—which they cannot do.

With my love to everybody on the Hill,

Affectionately yours,

W. H. P.

Mr. and Mrs. Waldorf Astor—since become Viscount and Viscountess Astor—had offered the Pages the use of their beautiful seaside house at Sandwich, Kent, and it was the proposed vacation here to which Page refers in this letter. He obtained a six weeks' leave of absence and almost the last letters which Page wrote from England are dated from this place. These letters have all the qualities of Page at his best: but the handwriting is a sad reminder of the change that was progressively taking place in his physical condition. It is still a clear and beautiful script, but there are signs of a less steady hand than the one that had written the vigorous papers of the preceding four years.

Memorandum

Sandwich, Kent, Sunday, 19 May, 1918.

We're at Rest Harrow and it's a fine, sunny early spring Carolina day. The big German drive has evidently begun its second phase. We hear the guns distinctly. We see the coast-guard aeroplanes at almost any time o' day. What is the mood about the big battle?

The soldiers—British and French—have confidence in their ability to hold the Germans back from the Channel and from Paris. Yet can one rely on the judgment of soldiers? They have the job in hand and of course they believe in themselves. While one does not like in the least to discount their judgment and their hopefulness, for my part I am not *quite* so sure of their ability to make sound judgments as I wish I were. The chances are in favour of their success; but—suppose they should have to yield and give up Calais and other Channel ports? Well, they've prepared for it as best they can. They have made provision for commandeering most of the hotels in London that are not yet taken over—for hospitals for the wounded now in France.

And the war would take on a new phase. Whatever should become of the British and American armies, the Germans would be no nearer having England than they now are. They would not have command of the sea. The combined British and American fleets could keep every German ship off the ocean and continue the blockade by sea—indefinitely; and, if the peoples of the two countries hold fast, a victory would be won at last—at sea.

To Ralph W. Page

Rest Harrow, Sandwich, Kent.
May 19, 1918.

DEAR RALPH:

I felt very proud yesterday when I read T. R.'s good word in the *Outlook* about your book.[1] If I had written what he said myself—I mean, if I had written what *I* think of the book—I should have said this very thing. And there is one thing more I should have said, viz.:—All your life and all my life, we have cultivated the opinion at home that we had nothing to do with the rest of the

---

[1] "Dramatic Moments in American Diplomacy," by Ralph W. Page, 1918.

world, nothing to do with Europe in particular—and in
our political life our hayseed spokesmen have said this
over and over again till many people, perhaps most people,
came really to believe that it was true. Now this aloofness, this utterly detached attitude, was a pure invention
of the shirt-sleeve statesman at home. I have long concluded, for other reasons as well as for this, that these men
are the most ignorant men in the whole world; more ignorant—because they are viciously ignorant—than the Negro
boys who act as caddies at Pinehurst; more ignorant than
the inmates of the Morganton Asylum; more ignorant
than sheep or rabbits or idiots. They have been the
chief hindrances of our country—worse than traitors, in
effect. It is they, in fact, who kept our people ignorant
of the Germans, ignorant of the English, ignorant of our
own history, ignorant of ourselves. Now your book,
without mentioning the subject, shows this important
fact clearly, by showing that our aloofness has all been a
fiction. *We've been in the world—and right in the middle
of the world—the whole time.*

And our public consciousness of this fact has enormously
slipped back. Take Franklin, Madison, Monroe, Jefferson; take Hay, Root—and then consider some of our
present representatives! One good result of the war and
of our being in it will be the restoration of our foreign consciousness. Every one of the half million, or three million,
soldiers who go to France will know more about foreign
affairs than all Congress knew two years ago.

A stay of nearly five years in London (five years ago
to-day I was on the ship coming here) with no absence
long enough to give any real rest, have got my digestion
wrong. I've therefore got a real leave for two months.
Your mother and I have a beautiful house here that has
been lent to us, right on the Channel where there's nothing

worth bombing and where as much sunshine and warmth come as come anywhere in England. We got here last night and to-day is as fine an early spring day as you ever had in the Sandhills. I shall golf and try to find me an old horse to ride, and I'll stay out in the sunshine and try to get the inside machinery going all right. We may have a few interruptions, but I hope not many, if the Germans leave us alone. Your mother has got to go to Newcastle to christen a new British warship—a compliment the Admiralty pays her "to bind the two nations closer together" etc. etc. And I've got to go to Cambridge to receive an LL. D. for the President. Only such things are allowed to interrupt us. And we are very much hoping to see Frank here.

We are in sound of the battle. We hear the big guns whenever we go outdoors. A few miles down the beach is a rifle range and we hear the practice there. Almost any time of day we can hear aeroplanes which (I presume) belong to the coast guard. There's no danger of forgetting the war, therefore, unless we become stone deaf. But this decent air and sunshine are blessings of the highest kind. I never became so **tired** of anything since I had the measles as I've become of London.

My Lord! it sounded last night as if we had jumped from the frying pan into the fire. Just as we were about to go to bed the big gun on the beach—just outside the fence around our yard—about 50 yards from the house, began its thundering belch—five times in quick succession, rattling the windows and shaking the very foundation of things. Then after a pause of a few minutes, another round of five shots. Then the other guns all along the beach took up the chorus—farther off—and the inland guns followed. They are planted all the way to London —ninety miles. For about two hours we had this roar

and racket.   There was an air raid on, and there were
supposed to be twenty-five or thirty German planes on
their way to London.   I hear that it was the worst raid
that London has had.   Two of them were brought down
—that's the only good piece of news I've heard about it.
Well, we are not supposed to be in danger.   They fly over
us on the way to bigger game.   At any rate I'll take the
risk for this air and sunshine.   Trenches and barbed wire
run all along the beach—I suppose to help in case of an
invasion.   But an invasion is impossible in my judgment.
Holy Moses! what a world!—the cannon in the big battle
in France roaring in our ears all the time, this cannon at
our door likely to begin action any night and all the rest
along the beach and on the way to London, and this is
what we call rest!   The world is upside down, all crazy,
all murderous; but we've got to stop this barbaric assault,
whatever the cost.

Ray Stannard Baker is spending a few days with us,
much to our pleasure.

    With love to Leila and the babies,

Yours affectionately,

W. H. P.

To Arthur W. Page

Rest Harrow, Sandwich Beach,
Sandwich, Kent, England.
May 20, 1918.

DEAR ARTHUR:

    . . .   I can't get quite to the bottom of the anti-
English feeling at Washington.   God knows, this people
have their faults.   Their social system and much else here
is mediæval.   I could write several volumes in criticism
of them.   So I could also in criticism of anybody else.

But Jefferson's[1] letter is as true to-day as it was when he wrote it. One may or may not have a lot of sentiment about it; but, without sentiment, it's mere common sense, mere prudence, the mere instinct of safety to keep close to Great Britain, to have a decent respect for the good qualities of these people and of this government. Certainly it is a mere perversity—lost time—lost motion, lost everything—to cherish a dislike and a distrust of them —a thing that I cannot wholly understand. While we are, I fear, going to have trade troubles and controversies, my feeling is, on the whole, in spite of the attitude of our official life, that an increasing number of our people are waking up to what England has done and is and may be depended on to do. Isn't that true?

We've no news here. We see nobody who knows anything. I am far from strong—the old stomach got tired and I must gradually coax it back to work. That's practically my sole business now for a time, and it's a slow process. But it's coming along and relief from seeing hordes of people is as good as medicine.

Affectionately,

W. H. P.

To the President

Sandwich, May 24, 1918.

DEAR MR. PRESIDENT:

Your speeches have a cumulative effect in cheering up the British. As you see, if you look over the mass of newspaper clippings that I send to the Department, or have them looked over, the British press of all parties and

---

[1] The reference is to a letter written in 1823 by Thomas Jefferson to President Monroe at the time when the Holy Alliance was threatening the independence of South America. "With Great Britain," Jefferson wrote, "we should most sedulously cherish a cordial friendship and nothing would tend more to knit our affections than to be fighting once more, side by side, in the same cause."

shades of opinion constantly quote them approvingly and gratefully. They have a cumulative effect, too, in clearing the atmosphere. Take, for instance, your declaration in New York about standing by Russia. All the allied governments in Europe wish to stand by Russia, but their pressing business with the war, near at hand, causes them in a way to forget Russia; and certainly the British public, all intent on the German "drive" in France had in a sense forgotten Russia. You woke them up. And your "Why set a limit to the American Army?" has had a cheering effect. As leader and spokesman of the enemies of Germany—by far the best trumpet-call spokesman and the strongest leader—your speeches are worth an army in France and more, for they keep the proper moral elevation. All this is gratefully recognized here. Public opinion toward us is wholesome and you have a "good press" in this Kingdom. In this larger matter, all is well. The English faults are the failings of the smaller men—about smaller matters—not of the large men nor of the public, about large matters.

In private, too, thoughtful Englishmen by their fears pay us high tribute. I hear more and more constantly such an opinion as this: "You see, when the war is over, you Americans will have much the largest merchant fleet. You will have much the largest share of money, and England and France and all the rest of the world will owe you money. You will have a large share of essential raw materials. You will have the machinery for marine insurance and for foreign banking. You will have much the largest volume of productive labour. And you will know the world as you have never known it before. What then is going to become of British trade?"

The best answer I can give is: "Adopt American methods of manufacture, and the devil take the hindmost. There will be for a long time plenty for everybody to do; and let us make sure that we both play the game fairly: that's the chief matter to look out for." That's what I most fear in the decades following the end of the war—trade clashes.

The Englishman's pride will be hurt. I recall a speech made to me by the friendliest of the British—Mr. Balfour himself: "I confess that as an Englishman it hurts my pride to have to borrow so much even from you. But I will say that I'd rather be in your debt than in anybody else's."

To Edward M. House

May 27, 1918.

MY DEAR HOUSE:

. . . I can write in the same spirit of the Labour Group which left for home last week. Nobody has been here from our side who had a better influence than they. They emphatically stuck by their instructions and took pleasure, against the blandishments of certain British Socialists, in declaring against any meeting with anybody from the enemy countries to discuss "peace-by-negotiation" or anything else till the enemy is whipped. They made admirable speeches and proved admirable representatives of the bone and sinew of American manhood. They had dead-earnestness and good-humour and hard horse-sense.

This sort of visit is all to the good. Great good they do, too, in the present English curiosity to see and hear the right sort of frank, candid Americans. Nobody who hasn't been here lately can form an idea of the eagerness of all classes to hear and learn about the United States. There never was, and maybe never will be again, such a chance to inform the British and—to help them toward a right understanding of the United States and our people.

We are not half using the opportunity. There seems to be a feeling on your side the ocean that we oughtn't to send men here to "lecture" the British. No typical, earnest, sound American who has been here has "lectured" the British. They have all simply told facts and instructed them and won their gratitude and removed misconceptions. For instance, I have twenty inquiries a week about Dr. Buttrick. He went about quietly during his visit here and talked to university audiences and to working-men's meetings and he captured and fascinated every man he met. He simply told them American facts, explained the American spirit and aims and left a grateful memory everywhere. Buttrick cost our Government nothing: he paid his own way. But if he had cost as much as a regiment it would have been well spent. The people who heard him, read American utterances, American history, American news in a new light. And most of his talk was with little groups of men, much of it even in private conversation. He did no orating or "lecturing." A hundred such men, if we had them, would do more for a perfect understanding with the British people than anything else whatsoever could do.

Yours sincerely,
WALTER H. PAGE.

To Arthur W. Page

Sandwich, May 27, 1918.

DEAR ARTHUR:

. . . I do get tired—my Lord! how tired!—not of the work but of the confinement, of the useless things I have to spend time on, of the bad digestion that has overtaken me, of London, of the weather, of absence from you all—of the general breaking up of the world, of this mad slaughter of men. But, after all, this is the common lot now and I am grateful for a chance to do what I can. That's the true way to look at it.

. . . Worry? I don't worry about anything except the war in general and this mad world so threatened by these devil barbarians. And I have a feeling that, when we get a few thousand flying machines, we'll put an end to that, alas! with the loss of many of our brave boys. I hear the guns across the channel as I write—an unceasing boom! boom! boom! That's what takes the stuff out of me and gets my inside machinery wrong. Still, I'm gradually getting even that back to normal. Golf and the poets are fine medicine. I read Keats the other day, with entire forgetfulness of the guns. Here we have a comfortable house, our own servants (as many as we need), a beautiful calm sea, a perfect air and for the present ideal weather. There's nobody down here but Scottish soldiers. We've struck up a pleasant acquaintance with them; and some of the fellows from the Embassy come down week ends. Only the murderous guns keep their eternal roar.

Thanks, thanks, a thousand thanks, old man. It'll all work out right.

. . . I look at it in this way: all's well that ends well. We are now doing our duty. That's enough. These things don't bother me, because doing our duty now is worth a million years of past errors and shortcomings.

Your mother's well and spry—very, and the best company in the world. We're having a great time.

Bully for the kids! Kiss 'em for me and Mollie too.

Affectionately,

W. H. P.

Make Shoecraft tell you everything. He's one of the best boys and truest in the world.

To Ralph W. Page

Rest Harrow, Sandwich, Kent.
June 7, 1918.

MY DEAR RALPH:

. . . I have all along cherished an expectation of two things—(1) That when we did get an American Army by conscription, if it should remain at war long enough to learn the game, it would become the best army that the world ever saw, for the simple reason that its ranks would contain more capable men than any other country has ever produced. The proof of this comes at once. Even our new and raw troops have astonished the veterans of the French and British armies and (I have no doubt) of the German Army also. It'll be our men who will whip the Germans, and there are nobody else's men who could do it. We've already saved the Entente from collapse by our money. We'll save the day again by our fighting men. That is to say, we'll save the world, thank God; and I fear it couldn't have been saved in any other way. (2) Since the people by their mood command and compel efficiency, the most efficient people will at last (as recent events show) get at the concrete jobs, in spite of anybody's preferences or philosophy. And this seems at last to be taking place. What we have suffered and shall suffer is not failure but delays and delays and bunglings. But they've got to end by the sheer pressure of the people's earnestness. These two things, then, are all to the good.

I get the morning papers here at noon. And to-day I am all alone. Your mother went early on her journey to launch a British battleship. I haven't had a soul to speak to all day but my servants. At noon, therefore, I was rather eager for the papers. I saw at a glance that a submarine is at work off the New Jersey coast! It's an awful thing for the innocent victims, to be drowned. But their deaths have done us a greater service than 100 times as many lives lost in battle. If anybody lacked earnestness about the war, I venture to guess that he doesn't lack it any longer. If the fools would now only shell some innocent town on the coast, the journey to Berlin would be shortened.

If the Germans had practised a chivalrous humanity in their war for conquest, they'd have won it. Nothing on earth can now save them; for the world isn't big enough to hold them and civilized people. Nor is there any room for pacifists till this grim business is done.

Affectionately,
W. H. P.

The last piece of writing from Sandwich is the following memorandum:

Sandwich, Kent.
June 10, 1918.

The Germans continue to gain ground in France—more slowly, but still they gain. The French and British papers now give space to plans for the final defense—the desperate defense—of Paris. The Germans are only forty miles away. Slocum, military attaché, thinks they will get it and he reports the same opinion at the War Office—because the Germans have taken such a large number of guns and so much ammunition. Some of these guns were meant for the American troops, and they cannot now be replaced in time if the German advance continues. But I do not know enough facts at first hand to form an opinion. But, if Paris be taken, the war will go on a long time —unless the English-speaking rulers make a compromise. And, then, in another form—and forms—it'll go on indefinitely.—There has been no more perilous or uncertain or anxious time than now.

The United States too late, too late, too late: what if it should turn out so?

But it did not turn out so.   Even while Page was penning these lines great events were taking place in France and the American troops were having a large share in them.   In June the Americans stopped the German troops at Belleau Wood—a battle which proved the mettle of these fresh levies not only for the benefit of the Germans but of the Allies as well.   Thus Page had the great satisfaction of returning to London while the city was ringing with the praise of these achievements.   He found that the atmosphere had materially changed since he had last been in the British capital; when he had left for Sandwich there had been a general expectation that the Germans would get Paris or the Channel ports; now, however, there was every confidence of victory.   Greatly as Page rejoiced over the new prospect, however, the fight at Belleau Wood brought him his last great sorrow.   His nephew, Allison M. Page, of Aberdeen, North Carolina, the son of his youngest brother, Frank, lost his life in that engagement.   At first the young man was reported "missing"; the investigation set afoot by the Ambassador for some time brought no definite information.   One of the most pathetic of Page's papers is a brief note addressed by him to Allison Page, asking him for news: "It's been a long time since we heard from you," Page wrote his nephew.   "Write how it goes with you.   Affectionately, Uncle Wat."   After travelling over a considerable part of France, this note found its way back to the Embassy.   The boy—he was only 19—had been killed in action near Belleau Wood, on June 25th, while leading his detachment in an attack on a machine gun.   Citations and decorations for gallantry in action were given posthumously by General Pershing, Marshal Pétain, Major-General Omar Bundy, and Major-General John A. LeJeune.

And now the shadows began to close in rapidly on Page. In early July Major Frank C. Page, the Ambassador's youngest son, came over from France. A brief glance at his father convinced him that he was dying. By this time the Ambassador had ceased to go to the Chancery, but was transacting the most imperative business propped up in a chair at home. His mind was possessed by two yearnings: one was to remain in London until the end of the war, the other was to get back to his childhood home in North Carolina. Young Page urged his father to resign, but the weary invalid insisted on sticking to his post. On this point it seemed impossible to move him. Knowing that his brother Arthur had great influence with his father, Frank Page cabled, asking him to come to England immediately. Arthur took the first boat, reaching London late in July.

The Ambassador's two sons then gently pressed upon their father the fact that he must resign. Weak as he was, the Ambassador was still obdurate.

"No," he said. "It's quitting on the job. I must see the war through. I can't quit until it's over."

But Sir William Osler, Page's physician and devoted friend, exercised his professional authority and insisted on the resignation. Finally Page consented.

To the President

American Embassy, London,
August 1, 1918.

My dear Mr. President:

I have been struggling for a number of months against the necessity to write you this note; for my doctors now advise me to give up all work for a period—my London doctor says for six months. I have a progressive digestive trouble which does not yield to the usual treatment. It's the war, five London winters, and the unceasing labour which is now the common lot. I am ashamed to say that these have brought me to something near a breakdown. I have had Sir William Osler as well as two distinguished London physicians for several months. The digestive trouble has brought other ills in its train; and I am assured that they will yield to freedom from responsibility and complete rest for a time in a dry, warm climate and that they are not likely to yield to anything else.

I see nothing else to do then but to bow to the inevitable and to ask you to be kind enough to relieve me and to accept my resignation to take effect as soon as I can go to Washington and make a somewhat extended report on the work here, which, I hope, will be of some use to the Department; and I ought to go as soon as possible—say, in September. I cannot tell you how great my disappointment is that this request has become necessary.

If the world and its work were so organized that we could do what we should like to do, I should like a leave of absence till winter be broken and then to take up my duties here again till the war end. But that, of course, is impracticable. And it is now a better time to change Ambassadors than at any time since the war began. My five years' service has had two main phases—the difficult period of our neutrality and the far easier period since we came into the war. But when the war ends, I fear that there will be again more or less troublesome tasks arising out of commercial difficulties.

But for any reasonable period the Embassy's work fortunately can now go on perfectly well with Mr. Laughlin as Chargé—until my successor can get here. The Foreign Office like him, he is *persona grata* to all other Departments of the Government, and he has had a long experience; and he is most conscientious and capable. And the organization is in excellent condition.

I venture to ask you to have a cable message sent to me (to be deciphered by me alone). It will require quite a little time to pack up and to get away.

I send this, Mr. President, with more regret than I can express and only after a struggle of more than six months to avoid it.

Yours sincerely,

WALTER H. PAGE.

Arthur Page took his father to Banff, in Scotland, for a little rest in preparation for the voyage. From this place came Page's last letter to his wife:

To Mrs. Page

Duff House, Banff, Scotland.
Sunday, September 2, 1918.

MY DEAR:

. . . I've put the period of our life in London, in my mind, as closed. That epoch is ended. And I am glad. It was time it ended. My job (*that* job) is done. From the letters that Shoecraft has sent me and from what the papers say, I think I couldn't have ended it more happily —or at a better time. I find myself thinking of the winter down South—of a Thanksgiving Day dinner for the older folks of our family, of a Christmas tree for the kids, of frolics of all sorts, of Rest, of some writing (perhaps not much), going over my papers with Ralph—that's what he wants, you know; etc., etc., etc.——

And I've got to eat more. *I* myself come into my thinking and planning in only two ways—(1) I'm going to have a suit like old Lord N.'s and (2) I'm going to get all the good things to eat that there are!

Meantime, my dear, how are you? Don't you let this getting ready wear you out. Let something go undone rather. Work Miss Latimer and the boys and the moving and packing men, and Petherick and the servants. Take it very easy yourself.

Nine and a half more days here—may they speed swiftly. Comfortable as I am, I'm mortal tired of being away from you—dead tired.

Praise God it's only 9½ days. If it were 9¾, I should not stand it, but break for home prematurely.

Yours, dear Allie, with all my love,

W. H. P.

On August 24th came the President's reply:

I have received your communication of August 1st. It caused me great regret that the condition of your health makes it necessary for you to resign. Under the circumstances I do not feel I have the right to insist on such a sacrifice as your remaining in London. Your resignation is therefore accepted. As you request it will take effect when you report to Washington. Accept my congratulations that you have no reason to fear a permanent impairment of your health and that you can resign knowing that you have performed your difficult duties with distinguished success.

WOODROW WILSON.

The news of Page's resignation inspired tributes from the British press and from British public men such as have been bestowed upon few Americans. The London *Times* headed its leader "A Great Ambassador" and this note was echoed in all sections of Great Britain. The part of Page's career which Englishmen chiefly recalled was his attitude during the period of neutrality. This, the newspapers declared, was Page's great contribution to the cause. The fact that it had had such far-reaching influences on history was the one especially insisted on. His conciliatory and skillful behaviour had kept the United States and Great Britain friends at a time when a less tactful ambassador might easily have made them enemies; the result was that, when the time came, the United States could join forces against the common enemy, with results that were then daily unfolding on the battlefields of France. "I really believe," wrote the Marquess of Crewe, "that there were several occasions when we might have made it finally impossible for America to join us in the war; that these passed by may have been partly due to some glimmering of common sense on our part, with Grey as its main exponent; but it was more largely owing to your patience and courtesy and to the certainty which the Foreign Office always enjoyed that its action would be set before the Secretary of State in as favourable a light as it conscientiously could be." That, then, was Page's contribution to the statesmanship of this crisis—that of holding the two countries together so that, when the time came, the United States could join the Allies. A mass of private letters, all breathing the same sentiment, began to pour in on Page. There was hardly an illustrious name in Great Britain that was not represented among these leave-takings. As illustrating the character and spirit animating them, the following selections are made:

From the King

The information communicated to me yesterday through Mr. Laughlin of Your Excellency's resignation of the Post of Ambassador and the cause of this step fill me with the keenest regret. During your term of office in days of peace and of war your influence has done much to strengthen the ties of friendship and good-will which unite the two English-speaking nations of the world. I trust your health will soon be restored and that we may have the pleasure of seeing you and Mrs. Page before your departure.

GEORGE R. I.

From the Prime Minister

10, Downing Street, Whitehall, S. W. 1,
30th August, 1918.

MY DEAR AMBASSADOR:

It is with the deepest regret that my colleagues and I have received the news that you have been forced by ill health to resign your office and that the President has consented to your relinquishing your ambassadorial duties. We are sorry that you are leaving us, all the more because your tenure of office has coincided with one of the greatest epochs in the history of our two countries and of the world, and because your influence and counsel throughout this difficult time have been of the utmost value to us all.

The power for good or evil which can be exerted by the occupant of your high position is at all times necessarily very great. That our peoples are now fighting side by side in the cause of human freedom and that they are manifesting an ever growing feeling of cordiality to one another is largely attributable to the exceptional wisdom and good-will with which you have discharged your duties. For the part you have played during the past five years in bringing about this happy result we owe you our lasting gratitude.

May I add that while you have always firmly presented the point of view of your own country, you have succeeded in winning, not only the respect and admiration of official circles, but the confidence, and I can say without hesitation, the affection of all sections of our people? It will be with universal regret that they will learn that, owing to the strain of the great responsibilities you have borne, you are no longer to remain among us. I earnestly trust that a well-earned rest will speedily restore you to complete health, and that you have many years of public service still in store for you.

I should like also to say how much we shall miss Mrs. Page. She has won a real place in all our hearts. Through her unfailing tact, her genuine kindliness, and her unvarying readiness to respond to any call upon her time and energy, she has greatly contributed to the success of your ambassadorship.

Ever sincerely,

D. LLOYD GEORGE.

From Viscount Grey of Fallodon

Glen Innerleithen, Scotland.
September 2, 1918.

DEAR MR. PAGE:

I have been out of touch with current events for a few days, but yesterday I read the two articles in the *Times* on your retirement. I am very grieved to think that you are going. There was not a word of eulogy in the *Times* articles that was not under rather than over-stated, and reflecting thus I thought how rare it is in public life to have an occasion that justifies the best that can be said. But it is so now, and I am filled with deep regret that you are going and with deep gratitude that you came to us and were here when the war broke out and subsequently. If the United States had been represented here by any one less decided as to the right and wrong of the war and less firm and courageous than yourself, the whole of the relations between your country and ours would have been in peril. And if the two countries had gone apart instead of coming together the whole fate of the world would be very different from what I hope it will now be.

I have often thought that the forces behind public affairs are so tremendous that individuals have little real, even when much apparent, influence upon the course of events. But in the early years of the war I think everything might have gone wrong if it had not been that certain men of strong moral conviction were in certain places. And you were preëminently one of these. President Wilson I am sure was another, though I know him only through you and Colonel House and his own public utterances. Even so your influence must have counted in his action, by your friendship with him as well as by the fact of your being the channel through which communications passed between him and us.

I cannot adequately express what it was to me personally in the dark days of 1914, 1915, and 1916 to know how you felt about the great issues involved in the war.

I go to Fallodon at the end of this week and come to London the first week of September—if you and Mrs. Page have not left by then I hope I may see you. I long to do so before you go. I wish you may recover perfect health. My eyesight continues to fail and I shall soon be absolutely dependent upon other eyes for reading print. Otherwise I feel as well as a schoolboy, but it is depressing to be so well and yet so crippled in sight.

Please do not trouble to answer this letter—you must have too many letters of the kind to be able to reply to them separately—but if there is a chance of my seeing

you before you go please let me have a message to say
when and where.

Yours sincerely,

GREY OF F.

A few months before his resignation Page had received
a letter from Theodore Roosevelt, who was more familiar
than most Americans with Page's work in London.   This
summed up what will be probably the judgment of history
upon his ambassadorship.   The letter was in reply to one
written to the Ex-President, asking him to show hospitality to the Archbishop of York,[1] who was about to visit the
United States.

(Office of the Metropolitan Magazine)
342 Fourth Ave., New York,
March 1st, 1918.

MY DEAR MR. AMBASSADOR:
I am very much pleased with your letter, and as soon
as the Archbishop arrives, he will be addressed by me
with all his titles, and I will get him to lunch with me or
dine with me, or do anything else he wishes!   I shall do it
for his own sake, and still more, my dear fellow, I shall do
it for the sake of the Ambassador who has represented
America in London during these trying years as no other
Ambassador in London has ever represented us, with the
exception of Charles Francis Adams, during the Civil
War.

Faithfully yours,

THEODORE ROOSEVELT.

The seriousness of Page's condition was not understood
in London; consequently there were many attempts to do

[1] See Vol. II, page 307.

him honour in which he was unable to participate. Cus-
tom demands that a retiring Ambassador shall go to
Windsor Castle to dine and to sleep; but King George,
who was very solicitous about Page's health, offered to
spare the Ambassador this trip and to come himself to
London for this leave-taking. However, Page insisted on
carrying out the usual programme; but the visit greatly
tired him and he found it impossible personally to take
part in any further official farewells. The last ceremony
was a visit from the Lord Mayor and Council of Plymouth,
who came to the Ambassador's house in September to present the freedom of the city. Ever since Page's speech of
August 4, 1917, Plymouth had been planning to do him this
honour; when the Council heard that the Ambassador's
health would make it impossible for him to visit Plymouth,
they asked if they might not come to London. The proceeding was most impressive and touching and the Ambassador's five-minute speech, the last one which he made in
England, had all his old earnestness and mental power,
though the physical weakness of the man saddened everybody present. The Lord Mayor presented the freedom
of the ancient borough in a temporary holder, explaining
that a more permanent receptacle would follow the Ambassador to America. When this arrived, it proved to be
a beautiful silver model of the *Mayflower*. Certainly
there could have been no more appropriate farewell gift
to Page from the English town whose name so closely
links the old country with the United States.

The last scene took place at Waterloo Station. Sir
Arthur Walsh came representing the King, while Mr.
Balfour, Lord Robert Cecil, and other ministers represented the cabinet. The Government had provided a
special railway carriage, and this was stationed at a convenient place as Page's motor drew up. So weak was

the Ambassador that it was with difficulty that his companions, the ever devoted Mr. Laughlin, on one side, and Page's secretary, Mr. Shoecraft, on the other, succeeded in supporting him to his chair. Mr. Balfour, Lord Robert Cecil and the others then entered the carriage, and, with all that sympathetic dignity in which Englishmen of this type excel, said a few gracious and affectionate words of good-bye. They all stood, with uncovered heads, as the train slowly pulled out of the station, and caught their final glimpse of Page as he smiled at them and faintly waved his hand.

Perhaps the man most affected by this leave-taking was Mr. Balfour. He knew, as did the others, that that frail and emaciated figure had been one of the greatest friends that Britain had had at the most dreadful crisis in her history. He has many times told of this parting scene at Waterloo Station and always with emotion.

"I loved that man," he once said to an American friend, recalling this event. "I almost wept when he left England."

CHAPTER XXVII

THE END

PAGE came home only to die. In fact, at one time it seemed improbable that he would live to reach the United States. The voyage of the *Olympic*, on which he sailed, was literally a race with death. The great-hearted Captain, Sir Bertram Hayes, hearing of the Ambassador's yearning to reach his North Carolina home, put the highest pressure upon his ship, which almost leaped through the waves. But for a considerable part of the trip Page was too ill to have much consciousness of his surroundings. At times he was delirious; once more he lived over the long period of "neutrality"; again he was discussing intercepted cargoes and "notes" with Sir Edward Grey; from this his mind would revert to his English literary friends, and then again he was a boy in North Carolina. The *Olympic* reached New York more than a day ahead of schedule; Page was carried down the gangplank on a stretcher, propped up with pillows; and since he was too weak then to be taken to his Southern home, he was placed temporarily in St. Luke's Hospital. Page arrived on a beautiful sunshiny October day; Fifth Avenue had changed its name in honour of the new Liberty Loan and had become the "Avenue of the Allies"; each block, from Forty-second Street north, was decorated with the colours of one of the nations engaged in the battle against Germany; the street was full of Red Cross workers and other picturesquely clad enthusiasts selling Liberty Bonds; in its animated beauty and in its inspiring signi-

404

ficance it formed an appropriate setting for Page's home-coming.

The American air seemed to act like a tonic on Page; in a short time he showed such improvement that his recovery seemed not impossible. So far as his spirits and his mind were concerned, he became his old familiar self. He was able to see several of his old friends, he read the newspapers and discussed the international situation with his customary liveliness. With the assistance of his daughter, Mrs. Loring, he even kept track of his correspondence. Evidently the serious nature of his illness was not understood, for invitations to speak poured in from all quarters. Most of these letters Mrs. Loring answered, but there was one that Page insisted on attending to himself. The City of Cleveland was organizing some kind of a meeting dedicated to closer relations with Great Britain, and the Mayor wrote Page asking him to speak. The last thing which Page wrote with his own hand was his reply to this invitation; and it is an impressive fact that his final written word should have dealt with the subject that had been so close to his heart for the preceding five years.

To Harry L. Davis, Mayor of Cleveland, Ohio

I deeply regret my health will not permit me to attend any public function for some time to come; for I deeply appreciate your invitation on behalf of the City of Cleveland for the meeting on December 7th, and have a profound sympathy with its purpose to bring the two great English-speaking worlds as close together as possible, so that each shall thoroughly understand the courage and sacrifice and ideals of the other. This is the greatest political task of the future. For such a complete and lasting understanding is the only basis for the continued progress of civilization.   I am proud to be associated in your thought, Mr. Mayor, with so fitting and happy an occasion, and only physical inability could cause absence.

Sincerely,

WALTER H. PAGE.

Page's improvement was only temporary; a day or two after this letter was written he began to sink rapidly; it was therefore decided to grant his strongest wish and take him to North Carolina.   He arrived in Pinehurst on December 12th, so weak that his son Frank had to carry him in his arms from the train.

"Well, Frank," said Page, with a slightly triumphant smile, "I did get here after all, didn't I?"

He lingered for a few days and died, at eight o'clock in the evening, on December 21st, in his sixty-fourth year. He suffered no pain.   He was buried in the Page family plot in the Bethesda Cemetery near Aberdeen.

He was as much of a war casualty as was his nephew Allison Page, who lost his life with his face to the German machine guns in Belleau Wood.

THE END

APPENDIX

PAGE was not methodical in keeping diaries. His documents, however, reveal that he took many praiseworthy resolutions in this direction. They include a large number of bulky books, each labelled "Diary" and inscribed with the year whose events were to be recorded. The outlook is a promising one; but when the books are opened they reveal only fragmentary good intentions. Entries are kept up for a few days, and then the work comes to an end. These volumes contain many scraps of interesting writing, however, which are worth preserving; some of them are herewith presented in haphazard fashion, with no attempt at order in subject matter.

1913

PETHERICK

PETHERICK: may he be immortal; for he is a man who has made of a humble task a high calling; and without knowing it he has caused a man of a high calling to degrade it to a mean level. Now Petherick is a humble Englishman, whose father many years ago enjoyed the distinction of carrying the mail pouch to and from the post office for the American Embassy in London. As father, so son. Petherick succeeded Petherick. In this remote period (*the* Petherick must now be 60) Governments had "despatch agents," men who distributed mail and whatnot, sent it on from capital to capital—were a sort of general "forwarding" factotums. The office is really out of date now. Telegraph companies, express companies, railway companies, the excellent mail service and the like out-despatch any conceivable agent—except Petherick. Petherick has qualities that defy change, such as an unfailing courtesy, a genuine joy in serving his fellows, the very genius of helpfulness. Well, since a governmental office once established acquires qualities of perpetuity, three United States despatch agents have survived the development of modern communication, one in London, one in New York, and the third (I think) in San Francisco. At any rate, the London agent remains.

Now in the beginning the London despatch agent was a mail messenger (as I understand) for the Embassy. He still takes the pouch to the post office, and brings it back. In ordinary times, that's all he does for the Embassy, for which his salary of about * * * is paid by the State Department—too high a salary for the labour done, but none too high for the trustworthy qualities required. If this had been all that Petherick did, he would probably have long ago gone to the scrap heap. It is one mark of a man of genius that he always makes his job. So Petherick. The American Navy came into being and parts of it come to this side of the world. Naval officers need help when they come ashore. Petherick was always on hand with despatches and mail for them, and Petherick was a handy man. Did the Captain want a cab? Petherick had one waiting. Did the Captain want rooms? Such-and-such a hotel was the proper one for him. Rooms were engaged. Did the Captain's wife need a maid? Petherick had thought of that, too. Then a Secretary from some continental legation wished to know a good London tailor.

He sought Petherick. An American Ambassador from the continent came to London. London yielded Petherick for his guidance and his wants. Petherick became omnipresent, universally useful—an American institution in fact. A naval officer who had been in Asiatic waters was steaming westward to the Mediterranean. His wife and three babies came to London, where she was to meet her husband, who was to spend several weeks here. A telegram to Petherick: they needed to do nothing else. When the lady arrived a furnished flat, a maid and a nurse and a cook and toys awaited her. When her husband arrived, a pair of boots awaited him from the same last that his last pair had been made on, in London, five years before. At some thoughtful moment $1,000 was added to Petherick's salary by the Navy Department; and a few years ago a handsome present was made to Petherick by the United States Naval Officers all over the world.

But Petherick, with all his virtues, is merely an Englishman, and it is not usual for an Englishman to hold a $3,000 office under appointment from the United States Government. The office of despatch agent, therefore, has been nominally held by an American citizen in London. This American citizen for a good many years has been Mr. Crane, a barrister, who simply turns over the salary to Petherick; and all the world, except the Secretary of State, knows that Petherick is Petherick and there is none other but him.

Now comes the story: Mr. Bryan, looking around the world for offices for his henchmen, finds that one Crane has been despatch agent in London for many years, and he writes me a personal and confidential letter, asking if this be not a good office for some Democrat!

I tell the story to the Naval Attaché! He becomes

riotous. He'll have to employ half a dozen clerks to do
for the Navy ill what Petherick does well with ease, if he's
removed. Life would not be worth living anyhow. I
uncover Petherick to the Secretary and show him in his
glory. It must be said to the Secretary's credit that he
has said nothing more about it. Petherick, let us hope,
will live forever. The Secretary's petty-spoils mind now
works on grand plans for Peace, holy Peace, having unsuccessfully attacked poor Petherick. And Petherick
knows nothing about it and never dreams of an enemy in
all the world, and in all naval and diplomatic life he has
only fast friends. If Mr. Bryan had removed him, he
might have made a temporary friend of one Democrat
from Oklahoma, and lasting enemies of all that Democrat's rivals and of the whole naval and diplomatic service.

November, 1914.

We have to get away from it—or try to—a minute at a
time; and the comic gods sometimes help us. Squier[1] has
a junior officer here to hold his desk down when he's gone.
He's a West Point Lieutenant with a German name.
His study is ordnance. A new kind of bomb gives him
the same sort of joy that a new species would have given
Darwin. He was over in France—where the armies had
passed to and from Paris—and one day he found an un-
exploded German bomb of a new sort. The thing weighed
half a ton or thereabouts, and it was loaded. Somehow
he got it to London—I never did hear how. He wrapped
it in blankets and put it under his bed. He went out of
town to study some other infernal contraption and the
police found this thing under his bed. The War Office
took it and began to look for him—to shoot him, the

---

[1]Colonel (now Major General) George O. Squier, Military Attaché at the
American Embassy.

bomb-harbouring German! They soon discovered, of course, that he was one of our men and an officer in the United States Army. Then I heard of it for the first time. Here came a profuse letter of apology from the Government; they had not known the owner was one of my attachés. Pardon, pardon—a thousand apologies. But while this letter was being delivered to me one of the under-secretaries of the Government was asking one of our secretaries, "In Heaven's name, what's the Ambassador going to do about it? We have no right to molest the property of one of your attachés, but this man's room is less than 100 yards from Westminster Abbey: it might blow up half of London. We can't give the thing back to him!" They had taken it to the Duck Pond, wherever that is. About that time the Lieutenant came back. His pet bomb gone—what was I going to do about it?

The fellow actually wanted to bring it to his office in the Embassy!

"Look here, Lieutenant, besides the possibility of blow-up this building and killing every mother's son of us, consider the scandal of the American Embassy in London blown up by a German bomb. That would go down in the school histories of the United States. Don't you see?" No, he didn't see instantly—he does so love a bomb! I had to threaten to disown him and let him be shot before he was content to go and tell them to unload it—he *would* have it, unloaded, if not loaded.

Well, I had to write half a dozen letters before the thing was done for. He thinks me a chicken-livered old coward and I know much more about him than I knew before; and we are at peace. The newspapers never got the story, but his friends about town still laugh at him for trying first to blow up Westminister Abbey and then his own Ambassador. He was at my house at dinner the other night and one of the ladies asked him: "Lieutenant, have you any darling little pet lyddite cartridges in your pocket?" Think of a young fellow who just loves bombs! Has loaded bombs for pets! How I misspent my youth!

February, 1915.

This is among the day's stories: The British took a ship that had a cargo of 100,000 busts of Von Hindenburg—filled with copper.

Another: When Frederick Watts was painting Lord Minto he found it hard to make the portrait please him. When he was told that Lord Minto liked it and Lady Minto didn't and that So-and-So praised it, he exclaimed: "I don't care a d—n what anyone thinks about it—except a fellow named Sargent."

And the King said (about the wedding[1]): "I have the regulation of the dress to be worn at all functions in the Chapel Royal. I, therefore, declare that the American Ambassador may have any dress worn that he pleases!"

E. M. House went to Paris this morning, having no peace message from this Kingdom whatever. This kind of talk here now was spoken of by the Prime Minister the other day "as the twittering of a sparrow in a tumult that shakes the world."

Lady P. remarked to me to-day, as many persons do, that I am very fortunate to be Ambassador here at this particular time. Perhaps; but it isn't easy to point out precisely wherein the good fortune consists. This much is certain: it is surely a hazardous occupation now. Henry James remarked, too, that nobody could afford to miss the experience of being here—nobody who could be here. Perhaps true, again; but I confess to enough shock and horror to keep me from being so very sure of that. Yet

---

[1]The wedding of Mr. Page's daughter at the Chapel Royal.

no other phenomenon is more noticeable than the wish of every sort of an American to be here. I sometimes wonder whether the really well-balanced American does. Most of them are of the overwrought and excitable kinds.

A conservative lady, quite conscientious, was taken down to dinner by Winston Churchill. Said she, to be quite frank and fair: "Mr. Churchill, I must tell you that I don't like your politics. Yet we must get on together. You may say, if you like, that this is merely a matter of personal taste with me, as I might not like your—well, your moustache." "I see no reason, Madam, why you should come in contact with either."

My talk with Bonar Law: He was disposed to believe that if England had declared at once that she would go to war with Germany if France was attacked, there would have been no war. Well, would English opinion, before Belgium was attacked, have supported a government which made such a declaration?

Mr. Bonar Law thinks that President Wilson ought to have protested about Belgium.

He didn't agree with me that much good human material goes to waste in this Kingdom for lack of opportunity. (That's the Conservative in him.)

Friday, April 30, 1915.

Sir Edward Grey came to tea to talk with Mr. House and me—little talk of the main subject (peace), which is not yet ripe by a great deal. Sir Edward said the Germans had poisoned wells in South Africa. They have lately used deadly gases in France. The key to their mind says Sir Edward, is this—they attribute to other folk what they are thinking of doing themselves.

While Sir Edward was here John Sargent came in and brought Katharine the charcoal portrait of her that he had made—his present to her for her and Chud to give to W. A. W. P.[1] and me. A very graceful and beautiful thing for him to do.

April 30, 1915.

Concerning Peace: The German civil authorities want peace and so does one faction of the military party. But how can they save their face? They have made their people believe that they are at once the persecuted and the victorious. If they stop, how can they explain their stopping? The people might rend them. The ingenious loophole discovered by House is— mere moonshine, viz., the freedom of the seas in war. That is a one-sided proposition unless they couple with it the freedom of the land in war also, which is nonsense. Nothing can be done, then, until some unfavourable military event brings a new mind to the Germans. Peace talk, therefore, is yet mere moonshine. House has been to Berlin, from London, thence to Paris, then back to London again—from Nowhere (as far as peace is concerned) to Nowhere again.

May 3, 1915.

Why doesn't the President make himself more accessible? Dismiss X and get a bigger man? Take his cabinet members really into his confidence? Everybody who comes here makes these complaints of him!

We dined to-night at Y's. Professor M. was there, etc. He says we've got to have polygamy in Europe after the war to keep the race up.

Friday, May 21, 1915.

Last night the Italian Parliament voted to give the Government war-powers; and this means immediate war

---

[1] Mrs. Page.

on the side of the Allies. There are now eight nations fighting against Germany, Austria, and Turkey; viz., Great Britain, France, Russia, Italy, Japan, Belgium, Serbia, Montenegro. And it looks much as if the United States will be forced in by Germany.

The British Government is wrestling with a very grave internal disruption—to make a Coalition Government. The only portfolios that seem absolutely secure are the Prime Minister's and the Foreign Secretary's (Sir Edward Grey's)—for which latter, many thanks. The two-fold trouble is—(1) a difference between Churchill (First Lord of the Admiralty) and Lord Fisher—about the Dardanelles campaign and (I dare say) other things, and (2) Lord Kitchener's failure to secure ammunition—"to organize the industries of the Kingdom." Some even declare K. of K. (they now say Kitchener of Kaos) is a general colossal failure. But the prevailing opinion is that his raising of the new army has been good work but that he has failed with the task of procuring munitions. As for Churchill, he's too restless and erratic and dictatorial and fussy and he runs about too much. I talked with him at dinner last night at his mother's. He slips far down in his chair and swears and be-dams and by-Gods his assertions. But his energy does interest one. An impromptu meeting in the Stock Exchange to-day voted confidence in K. of K. and burned up a copy of the *Daily Mail*, which this morning had a severe editorial about him.

Washington, having sent a severe note to Germany, is now upbraided for not sending another to England, to match and pair it. That's largely German influence, but also the Chicago packers and the cotton men. These latter have easy grievances, like the Irish. The delays of the British Government are exasperating, but they are really not so bad now as they have been. Still, the President can be influenced by the criticism that he must hit one side every time he hits the other, else he's not neutral! I am working by every device to help the situation and to prevent another note. I proposed to-day to Sir Edward Grey that his Government make an immediate advance payment on the cotton that it proposes to buy.

Unless Joffre be a man of genius—of which there are some indications—and unless French also possibly have some claim to this distinction and *perhaps* the Grand Duke Nikolas, there doesn't yet seem to be a great man brought forth by the war. In civil life, Sir Edward Grey comes to a high measure. As we yet see it from this English corner of the world, no other statesman now ranks with him.

March 20, 1916.

I am sure I have the best secret service that could be got by any neutral. I am often amazed at its efficiency. It is good because it is not a secret—certainly not a spy service at all. It is all aboveboard and it is all done by men of high honour and good character—I mean the Embassy staff. Counting the attachés there are about twenty good men, every one of whom moves in a somewhat different circle from any other one. Every one cultivates his group of English folk, in and out of official life, and his group in the diplomatic corps. There isn't a week but every man of them sees his particular sources of information—at their offices, at the Embassy, at luncheon, at dinner, at the clubs—everywhere. We all take every possible occasion to serve our friends and they serve us. The result is, I verily believe, that we hear more than any other group in London. These young fellows are all keen as razors. They know when to be silent, too; and they are trusted as they deserve to be. Of course I see them, singly or in pairs, every day in the regular conduct of the work of the Embassy; and once a week we all meet together and go over everything that properly comes before so large a "cabinet" meeting. Thus some of us are on confidential terms with somebody in every department of the Government, with somebody in every other Embassy and Legation, with all the newspapers and correspondents—even with the censors. And the wives of those that are married are abler than their husbands. They are most attractive young women—welcome everywhere—and indefatigable. Mrs. Page has them spend one afternoon a week with her, rolling bandages; and that regular meeting always yields something else. They come to my house Thursday afternoons, too, when people always drop in to tea—visitors from other countries, resident Americans, English—everybody—sometimes one hundred.

Nobody in this company is a "Spy"—God forbid! I know no more honourable or attractive group of ladies and gentlemen. Yet can conceive of no organization of spies who could find out as many things. And the loyalty of them all! Somebody now and then prefaces a revelation with the declaration, "This is in strict confidence—absolutely nobody is to hear it." The answer is—"Yes, only, you know, I have no secrets from the Ambassador: no member of his staff can ever have."—Of course, we get some fun along with our tragedies. If I can find time, for instance, I am going to write out for House's amusement a verbatim report of every conversation that he held in London. It has all come to me—from what he said to the King down; and it all tallies with what House himself told me. He went over it all himself to me the other day at luncheon.—I not only believe—I am sure—that in this

way I do get a correct judgment of public feeling and
public opinion, from Cabinet Ministers to stock-brokers.

December 11, 1916.

The new Government is quite as friendly to us in its
intentions as the old, and much more energetic. The old
Government was a spent force. Mr. Balfour is an agreeable man to deal with, with a will to keep our sympathy,
unless the dire need of ships forces him to unpleasantness.
The Prime Minister is—American in his ways. Lord
Robert has the old Cecil in him, and he's going to maintain
the blockade at any cost that he can justify to himself
and to public opinion, and the public opinion is with him.
They are all eager to have American approval—much
more eager, I think, than a large section of public opinion,
which has almost ceased to care what Americans think
or do. The more we talk about peace, the more they
think about war. There is no vindictiveness in the
English. They do not care to do hurt to the German
people: they regard them as misguided and misled. But
no power on earth can stop the British till the German
military caste is broken—that leadership which attacked
Belgium and France and would destroy England. Balfour, Lloyd George, the people, the army and the navy
are at one in this matter, every labouring man, everybody,
except a little handful of Quakers and professors and Noel
Buxton. I think I know and see all the peace men. They
feel that they can talk to me with safety. They send me
their pamphlets and documents. I think that all of them
have now become warlike but three, and one of them is a
woman. If you meet a woman you know on the street
and express a sympathy on the loss of her second son, she
will say to you, "Yes, he died in defence of his country.
My third son will go next week. They all die to save

us." Doubtless she sheds tears in private. But her eyes are dry in public. She has discarded her luxuries to put money in the war loan. Say "Peace" to her? She would insult you.

May 10, 1917.

We dined at Lambeth Palace. There was Lord Morley, whom I had not seen since his long illness—much reduced in flesh, and quite feeble and old-looking. But his mind and speech were most alert. He spoke of Cobden favouring the Confederate States because the constitution of the Confederacy provided for free trade. But one day Bright informed Cobden that he was making the mistake of his life. Thereafter Cobden came over to the Union side. This, Morley heard direct from Bright.

The Archbishop spoke in high praise of Charnwood's Lincoln—was surprised at its excellence, etc.

Geoffrey Robinson[1] asked who wrote the *Quarterly* articles in favour of the Confederacy all through the war —was it Lord Salisbury? Nobody knew.

The widow of the former Archbishop Benson was there —the mother of all the Bensons, Hugh, A. C., etc., etc.— a remarkable old lady, who talked much in admiration of Balfour.

The Bishop of—Winchester(?)—was curious to know whether the people in the United States really understood the Irish question—the two-nation, two-religion aspect of the case. I had to say no!

There is an orphan asylum founded by some preceding Archbishop, by the sea. The danger of bombardment raised the question of safety. The Archbishop ordered all the children (40) to be sent to Lambeth Palace. We dined in a small dining room: "The children," Mrs. David-

---

[1] Editor of the London *Times*.

son explained, "have the big dining room." Each child has a lady as patroness or protector who "adopts" her, i.e., sees that she is looked after, etc. Some of the ladies who now do this were themselves orphans!

At prayers as usual at 10 o'clock in the chapel where prayers have been held every night—for how many centuries?

At lunch to-day at Mr. Asquith's—Lord Lansdowne there; took much interest in the Knapp farm work while I briefly explained.

Lord Morley said to Mrs. Page he had become almost a Tolstoyan—Human progress hasn't done much for mankind's happiness, etc. Look at the war—by a "progressive" nation. Now the mistake here is born of a class-society, a society that rests on privilege. "Progress," *has* done everything (1) in liberating men's minds and spirits in the United States. This is the real gain; (2) in arraying all the world *against* Germany.

Tuesday, January 22, 1918.

Some days bring a bunch of interesting things or men. Then there sometimes come relatively dull days—not often, however. To-day came:

General Tasker H. Bliss, Chief-of-Staff, now 64—the wisest (so I judge) of our military men, a rather wonderful old chap. He's on his way to Paris as a member of the Supreme War Council at Versailles. The big question he has struck is: Shall American troops be put into the British and French lines, in small groups, to fill up the gaps in those armies? The British have persuaded him that it is a military necessity. If it were less than a necessity, it would, of course, be wrong—i.e., it would cut across our national pride, force our men under another flag, etc. It is not proposed to deprive Pershing of his command nor even of his army. The plan is to bring over troops that would not otherwise now come and to lend these to the British and French armies, and to let Pershing go on with his army as if this hadn't been done. Bliss is inclined to grant this request on condition the British bring these men over, equip and feed them, etc. He came in to ask me to send a telegram for him to-morrow to the President, making this recommendation. But on reflection he decided to wait till he had seen and heard the French also, who desire the same thing as the British.

General Bliss is staying with Major Warburton; and Warburton gave me some interesting glimpses of him. A telegram came for the General. Warburton thought that he was out of the house and he decided to take it himself to the General's room. He opened the door. There sat the General by the fire talking to himself, wrapped in thought. Warburton walked to the middle of the room. The old man didn't see him. He decided not to disturb him, for he was rehearsing what he proposed to say to the Secretary of State for War or to the Prime Minister—getting his ears as well as his mind used to it. Warburton put the telegram on the table near the General, went out, and wasn't discovered.

Several nights, he sat by the fire with Warburton and began to talk, again rehearsing to himself some important conclusions that he had reached. Every once in a while he'd look up at Warburton and say: "Now, what do you think of that?"

That's an amazing good way to get your thought clear and your plans well laid out. I've done it myself.

I went home and Kipling and Carrie[1] were at lunch with us. Kipling said: "I'll tell you, your coming into the war made a new earth for me." He is on a committee to see

[1] Mrs. Kipling.

that British graves are properly marked and he talked much about it. I could not help thinking that in the back of his mind there was all the time thought of his own dead boy, John.

Then in the afternoon Major Drain brought the copy of a contract between the United States Government and the British to build together 1500 tanks ($7,500,000). We took it to the Foreign Office and Mr. Balfour and I signed it. Drain thinks that the tanks are capable of much development and he wishes our army after the war to keep on studying and experimenting with and improving such machines of destruction. Nobody knows what may come of it.

Then I dined at W. W. Astor's (Jr.) There were Balfour, Lord Salisbury, General and Lady Robertson, Mrs. Lyttleton and Philip Kerr.

During the afternoon Captain Amundsen, Arctic explorer came in, on his way from Norway to France as the guest of our Government, whereafter he will go to the United States and talk to Scandinavian people there.

That's a pretty good kind of a full day.

April, 19, 1918.

Bell,[1] and Mrs. Bell during the air raid took their little girl (Evangeline, aged three) to the cellar. They told her they went to the cellar to hear the big fire crackers. After a bomb fell that shook all Chelsea, Evangeline clapped her hands in glee. "Oh, mummy, what a *big* fire cracker!"

---

[1] Mr. Edward Bell, Second Secretary of the American Embassy.

INDEX

INDEX